FIRE UNDER THE ASHES

JAMES McNEISH

FIRE
UNDER THE ASHES

The Life of Danilo Dolci

ETNA, an isolated active volcano . . . Its form is
a domed cone . . . The cone is not perfect . . .
The height and form of the crater constantly
change . . . According to age and composition,
some lavas and most ashes have disintegrated
into fertile soil . . .
    Chambers Encyclopædia

HODDER AND STOUGHTON

Printed in Great Britain
for Hodder and Stoughton Ltd.,
St. Paul's House, Warwick Lane, London, E.C.4
by Richard Clay (The Chaucer Press), Ltd.,
Bungay, Suffolk

for FLICKA
who helped, more than she knew

It is true that in other countries great men have also occasionally been persecuted and put to death. Nowhere else, however, has this happened with the same discrimination, regularity, and determination . . . Italy instinctively neutralised all the men who tried to foist moral greatness on their countrymen.

—Luigi Barzini (*The Italians*)

Acknowledgments

I AM indebted to the following for permission to quote copyright material:

Danilo Dolci, for the poems, letters, speeches and other private documents.
Ilys Booker and Professor Ross Walker, for their private letters.
Laterza & Figli, Bari, for *Banditi a Partinico.*
Giulio Einaudi, Turin, for *Processo all'articolo 4.*
La Nuova Italia Editrice, Florence, for *Fare presto (e bene) perché si muore.*
MacGibbon & Kee, for *Inchiesta a Palermo* and *Spreco.*

The line-drawing prefacing the three sections is from Borgo di Dio, drawn by one of the children of the men killed by bandits.

Quotations accompanying illustrations, where not from the text or obviously by a peasant, are by Dolci.

Grateful acknowledgment is made to the Danilo Dolci Trust, 29 Gt. James St., London W.C.1, for its constant help and the photographs of the clinic, saplings and the Palma church. Also to Nicola Scafidi, Palermo, for the photographs of Cardinal Ruffini, Dolci and father, Genco Russo, Goffredo Fofi, the two oratory scenes at the trial and the 1955 fast vignette; and to Publifoto, Milan, for Dolci in chains.

Scores have helped with this biographical excursion. My especial thanks are due to: Annie Kalldal, of Kallrör, Sweden; Robin Dixon, Oxford; Don Zeno Saltini, Nomadelphia; Giorgio Pecorini, Milan; Norma Slevison and Bill Pepper, Rome; Marcello Cimino and Gino Orlando, Palermo; Franco Alasia and Vittorio Geraci, Partinico. Also to Diana Fussell, of Wellington, New Zealand, who took the picture of Dolci playing the accordion, translated the poems and transcribed many tapes; and Elizabeth Morton, of Auckland, who typed the MS in record time. Lastly, my deepest gratitude—to Pasqualino, whose mill, wine cellar and genius at unscrambling the Sicilian dialect were always forthcoming; to Kerstin and Eyvind Hytten, who bravely entrusted me with Borgo di Dio—and even Amedeo—when the furies were at their height; and to Totò, of Cammarata, who finally managed to convince the district police officer I was not a Communist spy.

Contents

CONTENTS

PART III

Illustrations

Photographs are by the author unless otherwise
acknowledged.

Introduction

DANILO DOLCI is that rare person, the intellectual who does things.

At the age of twenty he was unknown. At thirty-one he was a world figure. Today, at forty, he is as controversial in Europe as T. E. Lawrence is in England.

Sicilians sometimes call him 'the professional misery man'. He is still attacked for having revealed Sicily's tragic under-side to the civilised world; indeed, he is still attacked for almost everything he does. It is partly the lot of the pacifist reformer. It is particularly the lot of the reformer who is brave enough, or daft enough, to choose this unresponsive soil as his seeding ground. Sicilians seldom forgive, and, as the prince in *The Leopard* points out, 'The sin which we Sicilians never forgive is simply that of *doing* at all.' 'Doing' is probably the simplest way of describing Dolci's philosophy of life.

Ever since 1956, when he led a group of unemployed peasants out to repair a broken-down Government road, gratis, and got put in prison for it, Dolci's prestige outside Italy has soared, in inverse proportion to that within it. Nowadays, the official Italian press hardly mentions him, except occasionally to applaud when there appears a likelihood of his going to prison again, being put on the Index or, as in a recent fast, of going into a coma. It is generally the way with saints and revolutionaries. We love them all, from a distance. Close to home they are embarrassing.

Many observers consider that the *Eminence Grise* behind much official hostility to Dolci is not the Mafia but the leading ecclesiastical authority on the island, Cardinal Ernesto Ruffini, Archbishop of Palermo and Primate of Sicily. I cannot vouch for the statement. When I called at the archbishopric on 7 September 1963 His Eminence declined to receive me. He said he did not consider it opportune and authorised his secretary, Monsignor Longhi, to speak on his behalf. Monsignor Longhi described Dolci as an upstart, a disgraced Christian, an impostor, a dishonest and ambitious man whose aims were evil, grasping and immoral. These remarks were tape-recorded. To put them in perspective it should be

xiii

remembered that the broad Church criticism of Dolci is that he is 'a defamer of his country and his people'. 'It is a Christian duty not to speak badly of your neighbour,' priests have told me.

Monsignor Longhi gave me a confidential report on Dolci, completed in 1962 by the Palermo police. It is eight and a quarter foolscap pages closely typed. Part of it seems based on a newspaper article by a former Partinico senator, Savarino, which the police attempted to use as evidence against Dolci during his trial in 1956. Monsignor Longhi said I was to treat the police report as His Eminence's 'personal opinion'. It is not actually libellous. I shall quote from it, from time to time.

Aldous Huxley has called Dolci 'the ideal twentieth-century saint'.

It is one of Dolci's misfortunes that he does not look the reforming type. He is a towering broth of a man who always seems on the point of bursting out of his clothes which are too small for him, and indeed is fated to split his trousers at the most awkward moments. He reminds me of an unorthodox provincial businessman, in the act of clearing his desk before flinging a shoe-lace round his neck in mistake for a tie and departing at a hand-gallop for a well-earned holiday. Dolci is a conventional reformer only in so far as he never takes a holiday. Only the strong hazel eyes, limpid and penetrating behind the cut spectacles, and the uncanny moral armoury limning the quiet reassuring voice, betray the poet and mystic and the man of conscientious action.

One of the paradoxical things about Dolci is that he is criticised most by those farthest from him—those who understand him least, or do not want to understand him at all—like Cardinal Ruffini; and by some of those who have been closest to him—those who, one would think, understand him best—like Giovanni and Gerrit and Bianca and Pasqualino, all former colleagues and once staunch advocates. This is part of the riddle of Dolci, the man. For these latter people the close-focus of the man himself, his shortcomings, especially his failure as an administrator, are paramount. Each of them could write a separate, perhaps equally valid book on Dolci. But they would be writing about a different Dolci. For me it matters less that his private figure often falls short of his public figure. For me his limitations ·are secondary. I am concerned primarily with the man and the gesture; with Dolci in a world context, with the man of ideas and the influence of these ideas. I see him as a symbol, as a positive living force.

To write about Dolci it is also necessary to write about the Centre. This is the curious organisation he founded in 1958 which, from a renegade warehouse visited officially only by policemen armed with revolvers, has become a sort of moral launching-pad visited today by world authorities in the social sciences and by Italian ministers of state armed with portfolios. But this is not a history of the Dolci movement. Many names are omitted; and for this reason the stories of Goffredo and Ilys should not be taken as isolated epics. Others (Raffaele Maiello, Riborg van der Felz, Mariapia Pieri, Fiorella Viola, Marco Marchioni . . . the list is a long one) have achieved as much, and suffered more. I would like to have written more about these people, for they, too, are symbolic—of young men and women everywhere who fire themselves for an ideal, only to find that the more sacrifices they make the more it blinds and exhausts them. It has exhausted Eyvind. It killed Teresio Bonini, the young statistician who was found dead in his room, the gas-heater still burning, a letter he had been writing to Professor Waller, half-finished, in his typewriter.

My own connection with the Centre is oblique—I am of it but not in it. The connection has grown from a casual meeting with Dolci four years ago to a present attachment in the mountains, a field study blessed jointly by the Centre and Stockholm University. I should also explain that I am not a sociologist or an economist and have not attempted a close appraisal of Dolci's technical studies or the scores of monographs his specialists have prepared. They belong to a different kind of book. I have also omitted Dolci's more theoretical writings on what he calls the technology of non-violence, for the same reason.

This is principally the account of a man's life. It is not exhaustive. I regard it as an extended portrait rather than a full-scale biography. It is official in that I have had Dolci's willing co-operation, though this is almost a euphemism. Latterly he has been travelling so much that the only occasions when we have been able to get together for more than a day at a time have been, significantly, when he has been flat on his back, starving. I never got over a guilty feeling that I had him at a disadvantage.

To delve into a man who has already changed course three times in his life and is still maturing may seem impertinent. But when I remember how Gandhi and Kennedy died, when I pick up a Sicilian newspaper and see almost every day how casually, and sometimes carefully, lives are shattered here virtually by force of habit; when I drive across the island to the Partinico plain, near Palermo, where Dolci lives—that is, the long valley road which begins in the hills behind Santo Stefano and passes through Corleone and San Giuseppe Iato, skirting graveyards where lie the remnants of over two hundred Mafia murders, all recent and almost all unsolved—then I am not convinced that this book is premature. It is one of Dolci's achievements that he is alive at all.

Perhaps nowhere do the social revolutionary and truth have such short lives as on this melancholy island. Sicilians say that the truth does not exist. Their torn and beautiful land is littered with the tombstones of rebels who have sought truth and tried to build on it to bring about justice and change. I can think of only one other would-be reformer who provoked the Mafia and lived. He is a priest and the Mafia doesn't usually kill priests, and in any case this young man was made to sign a confession, under duress, retracting everything he had said. Nobody is sure why Dolci has been allowed to live. 'I don't know,' he says. 'I really don't know.'

Eduard would say that this is overplaying the Mafia's role, and he may be right. But Eduard, who is Dolci's liaison officer with the German-speaking world and the extension work in Africa, is himself something of a vagabond from death. He is one of the few surviving organisers of the *putsch* against Hitler and he should know how slender is the hair-line between luck and oblivion.

Some of Dolci's life is already studded with myth. It is not too soon to get at the facts. I can think of no better reason for making them known than Dolci's own reason for publicising the facts about Sicily—'For when they are deeply known, other people may then work.'

J. McN.
Cammarata, West Sicily, 1964

PART I

There will always be the sound of thunder, and chaos and ruin and death, in the affairs of men and nations until they achieve God and enter into his tranquillity

—Lao-Tse

ONE

Beginnings

HE had always been a maker of dreams. They were the sort of dreams that had to do with a reality that was just round the corner, that had to do with people, always people, and with faith in people. Faith-dreams, you might call them. He didn't look like a dreamer. He had that pathetic formal seriousness of the small boy who listens gravely to the parental word of command, and then strides off to carry it out as if the Papal dignity were at stake. 'Oh, he is such a *good* boy,' an elder aunt used to say. When he was four he was standing on a balcony wearing his sailor's cloth cap when he noticed an even smaller boy standing on the pavement below, gazing wistfully up at him. He took off the cap and gave it to his threadbare admirer. He never understood why his father beat him so hard afterwards, because his parents had always told him it was right to help the poor. Once his father sent him round to the tobacconist with a letter and the money to buy the stamp. The tobacconist who sold the stamps was closed, but he posted the letter in the pillar-box just the same, and then he posted the money for the stamp. He got a whelping for that too. He was always dreaming: about seamen and spacemen and starmen, about his paternal grandfather, Pietro, who had travelled even to America (and that was *something*, in those days) —dreams about poets and painters and great musicians. When he was fifteen and studying at technical school his dreams took the form of phantasies, lie-phantasies; sometimes he told lies from fear to avoid another beating, but the dream ones, he always said afterwards, were a part of his own private world of evasion and he had a need to kiss phantasy. The worst dream of all began after he was 25 and had left university and the family home in North Italy and gone away to live in a paupers' community run by a thickset dumpy man whom people called 'the mad priest of Nomadelphia'. This dream had outlasted even the revelations of Nomadelphia and had followed him down to Sicily. 'For several years I went on having this dream, until I was about thirty. I dreamed with anguish that I hadn't taken my architectural degree, a sort of guilt dream, afraid of not being strong, of not building these things.' The interesting thing is that the dream was true. In fact, he hadn't taken the degree.

Some ten years later, during a hunger strike, he had a different type of dream. It was short and, apparently, vivid. It was 14 September 1962. He was almost at the end of a nine-day fast in a poor part of the Sicilian town of Partinico. I was sleeping between his bed and the door, which was shut, and Franco his secretary was sleeping on the other side of the room. He'd put the light out about ten o'clock, and we lay back talking. He was worried and weak from lack of sugar. We all dropped off. It must have been about two in the morning when he woke suddenly and shouted to Franco, 'Quick! There's a police car out there.' I'd heard nothing, nor had Franco. Franco bolted outside in bare feet, holding his pyjama pants up with one hand and rubbing his eyes with the other. After a few minutes Franco was back. Yes, it was a police car, he said. The carabinieri had called at a house 60 yards down the street and taken a man away.

I am not sure if these dreams, if you can call them dreams, have any great significance. If they have, though, they belong more to the Pirandellian world of reality intertwined with illusion than to any Kafkaesque world of nightmarish hallucination. Perhaps this is just to say that they belong very much to the private world of Danilo Dolci.

He was born on 28 June 1924, at Sesana, a village near Trieste, which is today in Tito's Slovenia. He grew up in a typical middle-class Italian environment, or rather a series of environments, in which there was great affection, without real intimacy, and rather too much religion. The religion came from his mother who was Slav: Meli Kontely. His mother first spoke to him in Slovenian, and the prayers that were said every morning and evening were in that language. She gave him a Slav name, Danilo. As a boy he spoke Slovenian, the only foreign language he has mastered. From his mother he inherited a gift for music and a balanced artistic temperament. His father, Enrico Dolci, was a railway employee, of Italian and German blood, and, by reaction against Mrs. Dolci, a religious abstainer. The veil of astringent Catholicism, formal and uncritical, which tinged the family atmosphere had no influence at all over Signor Dolci's heavy hand which always seemed on the point of rising or falling, usually in the direction of Danilo. Yet Danilo was closer to his father, and from him gained a love of the country and of walking. Signor Dolci was a wiry, handsome man. Being attached to that vast machine, the Italian State Railways—which, like the state police, was in the habit of suddenly transferring its employees from one end of the republic to the other—he kept his family in a sort of perpetual motion, steering them on his modest railwayman's

salary through a succession of self-contained four-roomed bunga-
lows, with and without flower gardens, from Trieste to Lake
Maggiore, to a town near Alessandria, and to points south. Otherwise, apart from the weekly rows that civil servants the world over
have with their wives over matters of upbringing, life held no
major problems for Enrico Dolci. He was not an ambitious man.
There was no aspidistra in the Dolci bungalow. The only status
symbols were the upright piano in the living-room and a battered
leather suitcase which had belonged to Grandad Pietro, the traveller.
Danilo recalls the musical evenings as 'nice moments'. Mrs. Dolci
sang and played, Danilo played and sang, and two or three uncles
were usually on hand to ballast the choruses. When Danilo was
eight a sister appeared, Miriam, who thereafter seems to have become becalmed in the Italian middle-class existences of doing exactly
what was expected of you, which was what everyone else did. Life
was quiet, modest and 'traditional'. The household of Mr. and Mrs.
Dolci appears as a warm suburban snug, an oasis of conventionality
rising out of the unorthodox past of their fathers and leading into
the outrageous future of their only son. Both Danilo's grandfathers
were rugged men, with the spice of originality. Both travelled.
Josef Kontely, his maternal grandfather, was a law clerk. He was a
linguist, a 'cellist and a man of fiery honour. In 1928, when Danilo
was four, Josef refused to doff his hat before a fascist banner at
Brescia, and for that was beaten and made to drink castor oil, the
stock fascist purgative. Josef returned to Yugoslavia and never set
foot in Italy again. Danilo never knew his paternal grandfather,
Pietro. He only knew there was a famous leather article in the
house known as 'Grandad's case' and from time to time messages
would arrive from the most improbable places, saying 'Send the
case—I'm off to America.' Grandad Pietro was a cheese traveller.
He came from Rovato, near Brescia, married a German woman from
Nuremberg and travelled half the world in the cause of *caciocavallo*.
He was in partnership with a man called Arrigoni. Pietro died
young and left a modest sum to be divided among ten children.
Enrico, who had wanted to study, started work at seventeen and became a railwayman by mistake. He determined that his son would
study and get an important post.

Danilo was more interested in music. At six he began with
Marusi, the organist at Milan Cathedral, and fell in love with Bach.
By his mid-teens he was accomplished on three instruments. If he
didn't play well Marusi used to rap him over the knuckles. An un-
stated hatred of violence was instilled early. His education was
formal and undistinguished, though occasionally his essays were

read aloud to the class. But he was not an outstanding pupil. He was not always present. If he didn't like the teacher he used to wander off into the fields and sit, through the long enigmatic afternoons, staring at the pebbles of a favourite stream-bed. He would take a book and read, or he'd just sit, staring. His father reacted typically when he found out, but the beatings Danilo received only drove him farther into his books. He read old library books, his father's books, anything he could lay hands on; all his savings went into books or music. He had his first calf-love affair (with a teacher) at nine, went through technical school in three different towns, played basketball, clambered up mountains and became an excellent swimmer. It was all 'very normal', he says. Above all through his adolescence, he read.

Born into the cynical twenties, he was growing up in a world slowly emptying itself of spiritual values, against a background of mounting violence and empty slogans. Education glorified male supremacy, fighting terms and the state. Along with millions of other Italian children he learned by rote the slogans, 'Mussolini is always right', 'With book and gun, true fascist son', and 'Better to live one day as a lion than a hundred years as a sheep'. At six he put on the black shirt, black belt, black fez and grey-green socks of the *balilla* and at fourteen became a *marinaretto*, the sea-scout version of the *avanguardisti*, by means of which Mussolini was spinning a paper web of efficiency for the first time in the history of a united Italy. His father was an early conformer to the facile acceptance of a dictatorship few believed in or even understood, and as the mood of life subtly altered through the thirties, and youth took sides, Danilo acquiesced, without criticising. But he remained uncommitted. In 1939 when Hitler marched into Czechoslovakia and Mussolini, not to be outdone, invaded Albania, Danilo was flirting with the heroes of Jules Verne. He experienced his first instinctive revulsion for the régime at sixteen, shortly after Italy entered the war. His father refused to let him listen to the BBC in London. They argued bitterly. Then there occurred a small, almost routine event which was later to reshape his life. His father was sent from Tortona near Alessandria, where they were living, to become stationmaster in a remote village at the other end of Italy, the village of Trappeto in Sicily. It was rather like being promoted from pointsman on the Exeter bypass to be chief traffic officer at Barra in the Outer Hebrides. None of the family had ever heard of Trappeto before.

Mrs. Dolci and the children remained in the north. Danilo studied mathematics and drawing at school and at home plunged deeper into his reading. It had become a ritual. He would rise at four, slip an overcoat over his pyjamas and read for two hours; after a break for a hot drink he would go on reading until it was time for school. In three, three and a half hours, he would assimilate a major work. In his sixteenth year he read close on three hundred titles—all the Italian classics, Goethe, Schiller, Tolstoy, Ibsen, Shakespeare. Simultaneously he studied the history of art and crossed into fresh religious worlds, wanting to understand how so many other millions outside Italy might live according to vastly different, yet firmly established patterns of conduct. He read the Bible and the Koran, turned to Tao, Confucius and the teachings of Buddha. He read all seven hundred stanzas of the *Bhagavad Gita*, the work which half a century before had become Gandhi's spiritual reference book. The great minds of the past devoured him. He soaked up knowledge drunkenly. But there was no correlation between theory and the practice; the growing intellectual had no platform.

In the summer of 1941, when he was seventeen, he took a sketch-pad and went south with his mother and sister for a holiday. After two nights and a day on the train they came to the fishing village of Trappeto, in western Sicily, where his father was stationmaster, and rented a house by the sea.

Trappeto, like most southern villages, was half-starved. People were living on locust and carob beans and whatever herbs they could scratch from the countryside. There was no grain for bread—it had either been requisitioned by the military or hoarded by the rich. But as the war had so far not ruffled Danilo's conscience, so the poverty of Trappeto failed to touch him. He read and sketched the painted boats, made friends with the black-garbed fishermen, with Paolino and Toni and Peppino and Leonardo, 'son of the blind one'. They spoke a loud gravelly dialect he couldn't understand, took him fishing at night, and Toni 'the philosopher' talked of Alaska, showed him the stars and introduced him to the magical world of the Biblical night fisherman. It was the world they lived and the world of *Moby Dick*, and it excited him. 'They translated what I'd read into reality, gave me a new dimension of the world.' But it was an artistic dimension. The primitive boats, the crusts of bread, the tumbledown dwellings—he saw it all pictorially.

His dad was a bit of a hero, he discovered. Fishing was officially prohibited in wartime right round the coast. 'We told your dad, Signor Dolci, we couldn't take the boats out when he came,' Paolino said. 'And off he goes and speaks with the carabinieri [the state police]. The carabinieri sent him to the military and the military sent

23

him to the mayor and the mayor sent him back to the carabinieri . . . what a business. But he sorted it out, your dad. He came down one night and he says, "It's all right, lads, you can take your boats out." He fixed it.'

Danilo felt no longing to emulate his father. He knew him to be a *good* man. It was enough. His father wanted him to get on quickly, pass his surveyor's exams and take a job with a big construction firm, perhaps in Africa. Danilo read *The History of Italian Art* and went on a pilgrimage to the south-western corner of the island, to Selinunte and Segesta, to study the Greek glories of the past. He saw the temple of Segesta alone on a summer's morning. The massive frontal columns, set starkly on a hill above the cavernous goat country which fell away behind, seemed far more important to him than Trappeto. He saw the temple, above the blue thistle and the sombre green esparto grass, with a kind of greedy curiosity, made several sketches and went away. He was in love with the idea of becoming an architect.

He returned north with his mother, jumped a year to take his surveyor's diploma and gained a cultural diploma as well at the Brera Academy, Milan.

By autumn 1942 the tide of war was turning. German troops were taking over the north, anti-fascism was spreading and Mussolini was losing control: his mistress' relatives were rumoured to be sidling into the country's affairs, from posts in the diplomatic service to professorships at Milan University and the Polytechnic, where Danilo was now a first-year architectural student. Fascist leaders began listening to the BBC in London to find out what was happening, and Danilo began his first serious love affair. But study remained his real passion. Against a background of mounting chaos he continued the early morning ritual, rising at four, reading the Greek dramatists and the Utopians. He earned his first money, teaching in the evenings. By the late spring of 1943 half Mussolini's armies in Russia were lost, his forces had surrendered in North Africa and, with the allies about to invade Sicily, Signor Dolci had left the Sicilian railways to their fate and returned north. Before he did so, however, he cemented the Dolci prestige in Trappeto by persuading the carabinieri to break into the warehouses of the landowners and distribute the hoarded grain among the fisherfolk.

Danilo, studying fifteen hours a day, collapsed from overwork. His parents found him in a faint on the sofa. It was the first of a series of frights he gave them. The Allies landed in the south, the Nazis occupied Rome and Mussolini set up his puppet state in the

24

'People must realise that public and private charity . . are no longer remedies for the ills of today'

'They give the impression it is a holiday, as indeed it is, an almost perpetual holiday'

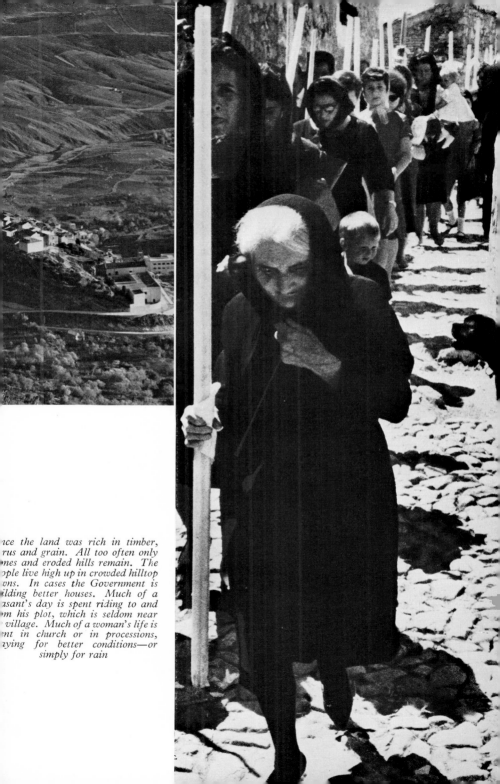

...ce the land was rich in timber,
...rus and grain. All too often only
...nes and eroded hills remain. The
...ple live high up in crowded hilltop
...ns. In cases the Government is
...ilding better houses. Much of a
...asant's day is spent riding to and
...m his plot, which is seldom near
...village. Much of a woman's life is
...nt in church or in processions,
...aying for better conditions—or
simply for rain

'If we hadn't been baptised we'd be no better than animals that talk.' Dolci heard this expression at Trappeto in 1952. It is common in 1964, from Alcamo to Enna. A third of a sample of peasants interviewed at Cammarata, where this picture was taken, said that landslides and soil erosion were due to magic spells or acts of God north centred on Salò. It was late 1943. Rebellion was in the air. At nineteen Danilo, sympathetically involved in the growing resistance, was picked as officer material and knew he would soon be called up. Emerging from the idealism of Plato's *Republic* he realised he wanted nothing to do with Mussolini's so-called Republic of Salò. He saw himself as a combatant in a hypocritical school of murder. He went round ripping down Nazi posters—'those horrible Nazi posters'—wherever he saw them. His parents were terrified. Danilo went on ripping down the posters. Then he decided to reach Rome. He left a note for his father, with the money he had earned from teaching, and took a train south. He had two books with him, Mazzini's *The Rights and Duties of Men* and Thomas à Kempis' *Of the Imitation of Christ*. Before Genoa there was a train check by the Nazis. He was arrested, handcuffed and taken to Sturla jail where he spent the next ten days in a cell, 18 feet by 9 feet, sleeping under straw and blankets with twelve others and a small army of lice. His companions were port thieves and partisans, and included a Jewish factory owner who had tried to escape by jumping out of the window when the Germans arrived. The Jew was taken away from the cell and not seen again. Danilo got out curiously. At the prison hearing, he mentioned casually to the officer-interpreter the name of an obscure German sculptor he'd read about in a doctor's waiting-room. The interpreter was impressed: he knew the sculptor. Danilo played his advantage and appears to have convinced the interpreter that he himself was an architectural genius, for the latter spoke to a superior, handed Danilo a *laissez-passer* note, and Danilo walked out of the gate.

He walked up into the Ligurian mountains, went south by lorry and foot, came to the Abruzzi and again took to the mountains. He passed Gran Sasso, the highest peak in the Italian Apennines, and above L'Aquila was chased by a German patrol. He hid in the snow. He had a close shave with a fascist patrol and then in the woods found a loaded pistol. It came in handy, scavenging for food. Then he thought about it and threw the pistol away. For a week he lived on diseased and dying hens which the peasants had thrown out. 'I skinned them and boiled them. I had chook for breakfast, chook for dinner and chook for supper. I never had so much poultry in all my life.' He was sheltered by a shepherd family in the village of Poggio Canelli, where escaped British prisoners were also lying up, and learned his first words of English from a New Zealand infantryman who'd just captured a runaway pig. 'Such is life,' the Kiwi said with a grin, and proceeded to slaughter the pig. The Germans were now retreating north from Naples, but were still in charge of

Rome, as Danilo discovered when he drew near. He returned to Poggio Canelli and stayed with the same shepherd family, giving their son Italian lessons in return for food. Early in 1944 he crossed over the lines, hidden in the back of a truck carrying merchandise, and reached Rome. The war for Italy was virtually over.

TWO

The First Fever

A PHOTOGRAPH taken about 1947 when Danilo was 23 and in his
fourth year of architecture in Milan shows a shock of wavy brown
hair, a lean dedicated face, impeccable collar and tie and expensive
rimless spectacles. There is an air of groomed, assured professional-
ism. There is no hint of an internal struggle which had begun a
year or so before, a poet's rebellion against the sophisticated society
in which he was living. He'd given up reading altogether and begun
writing poetry, seeking in the battle for the control of words themselves a way out of rhetoric and into reality. And then, one October, he
went out into the country. Years later he told me of the experience:

'I went out from one October to the next, because I wanted to
verify directly the things I'd been reading. I saw all things born and
I saw all things die. And I realised that everthing became, could
become, a parable. I saw that when the leaves fell from the trees you
could see farther. I saw that you could see the sun only when it was
hidden by mists. I saw, as we all do, that from afar the grass seems
luxuriant and it's only when you're close that you see the patches of
dry earth. I saw that when the leaves fall only the seeds remain, that
the seeds then return to the earth. I saw that in the act of wasting
away they become reborn. And continuously the seeds fell and became fruit, ready for eating. And I saw all the seasons like this, from
inside, as it were. I forgot everything else. I wanted to live them,
just once; and I did. I saw the whole cycle of life. I *felt*, I didn't
reason it, that nature, that everything, was a tragedy where the
living devoured the dead. I didn't know why, I only knew it was so.
And then slowly, very slowly, I felt the need to be consumed, like
the seeds, to become manure myself.

'And then I understood the value of communion, that everybody
must be together. I understood God's purpose in creation.'

Out of a synthesis of bookish culture and mystical experience he
had discovered a meaning in life. But he was not yet to collaborate
with it. His head continued to go one way, his body another. As he
wrote in a poem, there were

daemons of the flesh
placed in positions of command.

27

Yet the Hyde of his dual personality wasn't a very ribald fellow. At parties he was often to be found at the piano, playing Bach. He had the body of an athlete and warm friendly eyes which his girl friends found endearing, but he had a disconcerting Edwardian mode of expressing his feelings. According to a contemporary account, one affair ended rather abruptly when he turned up to a rendezvous on a crowded Milan thoroughfare at promenade time, pulled a piece of paper from his pocket, saying 'Just a minute, let's look at this poem', and with that sat down on the pavement and began to read it aloud. He became engaged to an attractive arts graduate, Alicia, and they courted formally—every Sunday, mostly by reading poetry together —talked increasingly of marriage, of property and children, and of entering the *società illuminata* of Milan when he had qualified and set up in practice. Alicia was the daughter of a well-to-do provincial building contractor. Danilo was well-endowed artistically and pressing to the front of the new generation of resourceful and energetic designers. They were both good Catholics and went regularly to church with their respective parents, Danilo going home to Tortona and visiting his fiancée in a nearby town every weekend. It seemed an ideal match. His parents in particular were delighted.

He had rented a room in Milan, filled it with a piano (on hire) and books and music, and was paying his way by teaching at the Milan Polytechnic at night and by giving lessons on the theory of construction to his architectural colleagues. He is 'ashamed to admit' nowadays that he took money from fellow students. It was at the Polytechnic that his rebellion against the shallows of intellectualism took hold. He began to admire qualities, such as the capacity for sweat and work, in ordinary people about him. He was teaching literature to lads of seventeen and men of thirty, all bunched together, mostly labourers and factory hands. Among them was a young mechanic, Franco Alasia. Franco was three years younger than Danilo, and working ten hours a day in a motor-assembly plant. He was a raw young man, handsome in a finely chiselled way, and gawkily enthusiastic for knowledge. He had come through the fascist education-mill of being taught not to think, and was trying to make up the gap at night school and also to overcome a deep-seated inferiority complex about girls who wouldn't dance with him because, he told Danilo, 'I'm not cultured.' Somewhere between the mechanic's striving to get up, and the intellectual's yearning to climb down, the two found a relaxed meeting point. Danilo was the first intellectual in Franco's life. 'I felt this respect on his part, this equality between teacher and pupils,' Franco relates. 'He had a humility before each person, irrespective of their amount of culture,

28

just because they were people. All I waited for were his lessons. Often he'd go well beyond the subject and we'd continue the discussion walking home.' A deep bond sprang up between them.

Danilo, meantime, was coming more and more to despise intellectualism for its own sake. He was restless. Ideas, he felt intuitively, should be made a function of life itself, not merely a means of analysing it. In the summer of 1948, not long after he met Franco, he heard of a Catholic community run by a man called Don Zeno—'the mad priest of Nomadelphia'. Nomadelphia was a self-supporting charity for destitute orphans in Emilia. Perhaps in community life he might find the transition he was seeking from theory to application. He decided to go and see.

In fact, he wasn't much impressed. Scattered over a few flat acres at Fossoli, near Modena, on the site of an old concentration camp, Nomadelphia had an air of desolation. Pictorially, it was a mess. It was far from being the perfect society he had imagined. He spent a day there and went back to Milan to prepare for his finals.

He had already published two architectural monographs, *The Science of Construction* and *The Theory of Reinforced Concrete*, had designed a church, been offered further commissions and was delving into research on tensile strengths and beam structures with a young engineer with whom he planned to go into practice. He was regarded as 'more than promising'. Friends predicted a bold career and his fiancée was enthusiastic. They began building, preparing to set up house by the park and he rented a studio in Corso Sempione, the Champs Elysées of Milan. But as the time for taking his finals approached fresh doubt arose. At lectures his mind wandered to Utopian visions, beam structures were blurred and behind them he saw the faces of the orphans of Nomadelphia and the crinkled leonine face of the priest who'd given them the first real home they'd ever known. He went about in a sort of coma. For two days, in fever, Nomadelphia tormented him. Did he really want to become an architect? To build houses for the rich, creating more privileges for those who were privileged enough already, while all around him . . .? 'The mad priest of Nomadelphia,' people said. Was it so? Was the priest mad?

Almost on the point of taking his final exams, Danilo said, No.

'I suddenly realised that I was about to become fossilised,' he says. 'I was about to bury myself in a materialist society which glorified intellect to the point where it killed feelings, those very feelings which could become actions. And I felt the *need* of action. I suddenly realised that reinforced concrete and drawing-boards weren't enough. A home, a car and all the rest—they weren't enough. Better to be penniless and in shirt-sleeves and a nobody, merely alive in the midst of life, alive in the midst of the perfect community which was still maturing within me.'

Alicia broke down when he told her of his decision. He asked her to come to Nomadelphia with him. She returned the engagement ring. Only Franco, the young mechanic, was sympathetic to the idea.

Mr. and Mrs. Dolci had always listened to their son's theories, his talk of a better world, with nods of approval, even with admiration. After all, the ideas had come from them in the first place. 'The true Christian, Danilo, is the one who lives for the next man,' his mother had always said. But now, at home in Tortona, faced with a 25-year old son about to act on these ideals, they rebelled. It was late one autumn morning in 1949 when Danilo took out Grandad's case and put it on the spotless drawing-room table where the flower-vase normally stood, and began to pack his belongings. Most of the town's prosperous farming community was in the fields, getting in the wine harvest, a few wives were nodding away the sultry morning in the market square, and Mr. Dolci was home from the railway station. He was standing by the sideboard mirror watching his son pack, shaking with rage and weeping. Danilo had never seen his father cry before; he went 'quite green'. Mrs. Dolci was in the kitchen, weeping and cutting up bread and salami so that her son might want for nothing on the journey. Mr. Dolci gripped his big-boned son by the shoulders and began shaking and abusing him. When Mrs. Dolci came in from the kitchen bearing a handful of salami and cheese her husband was swearing and pummelling the table so that the suitcase jumped. He grabbed the salami and stuffed it in with the underclothes and sweaters, and then the bread and the cheese, and all the time he went on swearing at his son and throwing things into the case and shouting that the world was what it was, and there was no sense in trying to change it. Danilo—tense, yet almost detached—spoke of renunciation and said you had to start somewhere. He kissed his mother goodbye.

His father went with him to the station. He bought a single ticket for Modena and waved to his father out of the third-class carriage window. It was a tearing away of the flesh on both sides. The older man remained standing on the platform. He felt emptied out, betrayed.

One of the last things Danilo did before he went home to pack was to go through all his books and music, and the hundreds of poems he'd written, at his digs in Milan. He kept the books and the music. When the next tenant moved in he found what was left of the poems in various corners of the room—so many pieces of paper, torn to shreds.

THREE

The Perfect World of Don Zeno

DON ZENO, the founder of Nomadelphia and, after 33 years, still its guiding light, is not a Gandhi. In moments of priestly anger he has been known to break chairs and lesser pieces of furniture across his knee and, in matters of community administration, to deliver judgment with a kind of brute spiritual violence verging on moral totalitarianism. Once he confronted a newly arrived young woman with twenty children, saying 'This is your family', announcing in a few seconds the sentence which was to seal the rest of her life. When Danilo arrived, wearing an old sweater and carrying Grandad's case, both traits—the moral and the physical force—were in full evidence and Don Zeno was, like his thriving community, in the prime of life.

Don Zeno Saltini was born in Emilia in 1900, one of ten children in a rich peasant family. He spent his youth skipping school and hobnobbing with delinquents, and almost became a penal lawyer; but he changed his mind and became a parish priest, deciding that instead of defending delinquents it was more sensible to try and prevent the delinquency. On the day he said his first mass in 1931 he adopted a nineteen-year-old orphan, just released from prison, who was in the congregation, and spent his entire inheritance on an orphans' home in his parish of Mirandola, near Carpi. He waited almost ten years before his first 'mother', an eighteen-year-old girl called Irene, turned up—she was given 46 children as her first family. When Italy entered the war, the 'little apostles', as they were then known, became flying angels. Don Zeno was arrested for his anti-fascist outbursts, and jailed, and the children became scattered. Then the people of Mirandola rose up and threatened to sack the village, and Don Zeno was released. He went on campaigning against the régime. Six of his followers, aged sixteen and seventeen, were caught in possession of his propaganda leaflets, and either shot or hanged, and Don Zeno had to flee with a price on his head. At the same time as Danilo was lying up with British infantrymen among shepherds in the central Apennines, Don Zeno was hiding somewhere in the Maremma, living rough with two escaped prisoners-of-war, one of them an Englishman. In 1946 he turned

32

up in his home country again with a crowd of orphans and a tinpan-alley band, piled on top of a truck full of bedding and old furniture. He took them across the fields and marshes of the Modena country-side to Fossoli, to an abandoned concentration camp where five hundred Jews and many British soldiers had lost their lives. With-out waiting for permission he led them on to the site and occupied the camp. They breached the walls, ripped up the barbed-wire enclosures and put dovecots on the four watch-towers, in place of the machine-gun posts, as a symbol of faith in their new world. Noma-delphia proper had begun. Nomadelphia was, by its name, the place 'where fraternity is law'.

From that day on children flocked out of the war-torn Emilian landscape into the ready arms of Don Zeno. Institutes made over their 'impossibles' to him and he combed the streets, bringing in coloured children, scavengers, thieves, the children of prostitutes. He rescued one child as the mother was about to throw it off the Fossoli bridge into the canal. When Danilo came back in 1949 he found fourteen hundred children in the care of sixty mothers and three thousand more abandoned children waiting to be admitted. 'This isn't a Boys' Town,' Don Zeno told him, 'but a reconstruction of ordinary family life.' Nomadelphia had its own pilot co-operative farm, church, school, store and recreation room. It was a creative society, a primitive work-and-prayer colony where everybody worked and money was never used, and there was one fixed point—great love.

For the first year Danilo was 'drunk' with the place. He worked as Don Zeno's secretary, borrowed his accordion and began a small orchestra, emptied rubbish, joined a wood-cutters' party in the scrub and then was put in charge of seventy of the rougher young-sters. He took his group on fortnightly camps to the woods above Grosseto and there he won their trust quickly. Occasionally he would read to them from the Gospels—some of them later com-plained he wore them out with religion.

'Sometimes I came to feel as if I had God in my hands,' he says, and this is evident in almost all the poems he wrote at Nomadelphia. They were published in 1951, as *Voices in the City of God*. Not masterly poems, but they show clearly the mystical intimacy of his thought:

> *In order to live I must be brother to You*
> *And father*
> *And wipe Your dripping nose*
> *Support Your faltering steps*
> *Build You a strong house of stone*

Solid and upright, and revive You
When Your helpless forehead
Burns on my knees
And get bread for You, soup,
And the honey and fruit You like:
This is my worship

Danilo regretted nothing. He got about in black—patched and torn pants, black jersey, black beret—and until they got to know him the mothers took him for 'one of them new-fangled American priests'. Priests who did come to Nomadelphia for the experience were put to work emptying septic tanks or scrubbing out latrines. A Professor of Holy Writ from Milan was given the job of overseeing the pig pen. Don Zeno was a great believer in Christian communism. Franco visited Danilo three times. Mr. Dolci came to see him. They were building a road at the time. 'If I'd known you were going to take to this sort of thing, Danilo,' he grumbled, 'I'd have brought you up to be a level-crossing attendant.'

Most nights he flopped into bed exhausted, almost too tired to eat. They were short-staffed, burdened with debts and the kids were far from angels. Some of them hid in a watch-tower, electrified the doors and roasted and ate every dove they could lay hands on. But he saw that nothing was hopeless. 'I discovered that even the dumbest, the most monstrous child, if I really loved him, became more beautiful, more intelligent. He became transformed.' After a time even the most dissolute youngster responded. 'I remember one essay, by a boy of about eleven. He wrote, "Our parents are the trunks and the roots and the branches. We are the leaves and the flowers. Without us they can't live." Usually we think that a child can't live without *us*, but this lad had understood perfectly the reciprocity of life. *Incredible* intuition.'

The whole environment created by Don Zeno nurtured intuition. Don Zeno became Danilo's *guru*. The two were almost always together. Don Zeno at fifty was a formidable figure, pouchy, squat, with a gnarled terrifying stance and the energy, in full cassock rig, to chase and catch a recalcitrant youngster less than half his years. He wore a thick black sweater, which emphasised his bulk, a beret pulled aggressively down over his thick brows and when he was angry retired to his room, tipped his beret slantwise over one ear and played the accordion. The kids loved him, and claimed that the moral impetus he radiated penetrated even the stoutest partition. Many a troubled youngster, about to knock on his door with a problem, would suddenly stop and then turn confidently away without entering, the solution having already 'arrived' across the threshold. Danilo loved him because of his rustic simplicity: when Don Zeno built his church, for example, he put the altar at one end and a cinema screen at the other, and on film nights had the smaller children sit on top of the altar to watch. The pair of them went for long walks, often out all night, railing under the stars, and Danilo tested the widening horizon of his ideas against the leathery sounding-board of the older man's profounder Catholicism. Once he rebuked Don Zeno for not admitting more children. 'Here we have order,' the priest rumbled. 'Open the doors out of blind love and we'll have chaos.' Danilo says, 'I made such acts of faith in him I lost the capacity to criticise, I began to think as he did. He was nearly always right.' Don Zeno talked of his vision, to construct *the* Christian Society, based on his three imperatives—love, brotherhood and justice—as an example to the world; and Danilo gave the vision substance, translating it into a kind of radial city on paper. As a first step he took forty of the older youngsters down to the hilly scrubland overlooking Grosseto, where Don Zeno had bought two hundred acres of wild pig country, and they began building a nucleus village.

The site was known as Ceffarello. It was a high wilderness, stony and rooted in tussock and heavy scrub, looking out over the olives and tidy vineyards of Grosseto plain to Elba and the north tip of Corsica. They tented down and worked by hand, quarrying their own stone, cutting a road up through the scrub, laying down foundations for eleven houses, a school, and a church, working like madmen, eighteen hours out of twenty-four. Don Zeno visited them, well pleased. He was beginning to feel he had found in Danilo someone who might eventually succeed him. Danilo said that some unemployed workmen from the village of Battignano had called, asking for jobs. 'We're not an employment agency,' the priest said, emphatically. A young labourer turned up and pleaded to be taken on. 'Either you take me, or I shoot myself,' he said. 'We can't take you,' Don Zeno said. Danilo argued with him. It was their duty to help *all* the poor, he said. 'That's your idea, Danilo. I don't even accept this principle; we're not a labour exchange.' Danilo persisted, stubbornly. The older man relented, almost huffily. 'All right then, give it a try—but that's not my line.' It was the first serious difference between them.

Danilo went ahead and engaged a dozen labourers, on contract. He was in his element, designing, supervising, surveying fresh sites, holding group discussions in the big recreation tent when it was too wet to work. Eleven buildings were rising and the electric-light tower was completed. The hillside swam with the hot sweat of fraternity in action. '*Men*, not merely stones,' he ruminated, looking out across the valley. Before him rose a vision of the city of the future.

> *High up, by the groves of marine olives*
> *In the scent from the vine-flowers*
> *We will build the city of God*

he wrote.

But Danilo was not, as it turned out, to be its architect. One of the reasons was that the world outside, the one he'd left behind, sent him a reminder notice, and he was called up to do his military service with the postponed 1924 class. Considering his state of mind it isn't surprising, perhaps, that when he reported to the barracks at Siena and was handed the regulation questionnaire, he filled it in:

PATERNITY: God
NUMBER OF BROTHERS: About a billion
NUMBER OF SISTERS: Ditto
PROFESSION: I'm learning to be consumed.

He was the strangest recruit they'd known. He told his superiors he considered military service a polite expression for organised murder, refused to do 'anything soldierly' and said, point blank, 'No shooting, no bayonet practice.' He stuck to his point, and won. He consented to do fire drill and gymnastics. After Don Zeno came to plead Nomadelphia's case Danilo was given liberal weekend leave. Once he came back a week late. He was called before the commanding officer, Colonel Sebastiano Camboso. He explained the needs of Nomadelphia and pointed out that Don Zeno was in trouble. Colonel Camboso was a cultured man and, by chance, had read some of the recruit's poems published in a national anthology. 'Never let it be said,' he remarked, 'that here brute force is a mightier weapon than the spirit.' He shook Danilo by the hand. What with Don Zeno's continued efforts, the help of friends at Siena University, the influence of the poems and Danilo's stubbornness, he did very little service of any kind. In desperation they put him to work as a designer and offered him a pip. Danilo refused the officers' course and stayed with the ranks. During the whole of the token three-months' course his single achievement appears to be an assignment carried out in Rome, abetted by friends from Siena, when he was ordered to design a new regimental standard. It was to show all the battalion emblems, mostly eagles' heads. He was given a car and a driver to go out and buy materials and paints. He finally produced a monstrous caricature—the eagles' heads were enormous, the talons fiercely predatory. Nobody noticed. It was hung proudly in the regimental officers' mess in Rome and, presumably, is still there.

Don Zeno was worried. In 1951, when Danilo was in camp, he had many enemies. He was not an anarchist, nor, as some cardinals in the Vatican and leading members of the new Christian Democrat Government considered, was he mad. He was a Catholic firebrand and a proud descendant of the unorthodox holy tradition of the Piedmontese Don Bosco and the Veronese Don Calabria and the most that could be said of him, in the political field, was that he was bizarre. He despised cant and clericalism, thought all the political parties were tarred with the same bourgeois brush—and ever since 1946 he said so, publicly. It did not endear him to the Vatican, especially after 1948 when the Christian Democrats, the official party of the Church, became all-powerful. Don Zeno, with seventeen Emilian priests, led a minor political revolt, on Nomadelphian principles. It failed. Emilia was militantly Communist. Mario Scelba, the equivocal Home Secretary and Minister of Police (1947–55), and the members of the Rome Curia were hysterically anti-Communist: it was the era when parish priests were encouraged to tell their congregations how the Reds would cut off small boys' heads and gobble up little girls with the *hors d'oeuvres*. Don Zeno's revolutionary Christianity—revolutionary, because actually put into practice—was too much of a bad thing. Inevitably he was suspected of being a Kremlin spy. In 1951, up to his eyebrows in debt, he asked the Government to help him settle his creditors, adding that he had rescued hundreds of children from crime and starvation whom no state institute had wanted or even known about. He had an ally in the Countess Maria Albertoni Pirelli, daughter of the tyre magnate, and to her Scelba made the enlightened statement that he did not approve of Nomadelphia 'from the moral, the social or the political point of view'. He tried to buy the priest out, offering to fix his debts if Don Zeno gave up Nomadelphia. Otherwise . . . the Minister made a firm threat. Don Zeno refused to be blackmailed or neutered, called the Christian Democrats 'heels' and 'anti-Christian' and quietly began ferrying some of the children from Fossoli down to Rosellana, a desolate woodland valley belonging to the Countess and directly underlying the hill of Ceffarello where Danilo was building. But he wasn't quick enough. The cold war with the Government became a hot one. Scelba sent a massive police force to Fossoli, blockaded the camp and, on a pretext of red tape, loaded the children on to lorries and took them to official religious colleges. Don Zeno lost a thousand children in a morning. His creditors took their cue and closed in; his assistant-priests, one by one, were recalled by their bishops. But Don Zeno had not trained as a lawyer for nothing. He spiked both Scelba's and the Vatican's guns by invoking the Italian decree which says it is against the law for a priest to go bankrupt—and promptly went into voluntary liquidation. 'Creditors can wait,' he thundered—'children can't!' He went to court, shouting, 'It's not Nomadelphia that's failed, but the State!', won the case, then threw off his cassock and became a layman. He dispersed the remaining children all over the north of Italy and then mustered them again at Rosellana where the Countess made him a gift of 2,000 acres. Nomadelphia is there today, a thriving creative colony, more than self-sufficient, and the nearest thing to non-marxist communism outside the *kibbutz* system in Israel. Don Zeno is once more a practising priest—he said his second 'first mass' in 1962—and Scelba is no longer in a post of importance.

Above the new Nomadelphia, near Grosseto, today can be seen the scored hill of Ceffarello, and on the skyline the ruins of Danilo's 'city'—the walls of eleven buildings, including the church, which he had intended to call Agape, and the completed light tower, on which someone has chiselled with a pick the motto of the Portuguese Catholic colonisers in South America, *Pasamos por aquí*—'We were here'. From time to time, whenever Danilo's name crops up, a shadow crosses Don Zeno's animated leonine face, and he says as though muttering to himself, 'If he'd stayed with us, he would have been precious.'

Danilo came out of camp in the summer of 1951 when the cold war between Don Zeno and the Government was at its height. A first colony of mothers and children from Fossoli was already tenting in the valley of Rosellana. They didn't use the dwellings at Ceffarello —Don Zeno had bought this land but never got round to paying for it, and when the credit squeeze took hold building stopped abruptly. Reluctantly Danilo dismissed the workmen and abandoned the site.

He took his building force on to the valley floor below, joined up with the others and they all began hacking a third Nomadelphia out of the wilderness. There were half a dozen mothers and a communal force of about a hundred and fifty, nearly all youngsters. The majority lived in tents. There was a farmhouse and one or two outbuildings. The rest was virgin bush and stone, hill scrub and fenland. The scrub ran for kilometres. 'We must have order!' Don Zeno pronounced. Boys of fourteen drove caterpillars, loaded stone on to lorries and assembled prefabs. ('Who knows?' Don Zeno told Danilo. 'We may have to move again.') Danilo's group grew to sixty and was the new agricultural arm. That autumn there were freak rains and throughout the district peasants walked off their land and declared the sowing of wheat and barley impossible. At Rosellana a tractor was bogged down and lost from sight. Danilo's group went on to the hillsides and sowed the entire crop by hand.

Gradually out of the wilderness came the breath of life: the children were repatterned into families, the stones became foundations of new houses, the scrubland became grain.

Don Zeno was then confident he could evacuate Fossoli completely in time to avert the coming storm. Danilo missed that battle. He was locked in a private war of his own. For the second time fever gripped him. 'Every day,' he reasoned, 'there are men from the villages with destitute families coming here and asking to be taken on. We have two courses—to accept or to refuse. We refuse them. Why? Because their moral convictions are different. We don't even *try* to solve their problem.' Finally, he went to Don Zeno and said, 'I'm thinking of leaving.' Don Zeno was sitting in his tent, writing. There was a brief exchange, pungent, not bitter. Danilo said he wasn't responding any more, that Nomadelphia was committed to a limited Catholic morality which argued only to the converted and which took no account of social problems outside. He felt he had to get out and help *all* classes of men. The older man snorted and advised him not to put the cart before the horse. 'You want social change—that's not a religious problem at all, Danilo. Everywhere you find social improvements and bad societies. We say—first, fraternity; then, social change. In that order. Don't mix them up. To build a social revolution *and* a new people there's only one way— and that's *here*.'

They were two obstinate men. Don Zeno took the young plant and nurtured it; Danilo wanted to straighten out the jungle. Their paths were quite different. It was painful for both of them.

Danilo said later: 'It wasn't so much that Nomadelphia excluded non-Catholics. Sometimes it seemed so good, so perfect, that bit by bit the children and adults formed the opinion they'd *achieved perfection*; and this perfection became enclosed, and a kind of pride— not in him, but in the others. It was mistaken, it was lost—and I felt empty.'

Don Zeno said later: 'We're not a closed shop—we're closed only to non-Catholics. With Danilo his idea was you could form a community even with different religions. It was a case of seeing and not seeing. But he had this driving force inside him, this force to be useful to humanity. And he *had* to go because of this—this in him.'

Danilo left Nomadelphia at the beginning of 1952. He gave all his books and music, several hundredweight of them, to Don Zeno for the library and caught a train, third-class, to Tortona. He went home, had a fresh row with his parents, and then north to look at the area round Ancona. But the villages he saw 'weren't poor enough'. He remembered Trappeto, in Sicily. He wrote to some of the fishermen to say he was coming.

He left Nomadelphia as he had come, quietly. The youngsters, who'd come to look on him as a kind of father, heard that he was not returning from Virgilio, one of the Ceffarello builders. They took Virgilio's news gloomily. 'He told me to tell Don Zeno not to worry. "Not to worry," he said, those were his words—"Tell him I'm going to become a priest." ' The group listened. Virgilio went on: 'All he had with him was a woman's basket, a skiddly *woman's* basket, and some olives and dried figs. And he got into third. I felt somehow ashamed, seeing him go off like that, like a——'

'Like a what?' someone said.

Virgilio hunched his shoulders and thought about it. 'Like a Gandhi,' he said at length.

PART II

Who shouts loudest, is right
                              —Sicilian proverb

FOUR

Among the Untouchables

DOLCI stepped off the one o'clock train at Trappeto in February 1952. He was wearing an old jersey and a pair of baggy strides and carried a few old clothes in Grandad's case. He had thirty lire in his pocket—fourpence. Some of the fishermen were there to meet him—young Paolino, Toni 'the philosopher', Leonardo, 'son of the blind one', Peppino Russo, Giuseppe Scardino and one or two others. They were all related. They embraced him warmly and he told them he'd come to stay. The fishermen scratched their ears. 'I've come to live among you, as a brother,' Dolci said.

They took him off round the village. He agreed, after persuasion, to spend the first few nights with the Scardino family. They squeezed him into a back alcove and he shared their single-room dwelling with the hens and three other sons. For the first two days he did nothing but walk round, talking to people. The knot of fishermen clung to him.

Trappeto, facing Castellammare Bay, thirty miles from Palermo, had some 2,800 inhabitants. People were living in conditions which no qualified vet would recommend for animals. He saw cubist patterns on sheets hanging over the alleys, looked closer and saw they were patches of patches of patches over patches. Rooms 4 yards square had beaten earth floors, ark-like sticks of furniture and no water. The word 'lavatory' was practically unknown. Antediluvian dressers leaned up behind pale fly-screens, laden with the monstrous bric-à-brac of the poor: old work-tools, outdated calendars, empty sauce tins, combs as big as rakes, clocks which had stopped when the Americans landed. Women who had never learned to sew sat mending on the step, using stitches half an inch long. Chairs which nobody used sat funereally round the walls. The rooms were dark and smelled. Most were partitioned for the mule or the pig; hens skittered under tables and larger animals emerged from the shadows. From behind the fly-screens the children and the elders watched. Everywhere blank faces, watching.

There was something else, something beyond the mere smell of poverty. Dolci couldn't put his finger on it.

A woman with five children said—Paolino was translating the

43

dialect into Italian: 'We eat twice usually—bread, straight, in the morning; at night a plate of spaghetti, sometimes coloured with sauce or beans. Today we haven't eaten yet.' It was a quarter to six in the evening. 'Do you ever have meat?' Dolci asked. The woman snorted. 'At Christmas.' She went on, 'At night we stand outside to get away from the smell. The kids play all weathers—over there, in the Vallone. It stinks there too, but it's a better stink than the one inside.'

The Vallone was an open canal, almost wide enough for a small boat, which ran through the middle of the village. It was drain, sewer, rubbish tip and children's playground. The kids played among hens and pigs at the bottom of the filth, often naked. 'Down there,' Paolino said, 'where Giustina's standing, the stuff often comes into the houses.' Giustina's husband was in prison, Paolino said. Dolci looked at her, nodded and went on walking round.

'If we hadn't been baptised we'd be no better than animals that talk,' someone said.

'Why were so many men in prison?' he asked. 'When the young ones cry we steal for them,' he was told.

A woman whose husband and four sons had earned a total of six pounds in the previous four months said they had been waiting to be put on poor relief for 29 years.

In one family of seven nobody had had as much as a day's schooling. 'I was barefooted, so the teacher used to send me home,' a girl of fifteen said.

'What do you do when you're not working?' Dolci asked everywhere. 'I go to bed,' one said, suspecting a trap; 'I'm not the sort of man who goes out to steal wood.' But the invariable reply was 'Nothing.'

'Do you have a bit of land?' he asked one man. 'Yes—in the cemetery, when I'm dead.'

Everywhere despair, a deep brooding on injustice, the feeling—real and imagined—of being forgotten, left out, of being put upon by the *signori*—the proprietors, the local authorities, the Government. By *them*. The feeling of being an untouchable.

Did they want anything then? he wondered. And if so, what? He asked, 'What do you want most?' A young girl smiled, without replying. A man of sixty seemed at first not to understand; then he decided: 'I'd like a pair of shoes, size nine.' A woman said: 'I want a new bed, complete with bedding.' A neighbour explained: 'Her husband died in it, you see, and they burned the bed and everything on it.'

Don Zeno had said: 'If you go south, Danilo, I think these are places you have to live in for a long, long time before you begin to understand them . . .'

Not everybody was poor. This too he noted, moving round.

He learned to talk with his mouth almost shut. 'When you walked along,' he says, 'the flies rose up and settled again after you'd gone. All the streets were streets and drains at the same time. People didn't know what a sewer was. And always a halo of flies. Black stains on the ground where the mules had passed. They rose and settled, rose and settled. You had to be careful how you opened your mouth . . .'

There was no chemist and no telephone, no library, no nursery school, no newsagent; and when he went into the only café it was unable to muster a cup of coffee. Children of seven regarded him curiously when he said 'Hullo', and he saw in their tired eyes the faces of adults of forty. Others, the spindly results of malnutrition, looked only half their years. He suspected that child mortality was high.

The fishermen took him down to the tiny rock beach. He remembered it well—the scrabbly coloured boats, drawn on to the shingle, painted and chipped with religious legends, the big kerosene lamps, the black nets. On the parapet above, fifty or sixty men gathered round him; there were warm words of recognition, handshakes, smiles—and general incomprehension when Paolino said he'd 'come to stay'.

They offered him tobacco. Dolci said he didn't smoke. 'Once I saw my father get in a rage because he'd run out of cigarettes, and I decided then I'd never take it up, for this reason.' They thought he was a bit odd.

They fished at night, they said, and sold their catch on the beach at dawn to the Palermo buyers. Most of the village took its livelihood from the sea. In winter they doubled as peasants. There were only the two jobs. Everyone did a bit of both.

Dolci explained his idea of opening a house where the needy would be fed and clothed and live together in brotherly love, which was the basis of true religion. A kind of community. There was silence. A community? What was that?

'You won't get far if you try to change things in this place,' someone said.

'Well, it sounds very fine to me, whatever it is,' Toni observed.

They began talking, all at once.

'If we're lucky we get fish on a hundred days of the year.'

'You see, Danilo,' Leonardo began, 'the Sicilian is born with this system, he——'

45

'A hundred and fifty at the most.'

'The fishing's being ruined by the trawlers.'

'He's born with this system, he grows up with this system, and——'

'They come within the limit, against the law.'

'Nobody cares.'

'We ask God for good health and providence, but nothing's ever done.'

'They come right inshore. Farther out they use bombs.'

'Bombs?' Dolci asked. 'How long's this been going on?'

'Ever since the war, since Mr. Dolci left.'

Leonardo said again: 'We're born with this system, we grow up with this system, and the responsibility for every darn thing falls on the man.'

For the hundredth time Dolci asked: 'What do you want most?'

'Work,' the fishermen said.

When Gandhi arrived back in India from South Africa in 1915 he spent his first year there with 'his ears open but his mouth shut'. It was the wisest thing he could have done.

Circumstances in Trappeto did not allow Dolci to follow Gandhi's example. He had little time to stop and consider his motives. Though he sensed, beneath the resignation, a kind of stoicism, his first reaction was that the situation was critical. He had to act, and act quickly.

When the confusing grains of evidence whirring in his brain had subsided, he picked out the two biggest bits. One was the desire for work. Of this he was convinced, in spite of a basic northerner's prejudice that southerners, especially Sicilian southerners, were 'idle'. The other problem was malnutrition. Children were wasting away in the alleys, were slowly starving. There was no money to buy medicines. Many were orphans. Food was needed, clothes, shoes, bedding, shelter. Quickly.

'We need a house to take in the needy,' he told the fishermen.

'Yes, yes, that's right,' they said.

'But there isn't one,' Paolino added, with Sicilian logic.

'We'll build one.'

'But you haven't got any money, Danilo.'

'I'll get some,' Dolci said.

They found him a site just outside the village. It was a wide shelf on top of a hill, harboured by olives and facing the sea. The owner wanted £210 for the land. Dolci borrowed enough money for his train fare and went north. He went home, and then to Milan where his former professor of architecture gave him sixty pounds. With this he returned to Trappeto, put it down as deposit, signed promissory notes for the rest and took possession of the land. He put up a tent and became a Sicilian 'resident'. From that day, in the spring of 1952, his troubles began.

The following Sunday many villagers came up to see the stranger in his tent. Even the mayor, and the archpriest of the next village, Balestrate, came. Describing this later, in *The Story of Borgo di Dio*, Paolino and Toni say: 'Everyone was pleased and they asked him what he planned to do. He told them everything and the mayor said he, for one, would do all he could to help.

'The next day Danilo fixed it with a mason to start on the house and the mason said he would work even if there were no wages—he was willing to wait on Providence, he said. ("Until it rains," as we say round here.) A man in Alcamo and another in Balestrate gave Danilo the lime for the mortar on credit . . . Two days later he went to Mazzara del Vallo for two wagon-loads of *tufo* building stone, asking them to send it COD, trusting that the money to pay for it would arrive about the same time as the stone did—otherwise he would have had to pay for the stuff to sit in the wagons at £2 7s. a day. But when the time came some friends lent him the money. And that's how it was with everything.

'When the stone was unloaded he was the first to grab a pick and start working, him and two others. There was a bit of a mule track up to the site, but when the horses were laden with stone they couldn't manage the last bit where the track petered out so Danilo and the others carried the stuff the rest of the way on their backs.'

Giovanni Piergallini, a wiry, drifting orphan from Lombardy, arrived out of the blue, and fresh from prison. This pallid foot-loose youth, an atheist, had had several stopovers in jail, for want of means and a fixed abode. He found his first spiritual home in Dolci's tent, and for more than three years gave himself to the work as no other volunteer did. Giovanni was the first veteran helper. He was followed almost immediately by Franco, the young Turin mechanic. Franco had written down, saying he was married and had a child, but little money. Dolci replied, saying, 'Come and look round.' Franco came for a month and stayed until his money ran out six months later. In 1956 he came back again, for good.

They worked on the house for a month and a half. As soon as the roof was on Dolci and Co. moved in.

He was in and out of the village every day, often sleeping there. He saw terrible quarrels. People fought each other in the ditches. A woman of 47 whose first daughter died of an abscess at eighteen months said: 'A year and a half later I lost a little boy of six. His throat was hurting and the doctor said it was meningitis, but at Palermo they said it was tetanus. When this one died I was pregnant and the shock took hold of the heart of the one unborn. Eight days after birth its feet were all swollen. The doctor said that it had a sick heart: "He'll die sooner or later," the doctor said. When the doctor came back he did die. Two years later I had another baby and as it was wartime, what hope was there of finding a doctor? At four months he got dysentery and sores all round the mouth. His sucking infected my breasts and the milk gave out altogether. At the children's hospital in Palermo they told me to leave him there, but I didn't want to leave him alone and brought him home again. I took him round the neighbours to be fed and after four days he was dead.'

Dolci began to believe it was possible for despair and hunger and blind feeling ignorance to drive people to anything.

He began fetching medicines from the chemist at Balestrate, five miles away. He told the chemist what he told everyone else—that he'd pay when God was willing. If the chemist refused him he'd bang on doors and badger people until he got what he wanted. Children now recognised his beret from a distance and would run after him, shouting 'Hullo, Danilo!' With the youngest he'd bend down and wipe their noses, as Don Zeno had done at Nomadelphia, and then he'd kiss them. The village watched and wondered.

He and Franco were sent for one day and brought to a basement at the bottom of the Vallone. The sewage water sludged past and seeped over the doorstep into the room. The room was dark. He made out humid stained walls and, in a corner, a slender young woman holding a baby a few weeks old. Her name was Giustina Barretta. She was 22. It was her first child. Since the baby was born she had eaten only a bit of bread and pasta the neighbours had given her. Her milk had dried up and the baby no longer had the strength to suck. Dolci ran to get powdered milk. They tried to give the milk to the baby, but at every attempt it vomited. They put the child on the bed, a palliasse laid on planks, and Franco went for the doctor. Dolci sat with Giustina.

While they were waiting for the doctor the child died.

The incident haunts Dolci still. 'I would never have believed if I hadn't seen it that a child might actually die of starvation,' he says. 'I can still see that woman—her hair, wild, her features, quite yellow, she no longer had the strength to shout or scream. She'd lost even the capacity to react. And this was the terrible thing—I didn't realise it till later, of course—that underneath ordinary misery was this hidden layer, a deeper stratum; and this was a mass thing, it had to do with the very *structure* of poverty.'

Although the incident, only one of a series of shocks, was not traumatically decisive for him—as is usually written—it was to affect his attitude to the whole Sicilian situation.

In the village people said Giustina's child had died of 'the black sickness'. It was 'just tiny', they said, as though there were some natural law by which tiny babies had to die.

FIVE

Borgo di Dio

OFTEN when Dolci went to Palermo for materials for the house he had to borrow his train fare from one of the fishermen. His father kept sending down money and toilet gifts, but just as he found it impossible to accept food from fisherfolk if it meant their going without, so he would not accept the gifts. He gave them away.

As the house grew so did his enthusiasm, and poetic fancy. Giovanni says: 'He'd told me there was already a co-operative of fishermen, a school, a house ready—everything. But when I got there in May there was a tent and two pieces of wall just off the ground, and nothing else. I didn't worry. I realised that the things he'd planned were still only in his mind.'

Dolci laid in beds, furniture, bathroom fittings, all on instalment. Initially, the local assistance board helped.

He was down in the village one day when he heard screams. A woman was holding a child with one hand and tearing at her hair with the other, shrieking in the street as her husband was being taken off to prison. He had stolen a bunch of grapes. Dolci persuaded the police to release the man and gave him a job.

They began work on a road up to the house. 'At first about twenty men came along,' Paolino and Toni relate, 'and he said to them: "I haven't a bean to pay you with, but if you want a job I'll give you wages just as soon as Providence sends me the money." The store-keepers staked the men in food, trusting that Danilo would eventually make good his promise . . . A few days went by and there were no longer twenty labourers but forty. In the end eighty men a day came to work there, until there was hardly enough room between them to swing a pick. There was no other work available . . .'

The house was low and L-shaped. It rose 150 feet above Castellammare Bay on a secluded shelf of carob and olive trees. It was simple and unostentatious.

He called it *Borgo di Dio*—Hamlet of God. It was constituted as an official organisation, with three aims: to house the needy, find work for the unemployed, and spread the Christian doctrine.

Even before Borgo was finished the first occupants moved in—Giustina and her husband Mimi. The following day Vincenzina

50

arrived with five children. Vincenzina Mangano was in heavy mourning. She was a peasant widow in her late twenties, handsome, with sturdy features and a resilient pose. Her tiny legs made her seem stockier than she actually was. Her husband, Luciano, had died at 34, following an attack by masked bandits. He was surprised in the fields while ploughing, made to lie down and heavily beaten when he refused to blackmail his employer. The shock, with recurrent fever, brought a slow and painful death four months later.

Vincenzina's five children were the first to be taken in. Within a week there were fifteen children at Borgo. They came from Trappeto and Partinico and Borgetto, the children of bandits and the children of the men the bandits had killed. When they saw whole loaves of bread on the table they took half a loaf and put it under their pillows to keep for the morning, because they couldn't imagine waking up and having still more bread the next day. 'These children,' Dolci says, 'you had to teach them to wipe their bottoms. When they were taken to the lavatory they screamed. To wipe their bottoms they used their fingers and then they cleaned their fingers on the wall. So we had to start their education from there.'

Giustina and Vincenzina kept house and looked after the children. The news of Borgo spread. So many women with husbands in prison brought their children that Dolci had to put them off until he had enough workers to start day sessions. Visitors from the north came and went, a little mystified by what Don Zeno's young revolutionary was hoping to achieve. Dolci yet had no clear idea himself. He was like a giant harbour of love, with the entrance lights constantly flashing, praying to God to send him cargo and no more freight charges. There were prayers daily, family visits to mass on Sundays and the Gospel of brotherly love. 'If we try to think and live as God wishes,' he told everyone, 'sharing everything alike, then we *shall* live together.'

The lesson didn't always go home. Giustina's parents came to Borgo, leaving their house in Trappeto empty. Dolci suggested they give it to another family whose house was falling down. The parents objected; the other family was 'dirty', they said. Giustina's parents went back to live in Trappeto.

Borgo was the first building in Trappeto to have a bath. When the furniture and fittings were finished half the village trooped up again to see.

Dolci asked the priest, Father Angelo Donato, if he might try the small organ in the church. The priest agreed. Dolci became the

official organist for mass. On other occasions he would slip down to
the church in the daytime, a score under his arm, and bestir the
wheezy cottage organ. The locals passing by would stop and listen,
marvelling at the sound coming from within, much as did the New
Zealand high country shepherds a century before when Samuel
Butler locked himself away in the South Canterbury ranges and
played fugues late into the night. The shepherds thought Butler
was balmy. The Trappeto fisherfolk were similarly puzzled. They
had never heard Bach before.

A nucleus of fishermen, however, was coming to regard Dolci as a
deeply religious man with high moral principles; a man of conti-
nence, who never smoked or drank and, most remarkable, in an environment where everybody shouted or screamed, never raised his
voice. He was always going somewhere, doing something, thinking
something, yet his unlined nordic face was almost always in repose.
He never seemed in a hurry. The fishermen saw him as someone
who could overcome any obstacle and his pensive voice gave them a
feeling of security. It had a saintly quality.

The children at Borgo found they were not neglected or beaten,
but were treated as individuals. Matteo, Vincenzina's second son,
was then about eleven. He had been in a religious college run by
nuns. He says: 'If we didn't say our rosaries right we were put to
bed without supper. One mealtime I was caught talking—or I
didn't like the food, I don't remember—and they made me come
out, me and another boy, and kneel down on the refectory floor in
front of everyone, with our hands cupped under our knees—like this.
Under our hands they put the shells of broken almonds. Then one
day my mother fetched me and brought me up to Borgo. I didn't
know how to take Danilo at first, but then suddenly I felt happy
there, lifted up—free.'

Dolci bought a second-hand accordion, on credit, and gave the
children music; he began to stock a library for the villagers in
Borgo's big room, 20 feet by 18 feet, and to plan another building to
house the volunteer helpers.

He acquired a blue motor-scooter, on which he and Franco,
sometimes both, swathed in old overcoats, berets and scarves, would
career over the low hills to Partinico and elsewhere on errands of
mercy. 'Once,' Franco says, 'we had to go to Palermo and there was
no money for petrol. I borrowed a litre here and a litre there and
put in a bit of olive oil, and in Palermo a friend lent us one and six
for a meal. Then we hadn't enough petrol to get back. So I found
four stamps in my briefcase—four threepenny stamps, right?—and
we sold them back to the tobacco shop and got a shilling's worth of

petrol. But it wasn't enough and we pushed the scooter the last few miles.'

Often they were days on end without money; bread was short at mealtimes, the children without shoes. Once their plight was so bad that when one baker refused credit Dolci wept at the counter, it is said, until he was given bread. His debts grew. Two men arrived from Palermo and demanded the furniture back unless he paid up on the spot. They grabbed him by the shoulders and tried to bang his head up against the library wall. Dolci, strong enough to hurl both men through the window, shook them off and told them they could have the motor-scooter as part payment. The men took the scooter and went off cursing. Later, when he was able to pay for the furniture, they gave him back the scooter, and he bought more fittings from the same shop.

The children were taken into the country, shown the flowers, the stars, were taught to design. The etchings young Matteo did then today symbolise the Dolci organisation on postcards which are sent all over the world. Matteo, the son of an illiterate peasant killed by bandits, is now a professional designer in Milan.

There was a danger in all this. Dolci had begun to create a kind of oasis, removed from the reality he was hoping to change. The revolution of Borgo, with its individual hand-to-mouth charity, its mixed bag of helpers, all untrained, all plunged urgently to work before they had time to understand the complex morality of the place, was to cost him dearly.

Giovanni and others had begun an inquiry in Trappeto and were bringing back incredible reports. People were living on as little as sevenpence a day. Children at ten or over didn't know how to write their own names or make the sign of the cross. Schoolteachers arrived halfway through the morning and some did not bother to come at all. Gaspare, a peasant, who had developed fluid on the lung, told them he had been given a cursory examination at Balestrate and sent back to Trappeto, where a local doctor came to draw off the fluid. 'He came along with his instruments, not a kitful, just a syringe and an old needle, and he began to poke into me. The first jab got me in the ribs. The second one was all right, but didn't manage to find the fluid immediately and he began to waggle the thing up and down until the needle broke off inside. Then he panicked so much he didn't even think to make a small cut to remove the other piece—you could see the broken bit. But he was terrified and had me sent off to the first-aid post in Palermo. There they X-rayed me for over two hours, twisting and turning me about until they located the needle. They said it meant an operation—they said they'd operate before midnight. Midnight came and they didn't operate. Nothing happened. The needle stayed put and I've had it inside me for more than five years . . .' In hospital, Gaspare said, he was treated for pleurisy. After twenty days he went home to help his wife through childbirth (the baby subsequently died of leukaemia) and took up cobbling. After a few months he had chronic TB. He went back to hospital and an operation was proposed, 'but neither the family nor any of my relatives would hear of it'. When Giovanni found him in Trappeto he was propped in bed in a narrow alcove, spitting up blood. The roof was falling in, and when it rained the water fell directly on to the bed. His wife was also ill. The family had no regular assistance and didn't know how to set about getting a pension.

Reports like these roused Dolci anew. 'Must we wait,' he wrote in his diary, 'until they rise up in revolt, maddened by hunger and misery, before we turn to and help them find work so they can save their families? Must we wait until they end up in the sanatoriums and the prisons?'

Autumn came, then late autumn, and the brief harvest of strong white wine led into the slack land season. 'The worst season of the year is still ahead; there are many unemployed; and what hope have they of finding work?' Unemployment rose. Sporadic crime increased. A middle-aged farmer, when he refused to pay two million lire (£1,200) extortion money, had his mule killed and a little later his vines cut down; above the limp vines was left a bamboo cross warning him not to go back to his land or he, too, would be killed.

And at Borgo: 'Oil, tomatoes, pasta, must be bought. Who cares? There aren't enough bunks; there aren't enough mattresses; there aren't enough sheets. Who cares?

'The tiny ones, who still mess in their pants, need several changes if they're to be kept clean. Who's going to buy the stuff? And the spoons and forks, if they're not to eat with their fingers? And the pens and pencils and the writing-paper, if they're not to grow into suspicious half-savages? Who *cares*?'

He saw that there was a solution to one of these problems, perhaps both. The people had only to use the waters of a stream, the River Iato, which ran to waste in the sea and there would be work for everybody. He drew up plans for an irrigation scheme. In summer, he reckoned, a forty-horsepower pump could raise the level of the water 180 feet in 150 seconds, irrigating 750 acres of dry land. Year after year the priest had been holding a special service, '*ad petendam pluviam*' (to pray for rain) and all the people knelt to pray '*ad petendam pluviam*', murmuring Latin words they did not understand, to solve a problem which a forty-horsepower pump could have solved in two and a half minutes.

Men *could* intervene to change things, he told the peasants.

For centuries they had been growing corn and beans on arid plain-land in unvarying rotation. 'Look,' he said, 'an acre of land growing corn needs only twelve working days a year. But if it's irrigated and produces vegetables it can stand perhaps as many as two hundred and fifty days a year. Don't you see?'

The peasants did not see. Irrigation and 'things like that' be-longed to the *signori*. Water belonged among the saints. 'Water is another God,' they said.

The priest did not see either. Dolci made application for the right to use the water. The local authorities were not interested.

Men came to Dolci asking for work, and kept on coming. He had none to give them. He called a meeting at Borgo and told the men there was no work and no possibility of any. In that case, they said, other children would die of hunger.

Dolci prayed.

Finally, he knew what he had to do. He sat down and wrote a letter. In it he asked for enough money to provide immediate work and relief for the village. Then he walked down to the village and into the basement that had been Giustina's house at the bottom of the Vallone. He lay down on the palliasse where the child had died and refused to eat until help, or death, came.

First Fast

Trappeto, 14 October 1952

Dearest friends,

I am a sinner but God will bear me out when I say I want nothing more than that I may die in order that you may all live . . .

We can stop these children being forced to leave school at seven or eight to become assistant-breadwinners.

We can very largely stop the prisons from filling up.

We can stop the ravages of death.

Would you pummel a person to cure him of pneumonia?

We must redeem and repent for this sin of omission towards our own brothers. We must save them and save ourselves by learning to love.

We must act at once. Urgent cases mean urgent treatment. I want to do penance in order that everyone may become more perfect. In the meantime rather than see another child die of hunger I would rather die myself. As from today I will not eat another mouthful until the £18,000 required to employ the neediest and help the most urgent cases has arrived.

When someone is about to shoot down a child, and there's no other way, shouldn't you throw yourself in front to save it? . . .

Then, at once! It is too late to go on waiting. Waiting only means more corpses.

If I, by living, cannot awaken people's love then by dying I will arouse their remorse.

Yours in God

DANILO

The letter was printed on a small hand-press in Palermo and sent off to a few friends.

Giustina's room was 8 feet below ground level. In the upper part someone had made a kind of window, an escape hatch in case the sewerage discharge should flood the place suddenly. The floor was earth. Dolci, clad in trousers and a sweater, spent most of the time lying under a blanket, meditating and talking to Franco. Franco had borrowed a bed and was sleeping in the same room.

'Danilo, you must get up and eat,' a woman said. 'You'll never get well lying down like that.'

Women came, with babies in their arms; some brought him food and when they saw he had no intention of eating they broke down and wept. He told them: 'If my own mother came I wouldn't want her in here crying. When you sow grain and the seed is scattered, and you know that the seed will waste away in order to bring forth fruit, aren't you cheerful then?' The women nodded. 'Well, then— a fast is the same. It's a strong thing, a joy.' He forbade them to come in weeping and told Franco to bring down the accordion from Borgo. Thereafter he played the accordion—dance tunes, mazurkas and waltzes—daily. He told everybody he felt calm and happy.

The village women never quite understood. They never got past the idea that he was doing penitence for the Madonna.

The news did not travel quickly or well. This was not surprising. Under fascism northerners seldom heard of the poverty of southern Italy and in 1952 they were scarcely better informed. Italian sociology and culture seldom probed beyond Naples. Sicily was that pernicious appendage at the bottom, land of robbers and police-men. Who in 1952 was likely to get worked up by skimpy reports about an accordion-playing crank, starving to save a tinpot village alongside Africa? The answer was, almost nobody.

On the third day Franco and others went to Palermo to try and raise the money. They came back downcast. 'There are other ways of setting about things than fasting,' officials told them. The Trappeto authorities were no help. They were not all there. The priest and the police sergeant had vanished, and were not seen in the village again until the fast was over.

Dolci was outwardly cheerful. He wrote, talked, got up, walked about, played the accordion and thought about everything except conserving his strength. As the days passed the villagers noticed that the tunes were becoming sadder and sadder. Women began to pray in the houses for him. 'He's too young to die,' they said. Vincenzina, the young widow, and Giustina took turns to visit him. Some of the fishermen proposed a public demonstration in the capital. 'Where is your faith?' Dolci said. They then pledged that should he die one of them would carry on fasting in his place. First Paolino, then Leonardo. 'Him first, and then us,' they said.

The mail brought little hope. Hardly any of those to whom the letter was sent bothered to reply. This upset him more than the in-difference of the authorities. 'It shows you, Franco,' he said, 'that we must put our trust in God, not in men.'

The only significant reply was from the pacifist, Aldo Capitini. Capitini had already founded at Perugia a movement for peace. He advised Dolci to stop fasting immediately. 'You've no right to throw your life away like this without first informing the public properly of the facts,' Capitini wrote, beginning a correspondence which was to have a big effect on Dolci's development.

Franco went to see Cardinal Ruffini, one of the most powerful men on the island. Not long before this, Ruffini had denounced the squalid conditions of many Sicilian families, granting land and money for rehousing in Palermo and calling for 'Christian action . . . to wipe a horrible reality *immediately* off the face of the earth.'

When he called at the archbishop's palace, Franco says, the Cardinal refused to see him because he was 'improperly dressed'.

After five days Dolci was visited by a young man called Mignosi, secretary to Alessi, an eminent Right-wing politician and a former Sicilian Prime Minister. Alessi (the present Senator) had a key post in the Christian Democrat party. Mignosi had read some of Dolci's poetry and, convinced he was not a crank, was moved to act. The case recalls that of Oscar Wilde whose *Salome* was produced in Paris while Wilde was in Reading Jail. On release Wilde said: 'In prison it had been entirely forgotten that I was a literary person; but when they saw that my play was a success in Paris they said to one another, "Well, but this is strange—he has talent, then." '

Mignosi told Dolci he had taken on too much and that nothing could be done unless he stopped fasting.

'Less than an hour's drive from here, where you've just come from,' Dolci said, 'there are bright lights, motor-cars and luxury by the windowful. Go for a walk round Trappeto and see the difference. He added: 'These people are all sons of God, like you and I, and children are dying here. Whoever knows this—and now the authorities *know*—and leaves them be, is an assassin.'

Mignosi said he would do all he could. 'But you must stop fasting.'

'Before anything will be done, someone's got to die,' Dolci said.

Dolci became weaker, and the accordion tunes petered out altogether. He continued to tell Franco that he was well.

Normally, given a relaxed body and adequate mental preparation, a fit person can starve for up to ten days without danger. Dolci had read *about* fasting. That was all. His preparation had been wholly religious. His technique was nil. This was a hunger strike in the raw and it frightened the wits out of young Franco. The Turin mechanic ministered to Dolci like a mother and grew pale with worry. Villagers hung about outside in small whispering groups. Many were now afraid to enter the room. Police constables watched the house day and night.

Towards evening on the seventh day Dolci became light-headed. It amazed him that he could still think lucidly—he said so to Franco. They put the light out at ten and dropped off to sleep with the noise of the sewage waters, rushing over the doorstep, in their ears. Dolci slept soundly. About half past two in the morning he woke suddenly and called out hoarsely to Franco.

'I turned on the light and went to his side,' Franco says. 'His hands were cold, his feet were cold, he was shaking all over. His breath came in gasps and his right arm and part of the right leg were paralysed.' Franco ran out in his pyjamas for the doctor. When the doctor arrived Dolci was unconscious. The doctor took the pulse and the heartbeats, declaring the one 'hanging by a thread' and the other 'imperceptible', administered some drops and a camphor injection and, when Dolci came round, harangued him at length about the need to begin eating. Dolci closed his eyes, opened them and said, No. The doctor sat down and wrote out a memorandum stating that the patient was dying and the fast had to be stopped immediately.

'How long . . .?' Franco started to say.

The doctor squeezed his upper body and jaw into one of those Sicilian gestures which disclaim responsibility, say nothing and everything at the same time, and went back to his bed.

Franco took the memorandum straight to Alessi. Late that afternoon, the eighth day, Dolci, resting fitfully, was roused by the arrival of Mignosi. With him was a welfare priest, Monsignor Arena, who said he was acting for the Prime Minister, Restivo.

'The Hon. Restivo wishes me to assure you of his full co-operation to relieve the desperate plight of this zone,' Arena said.

'Thank you,' Dolci said softly.

Arena said the Prime Minister guaranteed to grant £1,000 immediately, to care for the extreme needy whom Borgo could not accommodate, to open a work depot for 67 men, and to subsidise a project to harness the waters of the Iato for irrigation.

The last was the vital point. Above Trappeto the irrigation of a stony plain could transform 1,200 acres of sterile land into market gardens and orchards, providing work for over a thousand men and ending the unemployment.

Dolci thanked his visitors and asked them to wait outside while he talked it over with the others. A small group of fishermen came in. They had to strain to catch the words. 'Now don't accept this offer just on my account,' he told them. 'But if you're satisfied, I'm satisfied, and I'll get up and start eating.'

'What does it all mean?' Paolino asked.

Franco had scribbled down some figures. 'If these men are sincere,' Dolci said, 'the Government will meet nearly all the expenses of the works: Franco's worked it out—about £18,000, which is what we asked for. This is what they have promised.'

'We think it's fair,' Paolino said.

Dolci did too. He called the visitors back, accepted their pledge and said he would break the fast the following day.

'You're a brave man, Mr. Dolci,' Monsignor Arena said. 'The Prime Minister asked me to say also that when you are well he would like to meet you in Palermo.'

Dolci had not fasted merely to save Trappeto. He fasted for a creative principle—to redeem those who were blind to, or ignorant of, the sin of their own omission. There is a similarity to Gandhi's first fast in a public cause, in the foothills of the Himalayas in 1917. Gandhi fasted—his biographer, Fischer, writes—not so much to improve conditions for the textile workers as to cure the employers of their unwarranted objection to an arbitration system which would promote peace in the textile industry. 'I fasted to reform those who loved me,' Gandhi said.

More than anything Dolci's first fast was an act of love.

Villagers reported afterwards that when the two intermediaries, Arena the priest and Mignosi the state official, came out of the room, before walking up to their car they stood for a few moments looking across the mire of the Vallone where the children were playing; and that one of them made the sign of the cross. But whether in a spirit of blessing, or exorcism, the villagers said, it was too dark to tell.

SEVEN

The Two Dolcis

DOLCI returned to Borgo. After a few days he went to see Restivo and Alessi, both Christian Democrats. The Prime Minister said he would never have dreamed that a river might run to waste in the sea while, alongside, people starved. He praised Dolci's 'statesmanship' and said he had chosen a tragic area. Alas, he said, all of Sicily was poor.

It was to be more than six years before a Roman doctor, Silvio Pampiglione, revealed to both of them that, compared to the *miseria* of a town like Palma di Montechiaro, Trappeto was just a fleabite.

Works officials came to Trappeto and made preliminary surveys to pump the water from the Iato. Dolci drew up the deeds for a development syndicate among the farmers whose land would be irrigated. The promised thousand pounds arrived and in 1953 Trappeto got its first streets, its first drains, its first telephone and a chemist's shop.

At Borgo, they dispensed clothes, medicines and powdered milk which dribbled down from friends in the north. 'Simple charity,' someone said. A wagon-load of old clothes sent by Quakers arrived at the station one night. When they had sorted it the stuff filled the big room at Borgo, over 40 feet long. Next morning at six the villagers came up the hill at a gallop for their quota. Paolino attempted to distribute the parcels fairly, through a window, but got jammed and was nearly lynched.

Already there were two Dolcis in action, more or less irreconcilable. There was Dolci the apostle, community-builder, organist and good Catholic. There was Dolci the technician, irrigation-planner, sociologist and freelance trade union unto himself. In practical terms the only common meeting-point was his creed, '*Participate*, in order to understand.' It wasn't enough. A year after coming south he was still beside the same crossroads he had found on entering—one signpost said immediate Christian need; the other, long-distance social planning. Dolci, no longer directed by a Don Zeno, veered off on to a lone, if inspired, path of his own somewhere down the middle. Unwittingly, he compromised.

With anyone less single-minded it would have been fatal. As it was there were rifts. The do-gooders—in Dolci's words 'those who came to share but not to change'—were always at odds with him. They saw the contradiction in him and criticised his insistence on technological change *as well as* Christian charity. One or the other, they said, echoing Don Zeno. Carlo, a Roman helper, wanted to build a vast chicken hatchery; he thought you could combine meditation with making a living. Dolci pursued his own path. The critics invariably left. They said they did not understand him.

Reflecting now, he says: 'Nomadelphia—the fraternity ideal— matured inside me like a raging fire; and I imagined that at thirty I'd be dead. Then at Trappeto—I was already nearly thirty, and I realised that I was still very much alive, that what I had to do was long-term, that I had to reconsider a lot of things. This much is certain—I chose a path between that of giving myself to the people and putting my feet flat on the ground.'

In 1953 Dolci did not even realise there was a hard choice to be made. This ambivalence was to be his private bogey for years to come.

Even without this confusion of motives there were obstacles enough. Dolci's visitors, including the women, *bathed.* Before 1952 Trappeto had never seen a modern female bathing-suit. The people were scandalised. After the visit of Lamberto Borghi, Professor of Education in Florence and one of the leading pedagogists in Italy, Dolci was ridiculed. 'You told us he was a professor,' the Sicilians said, 'but he can't be. No professor would go walking on a beach in *bare feet*.' Dolci's own team contributed to the view that it was all a kind of circus-turn. Simply because he hadn't learned that it was sometimes important to refuse the needy stray (and many early volunteers were as much in need of help, one way and another, as the Sicilians themselves), hadn't learned tact, and selection—because of this Dolci found himself within a year surrounded by a collection of 'types' whose record cast impressive doubts on the sincerity of his aims. One, ironically enough from Nomadelphia, robbed Paolino of most of his money, then vanished. The first Sicilian helper was straight from prison. There was Carlo, a Roman orphan. A dedicated fascist at fifteen, Carlo had ploughed into trouble since, ending up at Borgo a thin, anarchical youth, out on his feet and spurred by a guilt complex and an indefinable blend of mysticism. 'There's good in everybody,' Dolci said. He was right, of course—in theory. As a working principle in Sicily it was calamitous.

'You, Mr. Dolci, I've no complaint about you personally,' the police sergeant said to him. 'But the company you keep . . . it doesn't, you might say, appear to heighten your own *honour-r-a-b-i-lll-i-t-y*.'

Thus whenever Dolci's helpers went to the priest to inquire about local customs or to the carabinieri to discuss the crime rate, they got nowhere. The priest replied that Mr. Dolci had no authority to take such a deep interest in the situation. The sergeant replied that he was not authorised to give a reply.

Sicilian officials have long been trained in the art of gentle rebuff. Additionally, Dolci came from 'the Continent'—that is, the mainland. He was a foreigner. And thus, automatically, an 'exploiter'. He found himself in a little Ireland. Much as the Irish used to resent prying English officials, so the encrusted layers of local bodydom resented Dolci. 'If you go to the town council,' he wrote, 'you find that member X is still on holiday, that his private secretary Y is nowhere to be found. Day after day. Is nobody deputising for them? The doormen as a rule behave like dumb beasts set to protect the tranquillity of their masters.'

Yet this was nothing to the barrier the villagers sent up when Dolci married the widow, Vincenzina, and adopted her five children. In any northern community the act would have been cheered, as indeed it was later overseas. In Trappeto it was resented. It is not easy for an outsider, and no more for an Italian, to grasp the stiff taboos of the Sicilian moral code, ingrained as they are with pagan and Moslem superstition. Normally, if it is known that a woman has been alone with a man for half an hour her reputation is ruined. If marriage follows at once, it is saved. 'To elope does not bring shame,' the proverb says, 'but preservation of life.' Vincenzina's first marriage was typical of many. She was a child bride at fourteen: a brief flight with her peasant-fiancé, Luciano, to relatives; enraged parents; return home, reconciliation, and a speedy marriage—and all was well. Luciano died in 1949.

When Dolci arrived in 1952 Vincenzina and the eldest boy, Turi, then eleven, were working in a sardine factory to keep the family. Between them they were earning 7s. 8d. for a fourteen- or fifteen-hour day. Vincenzina was desperate. Borgo was her salvation. She went there as housekeeper. Technically she had once again 'eloped'; but the role was eventually accepted. Now, more than a year later, there had been a delayed marriage. The villagers felt that their moral apple-cart had been upset twice over. Others had imagined Dolci to be the complete ascetic: 'We felt this way,' Leonardo says. 'He'd never said to us that he wouldn't get married, but he'd never led us to believe that he *would*, either. And somehow, by intuition we felt that he wouldn't. So when he did, it seemed wrong. I'd been away. I found him up at Borgo, planting tomatoes—and when he told me he'd married Vincenzina I got furious. "You'll have the whole village against you now!" I said. Then he got furious. We almost hit each other. After that I didn't speak to him for months.

'But now—that was years ago—now I see that I was wrong. He did well to marry Vincenzina. Now she's got a vocation, whereas before she was lost.'

Half-truths have recently appeared in Italian newspapers about the marriage. Many in Trappeto were against it at the time, especially the respective parents. On Dolci's part it was a sacrifice, even a necessary sacrifice, an earnest of his pledge to live among these people in brotherly love and share their conditions—and, in particular, to suffer with someone who spelled out in stark human terms his mission. That mission was Sicily, and Vincenzina, the uncomplaining yet volatile young widow, was every fibre of Sicily. Dolci told me: 'As a girl she'd saved up, lira by lira, for a small chest of drawers, and when she came to Borgo she wanted to have it up there too. It was everything to her. But her people objected. There was a scene. She didn't say anything, but I knew she was terribly upset. That dinner-time I didn't eat, again saying nothing. I couldn't, out of respect for her. When I saw her next she had two black eyes—the face of a pirate! She'd done it to herself, with her own fists. Why? Because she'd upset *me*. And that was what stunned me. This, I suddenly realised, was also Sicily, and I knew that if I was ever going to really understand this place I had to identify myself with it *thoroughly*.'

Dolci does not believe, with what he calls 'the big things', in doing by half-measures. 'Not in quality, not in love, nor in commitment,' he says. 'These three things with me are crucial. Quality —to give it you must make sacrifices, even sexual sacrifices. Love— you make love seriously, it's not a second-hand operation. Commitment—whatever your pledge, you carry it through.'

In Vincenzina there was a fusion of all three elements. Certainly Dolci did not marry for love in the conventional sense. He was poet, intellectual and mystic; she was a peasant woman, a year his senior and barely literate. At the same time there is a very deep and special bond with this heroic woman of alien culture. Vincenzina was two months pregnant when they married. The marriage would have taken place a lot sooner if family pressure on the priest had not caused him to 'lose' the papers. Father Donato succeeded in 'losing' them for some months and might never have found them again had Dolci not confronted him in the sacristy with an ultimatum. 'Are you going to marry us or not?' Dolci demanded. The priest managed to find the papers.

Father Angelo Donato's action plants him in illustrious company. Manzoni in *The Betrothed* created the archetype of the equivocal priest; 'Don Angelo' would do very well as a latter-day version of Don Abbondio.

Dolci and Vincenzina were married by Father Donato in Trappeto church in August 1953, and returned to Borgo to make of it a home and a creative community which would, they hoped, command the respect of the village. But the affair had driven a wedge between Borgo and a section of the people, and a few splinters would always remain.

They went on with the house-to-house inquiry, often under fire. 'We have even been spat on,' Dolci wrote. 'Real spit, saliva—not merely insults.' More than ten people worked on the inquiry, including Vincenzina and Giustina; with not more than seven years schooling between them, the pair became valuable helpers. The team memorised questionnaires which, with variation, were to become the blueprint for hundreds of Dolci workers: 'Do you usually read newspapers or books? Are you interested in the social conditions of the area, of the nation, of the world? Why? When is it holiday for you?' And so on. They discovered that nobody bought books or newspapers; that people were often resigned to things because they were told it was the will of God; that social and religious questions were not understood. One woman, asked how she tried to live religiously, answered abruptly: 'We're honest people. In all these years I've only been with my husband.' Only ten houses had running water. Infant mortality was nine times higher than in the north.

The facts alone were bad enough. They were underlined by a wide belief in the *maarie*, the spirits, who the people said always functioned; and wide disbelief in the *professori*, the state schoolteachers, who Dolci discovered almost never did.

Belief in the *maarie*, for example, led people to consult Ninuzzo rather than the doctor. Ninuzzo was of indeterminate sex and 'spoke' with the spirits. She, or he, had remedies for everything—especially love aches. On Ninuzzo's advice girls without suitors often mixed a little of their menstrual blood in some pasta or wine or in a cigarette, and gave or sent it to the man they wanted to marry. The alchemy is said to produce devastating results.

On the *professori*, Dolci noted: 'Not one of the ten teachers lives in the village . . . Today is 6 November. The schools began almost a month ago. This morning, out of ten teachers, two arrived. Yesterday, the same, and there are two hundred pupils. The children roam the muddy streets. It's been like this for weeks: out of ten masters two or three have turned up—exceptionally, four.' On 1 December he wrote: 'Soon it will be Christmas, and the schools have not yet begun properly.'

He sent an open letter to Alessi in Palermo, and another to the Italian Prime Minister, the Home Secretary, and the national secretary of the CD party in Rome. He told them it was the law itself which stood between an honest man and his right to eat. He said:

'In the Montelepre zone as far as Balestrate the four or five shillings a man earns for twelve hours' labour—since he can find work only for six months of the year—come down to two and six a day, which has to keep an average of five or six people; and this, as you well know, comes down to sixpence each; sixpence a day is not enough to keep one person.' He pointed out that banditry was increasing, and that carabinieri were risking their lives daily for starvation wages. 'Do you think you can resolve this problem by increasing the number of carabinieri? Do you think you can resolve it by increasing the wages of the carabinieri?'

He called for one, just one, agricultural expert to be placed at the disposal of the peasants in each of the 37 Sicilian communes; 'In a few years the agricultural face of the island would be transformed.'

Dolci told Alessi: 'A public administration which shirks dire needs is preparing tombs.'

The Trappeto inquiry was finished by Christmas and published in January 1954, as *Act Quickly (and Well) for People are Dying* [*Fare Presto (e Bene) perchè si Muore*]. It is the most spontaneous of Dolci's books and embodies the core of his religious thought. Small and tightly packed, it contains the open letters and a series of case histories, presented as running shorthand-autobiographies, and is remarkable for its head-on poetic accusation and a complete absence of rancour.

An Italian, looking at a forgotten part of the south, had dared to produce a document of shame and accusation. It was difficult for Italians to believe they were reading about their own republic:

Yesterday and today a woman told us that her husband got well by drinking a glass of urine; neighbours have praised this . . . therapeutic aid.

Meantime in a citrus orchard a couple of miles from here another man has been found shot dead.

And this is another day like all the rest.

Giovannino, aged five, left alone to shepherd a flock, when he got really thirsty used to drink his own urine.

We have taken in two more children: one of three, one of five. They were living in a pigsty less than three yards square with two young sisters (another child about to be born), their father and mother, and the pig, titleholder of the establishment. As well as several hens. The tiniest was wearing a piece of canvas so tight that to get it off we had to tear it: she had been wearing it for a long time.

The authorities were worried. There were signs that this man had big ideas. His fast had confined itself to 2,800 souls. Now he was talking about a whole *zone*; worse, he mentioned 'the Sicilian situation'. Had the Government not recently conducted its own parliamentary inquiry into southern destitution? It was embarrassing to have this very inquiry thrown in its face by a religious upstart who quoted, to his own advantage, the Government statistic that 'in these provinces about nine of every hundred children die among the poor, compared to one of every hundred among the rich.' The moral was clear: social insecurity killed eight children out of one hundred every year.

Here was a self-appointed missionary who had suddenly turned social detective; who spoke mystically of God as though they were fellow masons, and in the same breath called for agrarian *technicians*. What was he?

An agitator? Yes. But what *kind* of agitator? The authorities were not certain.

The fact that Dolci was not sure either did not console them. The missile was 'dangerous'. Intangibly, and quite suddenly, an official barrier of hindrances began to go up.

Dolci appealed for workers, in Churchillian tones: 'And whoever feels it in his bones to be consumed in order that these people might live, let him be prepared to find himself, almost isolated, dragged under water by those he is trying to save.'

At the end of 1953 he was desperately worried. He told a Florentine friend that though the promised money had arrived—every penny—the work depot had not been opened, the sixteen children in need of immediate care had not been provided for, the irrigation syndicate was still in bureaucratic limbo, and every day there arrived at Borgo more orphans, more widows, more unemployed, asking for help. 'We're building a kindergarten,' he said, 'but we need timber, we need whitewash, we need . . . everything. We need more helpers, men of courage. The furniture isn't paid up. We spend over a shilling a day for every child. The shopkeepers are too poor to give much credit. The baker says he can give credit only until the end of the week . . .'

Missionary or sociologist? The dilemma was clear. He was in a blind alley, caught between the fires of his own creation. He marched along it, confident of his path—and certain of his faith in the Sicilians. 'There is God in these people,' he wrote, 'like the fire that smoulders under the ashes.'

EIGHT

Sent to Coventry

TODAY at Borgo di Dio there is no community. There are some
outbuildings, including an enormous hall inhabited by rats and old
mattresses; there is squint-eyed, lovable Domenico, the peasant,
who patrols the grounds in the summer with a rusty shotgun, and
who, every time I stay there, promises to take me rabbit-shooting
but never does—for, he says, 'the rabbits are more cunning than
delinquents', and he hasn't got one himself yet; and alongside the
kindergarten, in Borgo itself, there is Eyvind, the Norwegian philosopher who is Dolci's valued colleague, his wife Kerstin, their three
children, a tame dog called Amedeo who understands Swedish and
a zebra-like donkey on whose back Eyvind may sometimes be seen,
thinking, and getting about the olives.

But for roughly eighteen months, between 1952 and 1954, there
were sixty children and adults here and Dolci's dogged faith in the
miracle of multi-religious brotherhood was not misplaced. When
the kindergarten was finished, Paolino and Toni relate, 'All of us
from Borgo went out and grabbed the poorest and the dirtiest and
the hungriest from among the hundred kids of kindergarten age.
We could only bring back thirty because there wasn't room for any
more.' More than a thousand villagers turned up to some of the
concerts in the great hall, called the People's University; repeat per-
formances were called for; Chekhov's *The Bear* was a big success.
Vincenzina called Borgo 'my garden'. From the prolific garden she
had an uninterrupted view of the whole gulf. The children had
health education on a Greek pattern under the olives. Volunteer
helpers donated books and teaching aids, chairs, tables and rubber
aprons, gramophone records and a hand-wound German gramophone. Doctors and musicians came regularly from Palermo. An
upright piano was freighted from Rome; legend says the instrument
reached Borgo still upright, but that the three-wheeled Vespa which
lugged it up the Borgo switchback was never the same again. All this
reached a peak in 1953 when there was a flood of private generosity
from the north. Giorgio La Pira, Mayor of Florence, cajoled friends
and journalists to visit the stone hamlet; Ignazio Silone, the novelist,
sent nine hundred pounds for the library and nursery-school;

and Elio Vittorini, author of *Conversation in Sicily*, donated the royalties of a fresh edition (they paid for the roof of Borgo). Maria Sacchetti-Fermi, sister of the Nobel scientist, sent her teenage daughter Ida to give a hand. Later, Maria Fermi came herself. She washed dishes. 'Whenever I feel depressed,' she told a friend in 1957, 'I simply take a trip down to Sicily and visit Dolci, and that always restores my sense of values.' A Swiss 'cellist, Claudio, arrived and went out with the fishermen every day for six months. He was the first foreign helper. Tullio Vinay sent a young Protestant couple from his alpine community in the north to staff the nursery. Vinay is Waldensian, the original Italian Protestant order. He is a Florentine. In the last war he saved the lives of scores of Jews and earned the nickname 'the Rabbi of Florence'. In 1953 Dolci was already turning to Vinay for spiritual help and then, Vinay says, 'was praying every night near his bed'.

Dolci's helpers were of both sexes and of every political and religious creed. When a dapper Palermo medical student, Vincenzo Borruso, turned up he found that segregation was strict and that when women stayed in Borgo, the men moved out and bunked in the People's University. Dolci went too.

The community had adopted fifty children, seventeen of whom lived at Borgo. It fed them, clothed them and doctors came fortnightly to examine them. The children, who lived by the sea, had been told that sun and salt air were 'harming'. When a party of them was taken to the beach the sun healed their running sores in a few days. Their designs and linocuts were collected and published to raise funds. And they were learning, slowly, when they quarrelled, not to reach for the nearest blunt object. Fraternity was sinking in.

Paolino explained it this way: 'When the sardine lamps for the boats came from the factory I read the instructions and couldn't get the hang of anything. But when someone showed me how to light them it was easy. It's the same with the Gospel—it was only when I saw them actually *living* it that Danilo's talk about brotherly love sank in.'

Dolci believed that all official attempts to repress banditry concentrated on attacking the symptom rather than the disease itself. The creative work at Borgo, among the children of the bandits, supported his theory that you had to begin underneath, with the disease itself. It was token proof, but it was a practical living expression for those who wanted to see.

When, in *Act Quickly* (*and Well*) he invited the reader to eavesdrop on the confidences of these children—the 'tremendous vendettas' some were brooding—he was speaking for the growing generation of a whole zone: four villages and a town, fifty thousand inhabitants. The Establishment remained puzzled by his intentions.

Democratic authority when puzzled is often deaf, and sometimes blind as well. Thus it was that it decided to close down Borgo di Dio.

There was no warning. They came at dawn in a small lorry, between 30 and 35 carabinieri from Palermo, commanded by a staff officer. They carried rifles and sub-machine guns.

On 22 January 1954, Matteo was up early. He says, 'I went into the garden and looked down the hill. It was cold. There was white on the trees. I saw one of the bushes move, and another, and then I saw the uniforms coming up the hill. I ran in and told Danilo. He was writing. He put down his pen and came out. He talked with the officer and then the officer and some of the men came in.' The children were roused and as the carabinieri entered they ran screaming down the corridor. They knew what 'police' meant. Some jumped out of the windows, but Borgo had been surrounded and they were brought back. The officer was the second Government representative to visit Borgo in an official capacity. The first was also a police officer; he had interviewed Dolci in the library with his pistol placed between them. The present visitor came straight to the point. He told Dolci that as there was no guarantee of financial security the premises were to be closed. Dolci replied: 'I've no intention of obeying any orders of the police or the prefect which contradict God's law.'

'We'll see,' the officer said.

He turned to the volunteers. He examined their papers, taking pains over Ida Sacchetti-Fermi and a young Tuscan teacher. The latter was bearded and had a bandage on one foot. 'What's wrong with your foot?' the officer said. The teacher replied, 'I cut it.' There had been an armed robbery on the Alcamo road and the culprits were at large. The teacher was told to remove the bandage. The officer peered closely at the cut and then tugged at the teacher's beard. He was disappointed to find both were genuine.

When the police left they took away those children whose fathers were in prison. Aged from seven to twelve, the children cried, screamed and fought all the way to the lorries. They were outnumbered, four to one. They were taken to Palermo and put into religious colleges. The parents were not consulted. Dolci learned later that at least two children were kept in a cell in a reform college where iron chains were set into the walls.

It is possible that had Dolci confined himself to schooling and medical aid he might have been left alone. But having finished the first inquiry, he had begun paddling in dangerous waters. He had begun campaigning against the pirate trawlers whose crews were destroying the livelihood of the local fishermen, from Trappeto to Castellammare del Golfo. Behind the trawlers there was a big business syndicate, and behind the syndicate was a branch of the Mafia.

The Mafia is the most single-minded organisation in Italy. It is also the most efficient. Concentrated in the west of the island, it has a cloak of mystique, fear and pseudo-legality, and a heritage of thousands of murders. Two-thirds of an officially estimated five thousand Mafia trials in history have come to nothing, for lack of proof.

Dolci had no idea the Mafia was a refined organisation of family cells, protected by Right-wing political forces. 'I'd heard of Mafia, of course, and I knew I was in a Mafia area,' he says, 'but like most northern Italians I thought of it as "robber bands" and "delinquency", nothing more.'

At the time of the police raid on 22 January piracy of the inshore fishing grounds had been going on for eleven years undisturbed, under the nose of Customs and Excise police. The law laid down a three-mile limit. Outside this, motorised boats from Palermo and Terrasini used bombs. Inside it, they used fine linen netting to cream off thousands of pounds of sardine fry in a night. 'And all the fry of the sardine mature,' Dolci noted. The fry were sold openly on the Palermo market. Dolci calculated that over forty days the earnings for the sixteen shareholders of one Trappeto boat amounted to 272 lire, a total of three shillings among sixteen families.

Many fishermen were too discouraged to take their boats out at all. Some were in an ugly mood.

Dolci went north to seek advice. In Perugia he met that cheery pacifist, Capitini, who, with Tullio Vinay, gave him great courage. 'It's a popular pastime to decry efforts towards spiritual regeneration,' the tubby professor of non-violence told him. Capitini's paternal interest in Dolci remains. In 1954 he did two things for him. He put Dolci in touch with a wide circle of distinguished lay friends—among them Einaudi the publisher, Calamandrei the lawyer, Calogero, the grand old man of Italian philosophy, and Levi the writer—so that Dolci was helped immediately by powerful intellectual forces. And he widened Dolci's intuitive Gandhism, planting the seeds of a more integrated Christianity. Writing to me, Capitini says, 'I think that these two elements, plus the backwardness of the Sicilian clergy, helped to enlarge Danilo's whole moral and religious horizon.'

On his trip Dolci kept a diary. In Turin he records: 'What a relief not to see carabinieri spying on you at every turning.'

In a series of public discussions he posed the problems, and said: 'Back there in two small towns of less than eight thousand people there are some fifty police, including ten Customs and Excise men, and a naval petty officer—although I get on very well with him I can't quite see what use he is. This means that every month £1,000 goes in police salaries alone. The local assistance board spends only twelve pounds a month for the whole of Trappeto.'

His facts were disputed. 'I don't wonder,' he records. 'Even in Trappeto people who live only a few yards from the grimmest poverty say: "It's because the brutes are too lazy to work." It's a question of getting your perspective right. . . . Revolution then? All right . . . But it's the form of revolution that counts. If we sow peas we don't reap fish. If we sow death and untruth we don't reap life.'

On 11 February at Vicenza he learned that the police had again visited Borgo, sending home the thirty nursery-school children and closing down the kindergarten. 'Why?' he asked. 'Ever since I was so high I never understood why Jesus was persecuted and murdered. Now I'm beginning to understand.'

The kindergarten was closed following the visit of a health inspector. He noted a mildewed stain on one wall and declared the place 'insanitary'.

Friends formed groups to send more funds. Everywhere he asked them, 'What do you advise me?' They answered, 'Go on.'

He returned to Sicily. Arriving at Borgo he found that the police had threatened to banish his helpers if they persisted in their inquiries among the fishermen. One had already been sent away—Ida Sacchetti-Fermi.

He wrote to the press. He called for speedy action on the Iato River project, publicised the fishing abuses and re-publicised the crucial facts, enclosing a petition covered with signatures stating that the situation described was 'the actual state of affairs'. To his surprise people began collecting signatures on their own initiative. 'It's perhaps the first spontaneous action of the kind here.'

In *Notes for Friends* he records: 'While I'm writing to you, fishermen and peasants are in the library listening to Bach's *Second St. Matthew Passion* . . .'

The 1954 raid on Borgo was a replica, in miniature, of the Scelbian police operation against Nomadelphia at Fossoli in 1952. Once again the Government only partly succeeded. Borgo was registered as a charitable institution and could not be wiped off the map. Dolci's marriage to Vincenzina gave him resident-status and he could not be served a *foglia di via*, the old fascist method of exiling 'prostitutes and other undesirables'. The kindergarten was soon re-opened. Dolci handed control to an official welfare organisation (who have it today), run by a friend, Senator Zanotti-Bianco.

Then he calmly resumed his attack on the fishing abuses. By March the local fishermen were so desperate they were breaking the law themselves, driven by hunger to use fine netting which all but scraped the sardine eggs off the sea bed. Dolci despaired. 'Why is it that certain people, instead of meeting our arguments with facts and figures, instead of treating us as colleagues, want us thrust aside and slandered? Why do they waste their time on flowery words when so much is crying out to be done?'

The answer was, in a word, Mafia.

Throughout this period his diary reads like a piece of Zola. But it was not fiction.

Sunday 21 March

The fishermen are walking the streets, their eyes lidded with sleep.

The night before last they were fishing until three-thirty in the morning. Some until four. Then they dried and repaired their nets: that took until eleven: the share-out was 8s. 2d. per man.

They ate some bread and a few sardines and went to bed at noon. Two hours later they were up again making ready the nets. At four o'clock they had some bread and pasta and at five they were at sea. They stayed out until three this morning. An hour later they began repairing the nets and they are still at it; it's now eleven o'clock. And so it goes on, day after day. Today's earnings were 5s. 10d. per man.

11–13 April

Two trawlers are fishing illegally. Last night a boat from Terrasini landed 100 cases of fry—1,400 pound of fish destroyed like this in a single night. Four other boats were fishing too . . .

10 May

A Customs launch appeared—at last—towards eleven o'clock and caught a trawler within the limit. Let's hope something happens. The locals are sceptical. 'They'll smarm their way out with a case of fish,' they say.

14 May

A trawler has been fishing illegally all day, only 300 yards out. We rang the Port Captain at Palermo: he promised to send a launch tomorrow morning.

15 May

A trawler fishing illegally all day long, undisturbed, a few hundred yards offshore. No sign of the Customs launch.

On 17 May Dolci wrote to the Port Captain: 'My dear Captain . . . After receiving ample evidence of the continued flagrant abuse of the fishing laws in Castellammare Bay; after being warned of the risk that the fishermen, losing patience, might start firing on their aggressors; after being advised that, thanks to you, Italy loses fully £90,000 a year in the Gulf of Castellammare alone—after all this, you continue to side with the culprits . . .

'This letter of ours is not meant as an insult: it is simply a recommendation that you should not allow things to get any worse.' The letter was signed by hundreds and, with documentary evidence, was sent to 22 of the authorities concerned in Italy.

18 May

A trawler is fishing a stone's throw from Trappeto beach. At Balestrate knots of fishermen are planning to board a trawler, beat the crew up and throw them over the side. Some want to tie the crew up and sink the vessel, others just want to cut the nets loose . . .

They're expecting a lawyer to talk the whole matter over with them at nine in the morning.

19 May

The lawyer did not turn up.

The lawyer came the following day. Three days later a Customs cutter arrived. But the trawler had been warned and was outside the limit. The captain of the cutter pointed out that the penalties, when applied, were inadequate anyway. He promised to return that night.

24 May

The cutter did not come back: but the trawler reappeared, it came almost on to the beach. First with lights doused and then, about ten o'clock, with all lights blazing.

The local fishermen, armed with knives, began circling round the trawler and prepared to board it. Dolci went out in a motor-boat and advised the trawlermen to clear off before blood was shed. They hauled in and went.

A month later the trawler was back. 'A few days ago,' Dolci wrote, 'the Head of the State was awarded the Order of Christ: "as a defender of Christian civilisation".'

In mid-August the Fisheries Board finally alerted all port captains in Sicily and called for 'decisive action' against the raiders. On 7 September Dolci records, laconically:

Three trawlers continue to fish illegally.

8.30 a.m.	Telephone the Fisheries Board. A girl's voice replies that the chairman is abroad and that, at this hour, nobody is able to speak for him.
8.40	Telephone the naval officer in charge at Balestrate.
9.00	Attempt to telephone the Port Captain; the book gives the wrong number. Various attempts over the next 70 minutes. We get the Deaf and Dumb Institute, a doctor, and other private numbers. Finally (at 10.15) the Balestrate naval man calls back: he'll go out tomorrow after the trawlers; today he's not feeling well.
10.30	The Port Captain's office, his deputy on the line: the captain isn't there. A sailor goes off to look for him. We hang on for five minutes. He can't be found but another person speaks to us who, on hearing what it's about, says he'll pass it on to Customs and Excise, as the Navy hasn't any vessels available.

Three days later Dolci was at the sea-front at dawn to see four trawlers fishing close in, undisturbed. When a fifth arrived he went straight to the head of police in Partinico. The inspector told him to submit a complaint in writing. The complaint, with 61 signatures attached, was submitted to the main police and port authorities of the province. 'We disown violence and bloodshed,' it ended, 'but we will not leave our families undefended. We beg you therefore to come to our aid *quickly and well*.'

That spring there were five murders in the area, several kidnappings, two armed robberies and an outbreak of petty thieving. By the end of the year trawlers had fished illegally for 350 out of 365 days without interference. Dolci had achieved nothing.

The complaint was archived.

(As I write these lines at Alcamo Marina, just round the coast from Trappeto, I am looking out on Castellammare Bay. It is late at night. The bay is lined with the kerosene lamps of pirate fishermen, working 250 yards from shore. I can count thirteen boats. None of the crews is local. The local fishermen are not to be found in the villages. They have gone away, northward, in search of work—untrained, unhappy, resentful. The population of Trappeto has fallen from 2,800 to barely 1,400. Almost all the able-bodied men have gone. The fishermen began leaving in the spring of 1954, after their collective complaint to the police went the way of all the rest.)

Such was, and is still, the power of a minor branch of the Mafia. It was the first and last time that Dolci was to limit himself to a protest that expressed itself entirely on paper. He had been rendered almost as impotent as the law itself. He was down, but not out. He would make more mistakes, but not again would he be so ingenuous as to tackle the Mafia single-handed without ascertaining first what Mafia actually was.

NINE

The Embattled Town

IN 1955 Dolci moved from Trappeto to Partinico.

There were many contributing factors. Vincenzina says they were under constant attack for living 'in a villa'. Many villagers continued to regard Borgo as a cross between a circus turn and comic opera. The kindergarten was flourishing again, but the fishermen had begun to drift away and the People's University had fallen silent.

There was the priest. Not to be outdone by Dolci's kindergarten Father Donato opened one himself, in opposition. Dolci sent 10,000 lire, more than he could afford, wishing the venture well. The money was returned. Dolci tried again. 'Please accept it,' he said. 'This is a good thing you're doing.' The money was refused a second time. 'We do not need your help,' he was told. Little by little, he was edged aside. Father Donato, bred in an antique reactionary mould, is a typical Sicilian figure. 'There's no poverty in Trappeto,' he told Dolci. 'It's only a few fishermen who aren't well off.' He came from another village where, he said, the poverty was far worse. That was hardly the point, Dolci said, suggesting, in vain, that the priest accept barefoot children in church. The priest suggested that Dolci ban non-Catholics from his community—also in vain. As Dolci's religious horizon widened, through Capitini, Vinay and others, he found no meeting-point with the other's limited Catholic view. It wasn't long before the latter was preaching openly against the 'godless foreigners'. Such is the distortion of gossip which follows village sermons in Sicily that locals came to believe not only that Dolci was in the pay of the Communists (Giovanni Piergallini was an atheist), but also that he was hand-in-glove with the bandits whose children he was attempting to succour. After Dolci's first child, Maria-Libera, was born in April 1954, and the baby was not baptised, the priest called him a heretic.

Of the Sicilian clergy Vinay has said: 'They are souls of their traditions and of their past. They are unable to understand that the task of the Church is to incarnate the words of God in the life of the people—are *unable* to understand. They are keeping, saving, preserving—and personally I think that the greatest sin of the Church is the sense of preservation; where there is preservation there is not faith.

78

'Danilo always considered himself a Catholic. But the Church denied it. How often it pushes out of the door the best men it has. And Danilo—little by little, he was out.'

By the end of 1954 Dolci had left the Catholic Church. But at Christmas he was given the *Premio della Bontà* (the Prize of Goodness), an award made annually by a group of Milan industrialists for Catholic social work.

The main reason for the move to Partinico, however, was practical. The Iato irrigation scheme, magnified now into a dam to serve the whole area, was based on Partinico, where lived the majority of farmers whose land would be flooded. Also, more and more bandits were coming from Partinico to blackmail the Trappeto folk. Partinico was the administrative and geographic centre of the whole homogeneous area, the headquarters of the police and the law courts as well as the bandits. Dolci wanted to get to grips with peasant suffering on a wide scale. If he was going to start with *gli ultimi*, the lowest, he had to live with them.

Partinico first shocked him, then drew him, irresistibly. Working, as usual, one step ahead of himself, he had already begun an inquiry here, with Giovanni and some graduates from Siena, travelling daily from Borgo by the seven a.m. train, on a spartan diet of bread-crusts, hot powdered milk and rock sugar.

The winter of 1954 brought more unemployment. Banditry flared. Behind the Partinican hills the crackle of machine-gun fire from police manoeuvres grew. On 13 December a man of 24 was shot dead ten yards from the square. A fortnight later Dolci and Giovanni were in Partinico, returning from discussing the dam in Palermo, and heard shots fired just in front of them. 'They sounded like squibs. Instead, they were three pistol shots, fired at a young notary. We saw him lurching about, his hands clasped to his abdomen. The evening promenade on the Corso—it was a Sunday —was momentarily interrupted, then, as soon as people saw he was "only shot", not dead, they went on promenading as if nothing had happened.'

By the time Christmas, and the Prize of Goodness, came along, Dolci knew he must break with the little oasis of goodness that was Borgo. It was the end of the Nomadelphian vision. It was inevitable. Slowly he was coming to feel the weight of Don Zeno's words: 'Fraternity and social change, they're two different things. Don't mix them up.'

There has always been something special about Partinico. The place has a martyred look. In 1955 the only standard things about it were an abiding preoccupation with death and a passionate mistrust of the outsider. The town is spread flat white in a broad basin. The basin is chequered in vines and olives and joins forces with the grizzled surrounds of Borgetto and Montelepre near by, and, farther out, with the fields of Trappeto, San Giuseppe Iato and Alcamo. From afar the houses appear herded together, in the shape of a tuatara lizard, uneasily united under the shadow of nude ochre mountains. They are of white and stippled blue wash. Above the houses tower the harsh reds and dun browns of King's Mountain, its shaggy pinnacle looming directly over the church and the town square. The Corso, the main street, is a mile long and dead straight. Every second shop seems to be a barber's, and every third a bar. The rest are mostly butchers. In summer when the flies appear and alight on the blood-red meat hanging outside, the flies are sometimes sprayed with DDT. Paunchy, white-frocked policemen stand about chatting in pairs, unbothered by the traffic jams of the mules, which outnumber the motor vehicles. Even today it is difficult to find a man about town who cannot produce a knife or a gun on demand. But for the absence of hitching rails, it is a classic Wild West setting.

For seven centuries Partinico has been a nerve centre of revolt. It is distinctly non-Christian, which may derive from Greek times, when its thick forests were sacred to Diana. The name itself either comes from the Greek, *Partenos* (Diana) or the Roman *Pars Iniquia* —under the Romans it was a penal colony. Only the Arabs, who planted sugar-cane and quilted the basin in market gardens, gave the Partinicans a sense of civic pride. None of the other invaders, spilling overland from Castellammare Bay or wreaking havoc on the plain-dwellers from the hills, except the Spaniards, stayed long enough to give the people anything but a rigid sense of social insecurity. For six centuries Partinico was an enormous church fief, a status-less ragamuffin outpost, and as late as the beginning of last century, when the Bourbon King, Ferdinand II, built his summer castle on King's Mountain, the only municipal authority was the archpriest's. The archpriest was everything from sheriff to undertaker. Ferdinand found the Partinicans scornful of church rule and pandered to them. He created the Great Royal Wine Cellars, planted a park with 3,600 rare trees and shrubs, and put a cross on top of King's Mountain which he visited, on a horse, whenever the heat of the plain grew oppressive. He made the town a commune, planted more dependants than he did trees and founded *The Academy*, where the local poets forgathered and fought out marathon battles of extempore verse.

Unfortunately, Ferdinand's dizzy patronage didn't last. The

castle, and the Great Royal Wine Cellars, fell into decay; and so, once more, did Partinico's civic pride. A rigid Bourbon régime settled. There was bitterness and unrest. Partinicans spat at the sight of a Bourbon tunic. By the time the century was out they had risen seven times against unjust land dues and each time had been savagely put down. Typically, in 1860, they did not wait for the invasion of Garibaldi and his Thousand, but rose spontaneously against the Bourbons almost a month before. When Garibaldi marched through Partinico and on to Palermo, to liberate the island and unite it to Italy, Partinicans had already baptised their new citizenship in blood. Cesare Abba, one of the Thousand, gives this description of Partinico:

18 May (1860), between Partinico and Burgeto

It would have been better to break our backs and cross the mountain rather than glimpse Partinico . . . The column we had routed at Calatafimi had run into the rebels of Partinico, heroic folk indeed. Having razed the village the Bourbons massacred the women and helpless of all ages. Corpses of soldiers and peasants, of horses and dogs, some with their guts torn out. As we rode up the bells were ringing, but whether in ecstasy or in rage I do not know; the houses were still smoking; the people in tumult among the ruins, priests and monks screaming frenzied 'Evviva!' The women were flailing their arms and around a funeral pyre of seven or eight singed and festering bodies large numbers of young girls were dancing in a crazed round, holding hands and singing. Those corpses were soldiers. The General spurred on through, wrenching his hat down over his eyes. We followed, all of us, deafened and miserable. Now we are far off, but the bells are sounding still. It is four-thirty. I would like to lie tonight among these olive groves and not lose from sight Castellammare Bay which sunset will shortly transform into who knows what heavenly radiance of colours.

From that day Partinico has been known as 'bandit town'. The *Giornale di Sicilia*, the Bourbon mouthpiece, called Garibaldi a bandit too, but changed its verdict to 'blond hero' when a few days later he slipped in by the back door and took the city by surprise.

Partinicans pinned their faith on the blond general and made him an honorary citizen. Garibaldi accepted 'with pride'. But his arrival, the end of one era of repression, only ushered in another, that of the Mafia.

Mafia had been conditioned by a gradual impoverishment of

the island under successive invaders, growing up as a peasant self-protection movement long before Garibaldi. Altruism soon vanished. The *mafiosi*, the bailiffs on the feudal estates, were happily placed—they blackmailed the absentee landlords on one hand, and terrorised with armed bands the peasants under them on the other. Garibaldi promised the peasants ownership of the land, and they followed him. So did the Mafia. It put its auxiliary police force at his disposal and then, having seen him safely off the premises, availed itself of his lieutenant, Nino Bixio, to shoot down the peasants. Under the soft new Kingdom of Italy it joined up with the reactionary landowners (both of them now had a vested interest in anaesthetising social revolt) and eased itself into power.

The so-called Liberation was the death-blow to peasant faith in the justice of the outsider.

'Change everything in order to change nothing,' says the prince in Lampedusa's Garibaldian novel, *The Leopard*. Garibaldi was not the peasant's saviour, but the Mafia's. It is from 1860 that organised Mafia as we know it today really took hold.

Sicilian peasants continued to revolt, without ever achieving a revolution. In the bloody nineties Partinicans were among the first to demonstrate, parading the streets with placards saying, 'BREAD, WORK, REFORM'. A Partinican woman of 35 led an invasion on the town hall, ejecting the mayor bodily into the arms of counter-attacking cavalrymen, and Crispi, the Prime Minister, was moved to confer on the zone the title, 'Crown of Thorns'.

A section in the *British Encyclopaedia* about 1900 notes that 'in organised form the Mafia survives only in isolated districts'. At the time the Mafia was entrenched throughout the four provinces of the west, its 'friends' resided in town councils, in police barracks, in law courts, and collusion flourished behind a mutually protective smoke-screen. In 1911 the economist, Lorenzoni, wrote: 'The scent of the orange groves in flower badly conceals the stench of gunshot smoke . . .' Political rivals were simply eliminated by hired Mafia assassins.

In 1918 a Partinican, Vittorio Emanuele Orlando, was Prime Minister of Italy. He became famous by uniting the people to drive out the Austrians and Hungarians and win the tail of the war; and in 1919 was one of the Big Four at Versailles with Lloyd George, Woodrow Wilson and Clemenceau. Orlando also granted favours to many Partinicans. Later, asked why he'd done nothing to improve his town's social conditions, he explained: 'You only asked me for jail passes and warrants to carry firearms—you didn't say anything about streets.'

As manifestoes in his electorate proclaimed in 1946, Vittorio Emanuele Orlando was '*l'amico degli amici*', or 'the friend of friends'. Everyone knew who the friends were.

On an island of the forgotten, Partinico stood out as a scabland of the iniquitous. Mafia fingered its wine, olive, citrus and market garden produce. Its death-roll was second to none. In 1924–5 there were some two hundred murders in Partinico. Emigration was restricted. Honesty meant starvation. Faced with the age-old dilemma, 'serf or bandit?', Partinicans chose banditry. This fringe activity naturally disturbed the Mafia. The Mafia declared war on the bandits. The state police were rendered almost superfluous.

During fascism, Mafia went underground. Mussolini's prefect, Mori, exiled or jailed many *mafiosi*, and tortured hundreds of innocents. In Partinico there were so many arrests the churches had to be used as tribunals. After the war the Mafia rose again, stronger than ever. As it had used Garibaldi, it used the American Seventh Army, paving the way for a smooth advance in 1943 and then, with the eager aid of the Americans, hoisting itself into key administrative posts. It entered the drug and contraband rackets, and politics. Mafia thugs came home from exile to become mayors and the Church did not publicly lament their appointment. An American officer nominated Don Calò Vizzini Mayor of Villalba. Don Calò was undisputed Head of the Mafia, a picturesque illiterate and a notorious criminal. On the day he became mayor priests and dignitaries, among them a representative of the Bishop of Caltanissetta and Dr. Calogero Volpe, the present CD deputy in Rome, greeted him with acclaim; and a select chorus of friends, lined up outside the police barracks, shouted tumultuously: 'Long live the Mafia! Long live delinquency! Long live Don Calò!' Don Calò opened his term of office by arranging for the extinction of the district police officer.

One of Don Calò's close associates was the head of the Partinico Mafia, Cavalier Santo Fleres. Fleres began life as a cowherd. His five-year reign, 1943–8, coincided with the rise of the famous Giuliano and an era of social banditry which gave the Trappeto–Partinico–Montelepre zone yet another title, 'Triangle of Hunger'. Fleres ran the town, and paraded the Corso in company with the local draper, the spaghetti merchant and others who are today prominent citizens. Giuliano worked from the Montelepre–Partinico hills. And whenever these two were resting there was always the Lombardo gang to keep up the terror of daily Partinico living. The Minister of Police, Scelba, tried hard to catch Giuliano—or said he did. Giuliano's men, under Mafia protection, walked the streets openly in their hooded cloaks, and Giuliano occasionally lodged with

Signor Giordano, the present draper, jeweller and church benefactor, who gave the outlaw-king the gold belt-buckle which appears
in so many photographs.

Fleres died, assassinated by Lombardo behind the municipal
bandstand in 1948. Giuliano died, betrayed by the Mafia, in 1950.
'When Giuliano died part of Sicily died with him' Herbert Kubly
wrote. Partinicans agreed. His band was recruited from Partinico.
Hunger drove the cowherds of the Via della Madonna to join him;
they followed his banner as a beacon in the long deluded search for
social justice.

Once again the peasants gained nothing, save a bad reputation and
long prison sentences.

The Mafia stayed in business. Having adopted Giuliano, then
cast him off, it returned to its old love, the forces of reaction, and
when Sicily was granted a form of home rule in 1948 backed the
Christian Democrats. The CD party adopted as its emblem the
cross. Half a superstitious peasantry was won over automatically—
'We always vote for the cross,' Dolci was told, 'because God told us
to carry the cross.' Others took the slogan 'Vote CD—or Starve' at
face value. Those who didn't see the cross as a political symbol of
divine justice had the theory explained from the pulpit. The Mafia
displayed 'friendship' in several ways. The elections coincided with
the peasants' symbolic occupation of the estates, under the new reform laws; and with the rise of a primitive Left-wing, largely in
support of peasant rights. Trade unionists had become popular
heroes, threatening to undermine the Mafia's rural dominion and a
CD majority. The Mafia began systematically to assassinate them.
In Partinico peasants were forbidden to enter the Left union, the
Camera del Lavoro, on pain of death; and on the Sunday preceding
the 1948 national elections, having murdered eleven key unionists
and socialists in three months, the Mafia conducted a punitive ex-
pedition which, beginning outside Palermo, took in Monreale,
Pioppo, Borgetto and San Giuseppe Iato, and ended in the centre of
Partinico with a hand bomb and bottles of benzine tossed into the
Communist headquarters. The death roll rose to thirteen. The
Mafia clinched its liaison with the Church party by rigging candidates and, in cases—where illiterate peasants needed a 'guide' to
mark the voting slips—also the polls.

In Sicily, in both regional and national elections, the CD party was
overwhelmingly victorious. In Partinico in 1947 the combined
Left-wing parties polled a total of 27 votes.

By 1955 when Dolci moved to Partinico the whole mutually protective network between Palermo and Rome, the foundation of

Mafia inviolability, had been stitched. Mafia was urbanised. Mafia was in building and banking, television, Government contracts, food distribution and water control. The only business it left alone was prostitution. In these few years social and economic progress on the west of the island was sterilised—indeed, if anything, it went backwards, for northern industrialists, to avoid graft and sabotage, were forced to move to the east. The *capo-mafiosi* wore lounge suits, frequented the Massimo Opera House and had 'friends' in the highest places—in the professions, in the Church, in the Regional Government and in ministerial office in Rome. Political murders by hired assassins could still be arranged for a mere fifty-pound tip. Palermo by now was a second Chicago of the Al Capone days. The murder rate was climbing to eight times that of any city in the north.

Around Palermo, outlying cliques were partly assimilated to the new urban pattern. Elements of these, the Water Mafia, the Mafia of the Gardens and so on, were to affect Dolci's later work.

There was a separate Mafia branch for every activity. Partinico boasted six, of a possible fifteen. The business end of these activities, the *lupara* shotgun, the traditional killing weapon, was presented by a series of middlemen—armed 'tax collectors' and reprisal merchants, able to turn their hand to an anonymous letter, a bomb or some other such ritual warning. The real *mafiosi* were few. They were the rustic heritage, the former rivals or bodyguards of Santo Fleres, and when not protecting their monopolies or leading religious processions were usually engaged in a tinpot vendetta among themselves. They were second-rate. The only figure was the absentee Frank Coppola. Francesco Paolo Coppola, after Orlando, is Partinico's most famous citizen. He was born there in 1899. As a youngster he went to America, became a gangster and was mentioned in the Kefauver congressional report on the American underworld. It is said he lost part of one hand while burgling a bank. The hand was jammed under a safe door just as the police sirens sounded, and in order to escape he cut off the trapped fingers. He was charged with drug-trafficking and extradited as undesirable, returning to Partinico in 1950 a conquering hero. On the welcoming committee were clergymen, among them the parish priest of the Church of the Holy Sufferers. Coppola then moved to Anzio, near Rome, spent some £42,000 acquiring and improving a 125-acre property and, as a gentleman farmer, was occasionally seen driving about in the company of a high-ranking Customs officer. His intimacy with Liberal and Christian Democrat politicians was not concealed; the successive Liberal and CD members for Partinico, Palazzolo and

Savarino (1953–8), addressed him by letter as 'My dearest Don Ciccio'. In 1951 Coppola was sought by Interpol as a growing rival (some say a partner) to Lucky Luciano, his Sicilian contemporary, who was the master-mind of the intricate drug-trade routes operating between the Middle East and the United States, via French and Italian pharmaceutical suppliers who refined the raw opium and morphine base into heroin. Luciano, jailed in America in 1936 on 62 charges of compulsory prostitution, was released and sent home in 1946 for his 'contribution to the war effort' (he arranged the bloodless American advance across Western Sicily in 1943 and the Americans in return arranged [unwittingly] the Mafia's return to power)—and resided in style at Naples where he rejoiced in the title of Ex-Whoremaster General of the United States. Luciano was suave and versatile. Coppola, operating from Anzio, was creased and brash but equally adept. In February 1952 one of his men was arrested at Alcamo carrying thirteen pounds of heroin for shipment to the United States in crates of salted fish; records found in the possession of his gang incriminated 23 prominent underworld figures, and a respected pharmaceutical dealer in Milan. Coppola was prosecuted, but evaded imprisonment. An official Italian Customs report of 15 May 1952 describes him, somewhat flatteringly, as 'supreme organiser' of the illicit narcotics traffic emanating from Italy. There is a photograph of Coppola taken about this time at an intimate gathering in Partinico where he was invited by the Partinico branch of FUCI, the Italian Federation of Catholic University Students. After that body had bestowed its honorary membership on him, he distributed spiced cakes to the gathering. In the photograph Coppola appears short and dumpy and somewhat tasselled, for he wears the white medieval tricorn of the Faculty of Philosophy. He lives nowadays at Pomezia near Rome, still farming. Since Orlando bequeathed Partinico to the nation as a safe Mafia seat Coppola has allegedly continued the tradition.* Italian newspapers denounce him repeatedly as the 'grand electoral patron' of the district; and an impressive number of affidavits before the present Parliamentary Commission of Inquiry into the Mafia link his fortunes more or less exclusively with the promotion of Right-wing senators. He is usually seen in Partinico only at election times.

* Mafia leaders have openly bragged about their support for CD and Liberal (extreme Right-wing) candidates. In *Vita di Capomafia*, Nick Gentile, former gangster of the Luciano–Anastasia–Capone school and today a gentleman farmer in Agrigento province, discusses his electoral campaigns for the former Sicilian President, La Loggia, and the Liberal senator, Battaglia. There are many more examples.

In 1955 when Dolci arrived, Partinico may have had only a second-rate Mafia, but it boasted first-class connections.

A CD administration ruled 25,000 inhabitants. Day-labourers, smallholders, cowherds, outlaws, dawn-scavengers. There was a small shopkeeping class, a smaller professional class, and a parasitical élite known as 'armchair Mafia'. The mayor was Mario Mancuso, a robust lawyer, friend of the police and also of Coppola. Senator Santi Savarino, also head of the powerful Government organ, the *Giornale d'Italia*, was in office.

Three years in the area had taught Dolci that the Honoured Society, as it is known, had a vested interest in social decay, and that, as a social *reformer*, his mere arrival in a town like this was tantamount to an open declaration of war. Trappeto fishermen tried to stop him going. Some called him a traitor. Most, like Leonardo, reminded him that there was such a branch as the Mafia of the Coffins. 'They pop men off like flies in that place,' Leonardo said. Dolci expostulated in his earnest way. 'Ah well, perhaps—but I'm going.' He had studied the island's history. He had studied the peasants and would study them further. He would understand them. He would continue to renounce violence. And he would work in only one direction, the way he believed to be right.

His belief was strong and profoundly Christian. This was the foundation of his own private inviolability.

On 16 May 1955 the last and greatest of the peasant leaders, Salvatore Carnevale, was murdered in the village of Sciara, not far from Palermo. Carnevale was thirty-two. He was the 38th trade union victim of the Mafia in less than ten years.

Dolci the outsider was slightly younger when he moved to Partinico in 1955. He arrived in June.

TEN

An Instrument for Action

HE found a house in Spine Sante, in the poor part. At first he lived alone, one of the workers cooking for him; he didn't believe in wasting time preparing meals. Spine Sante (Holy Thorns) was one of three emaciated quarters. On the north side was the Mulini area, where prostitution flourished. In the south-west, running off the Via della Madonna, were the outlaws and cowherds, the men who'd followed Giuliano, living in uneasy juxtaposition with the *mafiosi*. And just behind the church and square was the tight little bunch of smelly alleys known as Spine Sante. Even in Partinico Spine Sante was looked down on. Of a total of twelve quarters in all, it was the saddest, the retreat of the underdog, the half-bandit, the snail-picker, the mentally deficient. Half its numbers got by on expedients—one of Dolci's neighbours, for instance, kept his family by unbolting the brakes from the trains in the station yard and selling them for scrap-iron.

His rooms, at Number Ten, Via Iannello, were empty. The occupants had declared them haunted and cleared out. The 'ghosts' were a hen and her chicks who used to peck at their feet as they lay in bed. The rent was eight shillings a week. There were three rooms, two up and one halfway down the stairs. When Dolci's family arrived later in the year they all squeezed in—he, Vincenzina, Maria-Libera and their second child Cielo (born in June), Vincenzina's first five children, and six orphans: thirteen children in all. 'It could be worse, Sariddu,' Dolci told the Sicilian who lived opposite. 'There are fifteen people sleeping in the room just below us.'

The house was furnished by hard chairs, thirty-bob wire beds bought on instalment in Palermo, Vincenzina's girlhood dresser from Trappeto, giveaway oddments and one or two of Matteo's paintings. Dolci's office was the room off the first landing. It was divided by a curtain behind which he and Vincenzina and the two youngest slept. He rose every morning at four, when the peasants were beginning to clatter their mule-carts out for the two-hour ride to their plots. Upstairs, where the other children and occasional helpers slept navy-style round the walls, the rooms were divided by a toilet the size of a telephone booth. This was a luxury. Sariddu's

'It is time to stop siding with the strongest'

Last century Sicilian peasants rebelled seven times without ever achieving a revolution. Since the last war the people of Partinico have protested often against delays in building the Iato irrigation dam—in 1955, 1956, 1957, 1959 and 1961. Not until 1962, however, when Dolci fasted and marched with 3,000 townspeople in an historic procession openly challenging the Mafia, did despair turn to optimism and Rome acknowledge the appeal

Upper: *Dolci at his desk in Partinico*
Lower: *Giuseppe Genco Russo, acknowledged Head of the Mafia from 1954 to 1964, at the funeral of his predecessor, Don Calò Vizzini. By 1938 Russo had twelve penal charges against him, including homicide. After 1954 his alliance with the Christian Democrat (Church) Party prospered. He became party secretary and municipal councillor in his village of Mussomeli, intimate of priest and politician—supreme 'friend of friends'. He told Dolci, 'It is in my nature to do favours for others'*

E R N E S T O
DEL TITOLO DI S. SABINA
CARDINALE PRETE DI S. R. C. RUFFINI
ARCIVESCOVO DI PALERMO
E
AMMINISTRATORE APOSTOLICO DI PIANA DEGLI ALBANESI

INGIUSTA DIFFAMAZIONE DELLA SICILIA

Mi trovo in Sicilia da 18 anni e ritengo poter dire di conoscere abbastanza questa grande e splendida Isola nonchè il suo popolo, intelligente, generoso e buono. Quindi per l'appassionato amore che mi stringe alla verità e la profonda stima che andò sempre crescendo nel mio spirito per questa terra privilegiata, sento di dover dire una parola che dissipi pregiudizi e rettifichi concezioni le quali più della carità offendono la giustizia.

In questi ultimi tempi si direbbe che è stata organizzata una grave congiura per disonorare la Sicilia; e tre sono i fattori che maggiormente vi hanno contribuito: l a m a f i a, il G a t t o - p a r d o, D a n i l o D o l c i.

3

Cardinal Ruffini, Primate of Sicily; and the opening page of his latest pastoral letter. The letter blackens Dolci and is notably less critical of the Mafia

Below: *The great church at Palma di Montechiaro where a Roman doctor found that 3,404 people shared their 700 rooms with 5,085 animals*

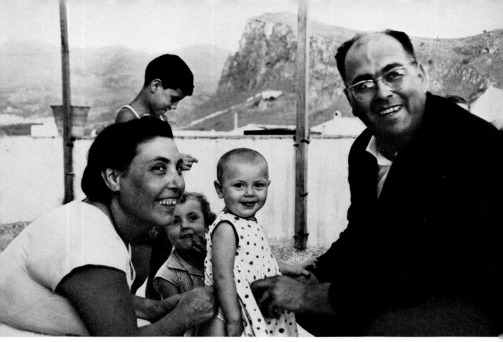

Dolci with Vincenzina and three of their five children on the roof of their Partinico home. Behind, King's Mountain

Signor Dolci with his son and the three eldest Dolci children

Don Zeno and Tullio Vinay

toilet, typical of the quarter, was a hole in the floor normally covered by the kitchen burner. The lavatories in Spine Sante, those that existed, went straight down into the 'drains' underneath. Dolci had left a Swiss and a young Italian graduate to carry on at Borgo; Giustina and her husband had found fresh quarters; the other volunteers, plus the seasonal Siena students, slept in another house in Via Iannello. But they ate at Number Ten. Vincenzina fetched water from the fountain, cared for the thirteen children and cooked on a three-ring gas-burner for the entire team. Pasta at noon, minestrone at night, wine on Sundays and when there were guests. At mealtimes half a dozen usually had to sit on the floor. For the next four years Vincenzina served a minimum of twenty people twice daily, kept house, did a good deal of the washing, parcelled out charity gifts and bore Dolci three more children. She never asked him for as much as a new dress.

From this base at the bottom of society they launched their new non-violent attack.

Dolci moved easily among the poor, a big man in a Basque beret and an old woolly sweater. He looked rather like a Quaker farmer. His clothes were too small for him, his trousers shabby, his gait ambling and a bit lopsided. Partinico was a noisy place, even for Sicily. The people expelled their dialect in ringing shouts. Beneath their gravelly poetic speech and extrovert manners he detected an individualism and an abrasive cynicism. Everywhere their history showed—anarchical pockets, religious action groups, street-corner informers, mental enfeeblement, insensitivity to violence, a wayward caste system. An Evangelist movement was almost tolerated. The men dressed up on Sundays, let their women go to church for them and rotated between the cinema, the card halls and the brothels as their main sources of escape. One brothel charged as little as sixpence a time. Knots of unemployed men were for ever glued to the stony Corso. A few yards off it, wherever he wandered, he was in a perpetual farmyard, where hens and goats wandered in and out over beaten earth floors. Mounds of dung and rubbish lay about like booby traps. The town seemed poised uncertainly between dumb narcotic stupor and revolutionary flashpoint. It was, as somebody said, a sociologist's dream.

His first foothold was with the chronically unemployed, the obdurate half-workers, who scrabbled a few lire from the wild life and herbs of the hills. Sariddu lived by gutting and spitting frogs and selling them in the square at threepence a time. 'It takes an awful lot of frogs to keep a wife and three children, Danilo,' he said.

Sariddu was a lithe young man with a vicious toothbrush moustache; he had been waiting nine years for a regular job. Dolci next concentrated on the outlaws. They were not the western kind. They were men who'd rubbed the police up the wrong way or got into trouble over a petty theft or a vendetta and had joined the bandits in order to stay alive, while their families were left to starve, or jailed. In many cases they were those who'd been questioned, beaten and tortured for no crime at all. 'Society bans them,' he told a friend. To him an outlaw was anyone who'd been banned from the possibility of living with others. They had chirpy Rhondda-type nicknames—Corn-eater, Three-day-Peppino, Shit-his-pants, Fifteen-lire (his mother sold him at three for fifteen lire), Donkey-dropper. But the loneliness of the great empty piazza by the town hall, leading to the Via della Madonna, was more intense than in the South Wales valleys. This was an introverted *town* misery.

It would be too much to say that the peasants trusted the Mafia. But it conditioned their behaviour pattern and commanded a sneaking respect. For if the state couldn't find their stolen animals (which it couldn't) the Mafia always could, provided it was paid well enough. He did not worry particularly about Mafia. When a trade unionist from Alia, Salvatore Comparetto, came to see him and said he was afraid to return to his village for fear of being murdered, Dolci hid him in a hay-loft, below his house, for a month. Comparetto was a close friend of Carnevale, the latest Mafia victim. Dolci was concerned with Mafia only as a state of mind contributing to the culture of the people and the repressive attitude of the police. The police sent for Dolci and invited him to clear out. 'You've come to the wrong place at the wrong time,' he was told. Dolci took no notice.

A Right-wing journalist of the day describes 'a lively charming town with white celestial houses . . . a modern rejuvenated little city'. The authorities had done 'their utmost' to relieve the sufferings of the poor, he says. The article appeared in *Voce Cattolica*, the voice of the Palermo archbishopric. The correspondent remarked on the 'calm, intelligent character' of the people, spoke with the mayor and, after a glance down the side streets for 'the terror of Partinico'—which, he said, he couldn't see—returned to the capital.

At the time two-thirds of the male population were unemployed, and the mayor was running a cosy gambling den among whose patrons were leading police officers of the district, Inspector La Corte and Lieutenant Petralito. The mayor's CD administration was spending over £30,000 a year on rural guards to watch over the acting-mayor's private herd of cattle; and municipal funds were augmented by a novel tax involving the creation of a ten-lire stamp bearing the image of the local Madonna. There was also a municipal tax on the brothels to help with the expenses of the annual religious *festa*.

Dolci bored into the facts. He noted that madmen, cripples and delinquents numbered more than a hundred, that illiteracy and absenteeism from school bordered on fifty per cent, and that public amenities—baths, lavatories, an efficient health service, a library—were nil. Infant mortality was nine per hundred—as against six for Italy as a whole and three for Britain. Residents of Spine Sante said they hadn't seen a street-sweeper for years, which was not surprising considering that two-thirds of the town rubbish-collectors had been diverted to wait privately on the mayor, his friends and the friends-of-friends.

Dolci's most startling discovery was that 350 outlaws had received from the state only 650 years of schooling as against a total of 3,000 years in prison. This simple juxtaposition of facts—documented, case by case—was to make the Government pink with rage.

'Moral pressure must be brought on the politicians from below,' he ruminated.

Some visitors did not want to believe what Dolci told them. He showed them just the same. 'Come and see for yourself,' he would say jauntily, propelling them to the handiest quarter. It saved hours of explanation, even if it did exasperate the English at the Palma di Montechiaro congress later. A British correspondent, hearing that there was a madman living in Spine Sante in the same room as his parents, asked the mayor if this were so. 'Oh yes,' Mr. Mancuso said, 'but the situation's much improved now. We've put a partition down the room.' The partition was a row of iron bars. Inside his cage Pasqualino, aged 32, paced up and down like a wild animal, roaring at intruders, black eyes flaming.

Volunteers came and went. Those who stayed were given questionnaires, rudimentary guidance, few questions asked and sent out as itinerant cullers-of-fact. Some complained of woolly instructions, others of autocracy—if they didn't come back with the right kind of information they were substituted. 'Danilo took almost anyone on,' one says. 'He wasn't fussy. He tried to direct the good in everybody. Sometimes he changed his mind ten times in a week, but as a team we got along.'

In his poky office Dolci began a kind of school where the men came assiduously in the evenings. He taught several of them to write, fathers of big families, and encouraged them to talk about their own lives. Some came begging. He gave his coat to a man who sold it and drank the proceeds. Vincenzina and the team continued to give out dried milk, medicines and old clothing. Half-samaritan, half-documenter, he was unable to say No, unable to break the vicious circle with which they were now utterly enclosed. Files grew, autobiographical accounts multiplied, and the police sent a couple of spies, got up as deadbeats, to discover exactly what the foreigners were up to. It should have been obvious. Dolci was diagnosing the disease points of the town. But even such a harmless task as mapping the municipal drains turned them into 'subversives'—the Siena students went out with an enormous sheet of blank card, to mark up all the sewers, fountains and amenities they could find: a few hours had elapsed, and then it was all round that Dolci was planning a 'foreign invasion'.

'Memories of Garibaldi and the Thousand,' Dolci chuckled.

'Or the Allied landings,' Giovanni grunted.

'Cretins,' one of the students said.

Finally, it was obvious what Dolci was up to. He was finding out too much and he was doing too much. Like the new recruit to union rules he was working far too hard and making the foremen feel uncomfortable. Dolci was called one day to an appointment at a warehouse. He went alone. He knew the men. Five of them were waiting for him, smoking, their berets pulled down hard at the corners. Two or three were relatives of a lad who was working for him, a local medical student; the others were their friends. One family had been instrumental in obtaining Coppola's safe passage home from America. Dolci had already been under pressure to release the lad. The men ushered Dolci to an inner room. One of them locked the door and pocketed the key. Dolci sat down on a crate and the men sat on crates facing him. They said the boy was degrading himself working amid poverty. They worked on Dolci for almost an hour, cajoling, threatening, raging purple. 'He's losing his *honour*!' they said. Dolci used simple moral arguments and repeated, 'The lad's free to do as he likes.' Both sides ran out of breath. They sat facing each other in sticky silence. Uncertain what to do next, Dolci reached down and took an orange from the crate he was sitting on. He began to peel it and when he had finished broke it into pieces and offered them round. The men took the segments and sat holding them. Dolci ate his and, after a bit, so did his captors. Not long after, mumbling something he didn't catch, they opened the door and went out. Dolci did, too.

He took the advice of a Palermo lawyer and for some time was careful not to go about alone at night.

It was a stock situation, the sort of warning appointment many had gone to, and then later disappeared. Dolci recounts the incident with an air of childish puzzlement. The student stayed with him, then gave up medicine. He is now a trade unionist in Palermo.

Mafia usually strikes when the atmosphere is still. Dolci was then working in comparative silence. It was a good moment to neutralise him. Yet the local Mafia hierarchy—whose opportunities for exerting friendly pressure on Rome were excellent—waited, well used to swatting inquisitive gadflies when the time came. They made a mistake. Soon Dolci would be more than a mere gadfly.

'When Danilo arrived,' Sariddu says, 'he and Vincenzina and all those children, they didn't have a lira. A few days after they moved in a woman brought along her baby, something like a year old. Imagine! A skeleton on legs. A ske-le-ton. You could pick up the skin in handfuls. When Danilo came downstairs and saw it he threw up his hands, and shouted to Carlo: "Carlo, how much've we got in the kitty?" "Just over a pound," Carlo yelled. "Bring it here," Danilo said. He gave the money to the woman and sent Carlo with her to see she got the right medicines. And that child, that piece of ragwort—it got better and better, it got so fat in the face it was like a *bull*!

'That night, after the woman came, I took Danilo and his family over some bread and cheese. They needed it. Because I saw that this was a charitable man.'

'Some families go for days on end without ever tasting bread,' Dolci told Carlo Levi. Levi, who was making his island trip that resulted in the book, *Words are Stones*, spent a day with Dolci. The latter said: 'I'd expected to find people who were brutal and shiftless. Instead, there's kindness and ignorance. They don't know what they need. The peasants don't know what a dam is. They've never heard of chemical fertiliser.'

Levi looked at some of the reports on Dolci's table. One stated that in a handful of houses there were seventeen declared cases of mental illness and epilepsy. Another, that at the start of the banditry in 1943 spacious premises which were being built as a hospital were converted to police barracks, leaving the whole zone without a hospital. In 1951 a 28-bed civic hospital was opened. It had no isolation ward, no delivery room, no child specialist on call. It served about seventy-eight thousand people. There was a maternity centre, but it hadn't enough dried milk for all the needy mothers and very many didn't know it existed.

In *Words are Stones* Levi, who is also a doctor, writes: 'We encountered the most elementary problems of a world slavishly confined within the limits set by hunger and disease; and once again, as had happened so many years before,* I was forced against my will to recall old and almost forgotten notions of medicine.' He found Dolci 'friendly and open . . . with a big, well-formed nordic head, and lively eyes behind his glasses; cheerful and full of internal energy . . .' Clouds of children called out 'Danine! Danine!' as he passed, 'as though they were uttering a magic formula.' Levi concluded that Dolci's chief quality was the confidence he aroused in others. He was to repeat the words in different circumstances the following year.

Late that summer of 1955 Dolci began to draw in the strings of the inquiry.

Several dealt with the treatment of outlaws in Partinico and in the Papirete Barracks, Palermo; the treatment known as the *cassetta*. One man told Dolci:

When I was arrested they put the mask on me twice. About ten minutes each time. The mask sucked up salt water from the bucket and then they yanked your head back so the water went down your throat. Your stomach swells up like you were pregnant.

They beat me nude, on the back, on the legs, all over my bare body. On the *cassetta* they wrench your genitals. But it's not only the beatings that are bad, it's the awful cold of the floor when they throw you down. The floor is soaking wet, they throw water and salt over you to stop up the bleeding and the swelling. And it's not that the warders do it secretly; they do it before their superiors who interrogate you and make out your statement while it's going on. Butchers!

In the meantime my family—I've three children—got no assistance from anyone.

'God knows how it sickens me to publicise such distress,' Dolci wrote, 'even though I know it is in defence of the weak, the ones at the bottom: *but it's up to us to ask forgiveness even from these people and make amends to them with immediate loving kindness.*'

He was not unduly confident about obtaining their forgiveness. But he knew it would never come as a result of empty pulpit speeches which spoke of 'work and human dignity' and emphasised the doctrine of St. Paul—He who will not work shall not eat—as though that alone would provide the remedy.

* *Christ Stopped at Eboli.*

'It isn't that these people don't want to work' he told visitors over and over. 'It's that they don't know *how* to.'

He turned to another report. A partial survey of nine hundred families showed nearly half to be destitute—161 of them because the father was, or had been in prison, had joined the outlaws or had been murdered. He was beginning to understand. Official theory was that all these irredeemable criminals had merely *happened* to gather in this one spot. He didn't believe it. He consulted the case histories of the 161 outlaws in the Madonna quarter. He found there wasn't one man among them he could classify as a pathological criminal.

Early one morning he pulled back the curtain of the bed-alcove where he and Vincenzina slept, switched on the lamp-bulb over the table and sat down on the planked ottoman before it, as he always did at this hour. Below, the peasants were starting to bump out in the darkness to their fields. The bumping of their carts over the cobbles rose as tiny shock waves, making the small table rock. He began to write:

'There is a world of condemned among us, condemned to death by us ourselves.

'It sometimes happens that it rises against injustice; then it is put down with the machine-gun and the prison.

'It is time to stop siding with the strongest, giving them leave to stifle the hopes of the others, as a cult, in broad daylight.

'I do not believe that we are all so barbarous that we want to go on killing, and let others do murder, like this. I will not believe it. Life, we know only too well, must go on.'

The words announced Dolci's stand in Partinico, as they were to announce the despairing town to the world. They became the introduction to *The Outlaws of Partinico*, an arrow of suffering shot into the ears of an obtuse society. It was published by Laterza that year.

The Outlaws had begun with a problem, and precise observance of that problem, grown through collective inquiry and understanding, and emerged as a human document binding the crucial facts.

It was to startle not only the Catholic world. A Welsh clergyman, the Rev. Wynne Jones, observed, after reading the French edition: 'Here is the *reductio ad absurdum* of what happens when crime and corruption are universal and unchecked: here is the blueprint for any country or state which wishes to allow the hoodlum a free hand to exploit his neighbour. Here poverty and the desire to earn an honest living are the only punishable crimes in the calendar.'

The Outlaws of Partinico soon threatened to become a best-seller.

95

Yet words alone, Dolci now knew, were not enough. Facts, however dramatically displayed, changed nothing. A book was not a
toy, a pleasant exercise in rhetoric. It was a tool, an instrument for
action. But action, seen from the lost playgrounds of the Partinican
alleys in the autumn of 1955, seemed as remote as a Roman tea-
party in the Via Veneto.

ELEVEN

Pause for Breath

FROM October in 1955 to Easter Day 1956, a period of five months, Dolci's life evolves, in perspective, as a patterned military operation. There is planning, a careful weighing of risk, there is skirmish, retreat, counter-attack and finally, success. But he did not arrange it like that. His instinct had a lot to do with it.

He knew in the autumn of 1955 he would have to act. Individual action was always possible. But individual action was no longer viable. 'Why is it in such grave situations it's always left to the individual to intervene on his own initiative?' he had wondered, in *The Outlaws*.

'As for "Christian Brotherhood", the less said the better . . . You find work for one of the sons only to hear the mother complain because the rest of her children are jobless; you help the sick only to get a grumble because you haven't brought the right medicine. And so on all day long, every day of the week. You can't blame them (the first thing they ask for, usually, is work) . . .'

Work. Wherever he went, that word. As at Trappeto everything seemed to resolve itself into those four letters.

Patchwork expedients by the state—work depots, housing schemes—had solved nothing. Hand-to-mouth charity by his own team only made things worse. The irrigation scheme was in cold storage. Help from outside? His northern friends were not industrialists and in any case no northern financier who valued his plant would come near West Sicily.

'What do you suggest?' he said to some trade unionists. 'March out and occupy the Sagana fief,' they said. This was the antediluvian slogan, heroic and witless, like Polish cavalry charging armoured regiments.

He fought for a solution.

He needed support. His own team was minimal—four adults and thirteen children. The only foreseeable backing was political. Here, Partinico was equipped. There were eleven political organisations, four trade unions and a Catholic Action group. They ranged from the dormant Left to the Right of beyond. He was encouraged by growing dissatisfaction among CDs with their own local

G   97

administration and canvassed hotly by the Left. But he didn't want to take sides. And he distrusted trade unions.

Party politics riled him. Boycotts, mass rallies, conventional strikes, class warfare did not interest him. They either confused the issue or led to violence, or both; and half the time the peasants didn't even know what the parties stood for. Where the Communists saw right and wrong he spoke of 'truth, which is above factions'; where they pounded the class struggle, he talked of 'collective responsibility' and 'love'; where they spoke of converting the masses and maximum jobs he declared he was not a missionary and didn't believe in political employment agencies.

Work, he said, was not an ultimate. The end was the moral redemption of man. A lasting solution was possible only if the initiative came from below, from the people themselves, and this presupposed a moral and spiritual revival which no coloured banner would ever inspire.

His hard moral core was unshakable. The Communists were mystified. Weren't they both on the side of the underdog? Here was a heaven-sent ally, an eloquent spokesman of the poor and a revolutionary to boot, who in the same breath was anti-Capitalist and anti-Communist as well. 'The idea of the class struggle ought to have preoccupied him,' the Communist writer, Franco Grasso, ruefully records.

Dolci was the Dresden Marxist who would sit on nobody's shelf.

He sympathised. He needed support. He did not wish to alienate any party. Inevitably, if only because he was a lapsed Catholic, he would be aligned with the Left whatever he did. But he felt intuitively that the moment he crossed into one political camp his hands would be tied.

He was treading on a pie-crust. Ostracised by the Right and wooed by the Left, he hesitated—and did not commit himself.

November came, and with it no solution. Winter is hard in a Sicilian community. In Spine Sante there were no fires and too much rain, earth floors and no drains. Dogs sniffed disappointedly for food scraps. The non-workers hugged copper lap-braziers, inspected their rising credit with the grocer and idly consulted the majestic clots of rubbish which the rains swept past their calico entrances. Robberies increased. Dolci's neighbour went out stealing lemons. A man was accused of murdering his brother for a couple of pounds. In a nearby street a baby girl of five months grew seriously ill from undernourishment; the mother sent an older daughter to Dolci for help, but on the way she stopped to talk to a friend and forgot her mission. By the time Dolci arrived it was too late. The child, weighing less than five pounds, died in convulsions, vomiting her intestines.

Unemployment rose. People came to Number Ten Via Iannello for help, not singly but in droves. There were too many for Dolci's team to handle.

Winter was only beginning.

By the end of November the situation was taut. Dolci fasted. On 27 November 1955 he appealed to the press and the main authorities in Italy. This is the essential part:

To all:

I invite everybody who feels a sense of public responsibility to fast for at least one day to refresh his memory, that is, if he has this kind of memory, of what it means to go hungry . . .

If at Trappeto, through the goodwill of friends, private people and the authorities, something has begun . . . here at Partinico we have to start from scratch. At least let us:

(1) Send every child to school until the age of 14; transform the present so-called schools,

(2) Help the families of the convicts and the 'bandits',

(3) Give work immediately to the jobless . . .

Meantime instead of our embracing the 'bandits' and seeking their forgiveness, above all by deeds, we shoot at them (and not only here).

Meantime by not building the dam and using the winter waters of the Iato River, up to £2·5 million goes to waste every year . . .

Starting tomorrow I shall not eat for one week. And I shall fast a week each year until the dam is built . . .

We cannot just sit back gaping at this habitual overturning of all our values.

Yours,
DANILO

Outwardly the fast served only to call attention to the problems and bolster local political initiative, and it might be argued that it was thus superfluous. *The Outlaws*, published in December 1955, put Partinico squarely in the public eye and Left-wing activity was slowly multiplying of its own accord. However, there were other reasons for the fast. Dolci was brooding a mass action. But the formula was vague. He wanted time—to sound, as well as stir local feeling. Like most men of conscience who, at flashpoint, go their own way whatever the consensus of opinion, he was humble enough —or human enough—to seek confirmation of his motives before the act.

Gronchi and Segni, the Italian President and Prime Minister respectively, and Alessi, the Sicilian Prime Minister, each received a personal note:

Gentlemen,

The action we are undertaking—aware that 'the Kingdom of Heaven and its Justice' are not easily brought among mortals—is intended as a serene contribution, the little we can, towards the efforts of all men of goodwill.

I am sure that you will understand the meaning behind these words.

Affectionately yours . . .
Danilo Dolci

Dolci fasted in a dark room at the end of Via Iannello. The title-holder was in prison and his wife, who lived with Vincenzina during the fast, without assistance. Vincenzina sat with him every day. He drank water, let the people talk, listened, and tried to convince everybody of the need for the dam. 'It will work wonders,' he said. Women said to him, 'Child, why do you starve yourself like this?' He replied, mystically: 'Exactness and truth melt, and destroy evil.'

As publicity mounted, reaction from the Right hardened. An American journalist was informally commissioned by the archpriest to see if Dolci was suffering. The journalist reported back that Dolci could stand and was not yet in a corpse-like condition. The archpriest concluded that the fast was a fake and spread the good news. At night the door was closed—chiefly because of the cold. Behind it, the critics concluded, Dolci was eating cheerfully. The mayor, the local senator, grafting public officials, leading Christian Democrats, landowners paying substandard wages, contractors supposedly constructing public works, joined the anti-Dolci movement. A well-known university don in Palermo, asked by a colleague, Professor Lucio Lombardo-Radice, to join a pro-Dolci committee, said he wanted nothing to do with 'that muck-raker'. The don added: 'Delinquents, bandits, madmen are born that way; the remedy is prison, the strait-jacket. That's what's needed!' His words echoed in the receptive crannies of conservative minds all over the island.

In Partinico signs of a moral change, a new civilising force, hesitant and tentative, were reflected in the kaleidoscope of visitors who hovered about the fasting room. Dolci noted an evident desire among the peasants to discuss non-violent remedies; to turn, for example, to the trade unions, to participate more sanely in the life of the community. He encouraged their talk. He pondered. He was hopeful.

The fast was a preparation, a necessary respite. It served as a moral brake on a situation which, in late November, was threatening to explode at any moment. It also opened the first crack in the barrel of mistrust towards outsiders.

Towards the end, on medical orders, Dolci took a little citrus juice squeezed into a glass of water to counteract ketonic poisoning. He addressed a second appeal to the nation. His workers explained it to the peasants. It was a plea for basic human rights and ended: 'We ask that the dam be built as soon as possible, for the immediate good of all.' On 4 December, the last day, thirty peasants joined him and fasted voluntarily. Hundreds filed through the tiny room and signed the appeal. It was sent off covered with crosses. Most of the fifteen hundred who signed were unable to write their names.

On the evening of 4 December Dolci drank a glass of milky coffee and ate some dry biscuits. His mind was clearer.

A few days later he picked up a copy of the Italian Constitution. It was only then that a solution came to him. God—and police reaction—willing, it was the right one. It was time for shock tactics.

TWELVE

The Plan that Failed

THE Italian Constitution is the fruit of the Italian Resistance movement of the last war. It is, in theory, perhaps the finest democratic
code in the world. Article I begins:

> *Italy is a democratic republic, founded on work.*

Article IV states:

> *The Republic recognises the right of all citizens to work and ensures
> the conditions necessary to make this right effective.*
>
> *It is the duty of every citizen to follow, according to his abilities and
> his own choice, such a calling or profession as shall contribute to the
> material and spiritual progress of the community.*

The solution lay in Article IV. It lay not in breaking the law, but
in *obeying* it. The idea had begun to coat his mind on the last day of
the fast, when Sarriddu said to him dismally: 'A hunger strike of a
few days isn't enough by itself.' 'I know,' Dolci said. 'You need a
thousand days.' 'You need a thousand men,' Sariddu said. From
there, to the peasant's suggestion that a thousand of them would
protest by lying full length on the railway track and thereby stop
all the trains going to Palermo.

Dolci was intrigued, but he dismissed the idea. It was too dangerous. And it was passive. He wanted action. 'Isn't there some
useful work we can do?' he asked. The peasants told him that one
of the country lanes behind the Madonna quarter, the Valguarnera
track, had become impassable after heavy rain. They couldn't get
their carts through. It was a public road. It was then that Dolci
picked up the Constitution.

Dolci decided on a plan of civil obedience. The state guaranteed
the legal right of every citizen to work. He would implement that
guarantee. The people wanted the road repaired. Very well; they
would repair the road. They would hold a 'strike-in-reverse'.

The strength of the plan lay in its simplicity and the near-certainty
of arrest. The shock lay in the method. Even if the other side
panicked there would be no violence from the demonstrators. This

negation of violence—a traditional value dear to every Sicilian—was the revolutionary aspect. Dolci was sure that the men had the right qualities. The doubt was in his own mind. He was not convinced that, alone, he possessed the moral fibre to rouse these qualities in the others.

On 15 December, ten days after the fast, he led about sixty unemployed men out to work. In a thin drizzle they began with picks and shovels to repair the road. They had been working for fifty minutes, shifting rocks and clearing caved-in verges, when the police arrived, 28 in all. Inspector La Corte ordered the men to stop working at once. 'You're committing an offence,' he declared. 'I'll have you all put in prison!' The men demurred. The inspector began swearing and threatened to baton-charge them. 'Enough of machine-guns—we want work!' the men shouted. The inspector promised to find them work and ordered them home. At that moment Dolci underestimated his own qualities of leadership. He conferred quickly with the men and called off the demonstration. The men obeyed the police and went home.

Dolci later said: '. . . it was a grave responsibility to act in the remote countryside without witnesses, where on one side were fathers of families and on the other, members of the police who are not used to strikes . . .'

The real reason was that he was not quite ready to go to prison.

Dolci's mind, even to those who know him well, has never appeared logical. It is continually turning in on itself, examining, re-examining, conducting a private tribunal in the realm of his own religious truth and moral convictions. This game of chess he plays, painfully, with himself is the inner spring which releases decisions and actions which at times appear wilful, contradictory and plain damn foolhardy. 'He goes along by zig-zag,' an Italian journalist observed. It is frustrating; it is inevitable; it is Dolci. But in practice he is nearly always consistent.

This time, however, he was not acting consistently. Having accepted the idea of 'disobedience to any police law which contradicts God's law', to be truthful—in his own phrase, to be *exact*—he was bound to act on that idea. For the first time, according to his own principles, he was guilty of dishonesty. He knew this. And it rankled.

According to his conscience, he was wrong. Tactically, as it turned out, he was right. He intended to obey the Constitution to the letter. The unwillingness of the police—or their inability—to grasp the spirit of the Constitution had demonstrated that this was a crime. He needed now a campaign, with wide publicity, national awareness and pressure from the top, as well as the bottom. A campaign, not merely a plan. In order to carry out a successful campaign of civil obedience he would have to adopt the rules of civil disobedience.

At last, and only in the face of defeat, did he come to the perfect solution. It was the result of experiment, compromise and a plan that failed.

THIRTEEN

The Road to Prison

IT was the harshest winter they could remember in that part of Sicily. A couple of emergency work depots were opened by the authorities and the Church, but the jobs were parcelled out by *mafiosi* to a few privileged friends. 'I will do everything in my power to find work for the jobless,' the mayor told Dolci. But two-thirds of the able-bodied male population remained unemployed.

In December 1955 Dolci wrote to Capitini: 'The people are beginning to understand that the act of signing there (in the fasting room) is tantamount to a pledge to renounce shooting.' He planned his campaign for the last days of January and the first week of February 1956.

One of the premises of civil disobedience is that you give the enemy all possible warning. You tell him the day, the hour and if possible the place. You welcome prison, receive sentence courteously, compliment the judge on his leniency and, if you are as generous as Gandhi was, you may even send your adversary—in Gandhi's case, Smuts—a handmade article which the latter will then cherish for the rest of his life.

When Dolci's first plan went off at half-cock the police were disappointed. Ever since the Borgo raid they had been waiting for a false move.

Dolci was almost ready to oblige. He prepared for a campaign to rouse the nation.

In Partinico he consulted with the families of the unemployed, wrote the text of a television talk he had been asked to give, put on the only respectable jacket he possessed and went north. In Rome the indefatigable Maria Sacchetti-Fermi embraced him and told him she had founded a national Danilo Dolci Committee. A few days later he was in Turin and on 13 January he gave his talk from the RAI television studios there. In it he returned to the principle of truth in creed and deed and announced his intentions to the nation. He said:

'In Partinico 2,500 out of 5,100 children do not go to school: they are above all the children of the bandits, the orphans. People say they've bad blood in them. Just for a moment, then, look at the drawings of Matteo, he's one of them (a dozen water-colours of Matteo, aged fourteen, are shown on the screen).

'Not only do they not go to school, the children: they cannot subsist. I would never have believed that suicide might become at times an act of reason. I always thought that to kill yourself you had to have "a screw loose". But ever since I began to see children—yes, children—watching me eat through the open door, their eyes starting, their lips drooling, only then did I start to think that to be consistent I should make sure their bellies are full before I take another mouthful myself. Let alone fast for one week in the year!...

'And when I go back what am I to tell those women who've said to me: "If you find us work we'll stop being prostitutes?"...

'Now when I return, if there are no other jobs to be had, while we're waiting for the dam to be built, we shall go to work on the track once again. I'm here to lay down to all of you, that no police charge will ever stop us from working...'

It was not Government policy to allow sociologists and writers freedom of the air to tell the truth about the south. The talk, toned down only slightly, went out more or less by accident. Dolci heard later that the two political editors who had dared to produce it, Michele Straniero and Furio Colombo, were sacked immediately. They have since become prominent in the Italian cultural world.

Dolci was given a surprise donation by a Turin benefactor. With the money he bought a car, a pre-war Lancia. It had wooden doors and held a bus-load. Friends who saw him off in Turin said that it wandered sadly down the Corso, pointed towards Milan, like a hearse in search of a funeral. Six days later it reached Rome, via Milan, Padova, Pisa and Florence. Everywhere Dolci explained his needs to friends, mayors, writers, students. They promised help. Embryo aid-committees sprang up in five centres. In Rome he told Maria Sacchetti-Fermi he was worried. All over the south, from Campania to Sardinia, labourers were demonstrating against feudal conditions. There had been clashes with the police. On the day he spoke in Turin hundreds of southern jobless had demonstrated at Venosa, in Puglia. The police had opened fire, killing a young peasant and wounding six others. It was not difficult to imagine a similar occurrence on the old Valguarnera track outside Partinico.

When Dolci drove back to Partinico he had a passenger with him, a sandy-haired teaching graduate from Gubbio. Goffredo Fofi had just finished his studies. He had read about Dolci in a French review and offered his services in Rome. Dolci's first news on return was that his other young teacher, Ugo Piacentini, a philologist left in charge of the People's University at Trappeto, had been sent away. Piacentini had applied to the Trappeto town council for a change of residence from Savona and been refused, 'on the grounds that your residence here is not justified by a remunerative employment or any other adequate reason.' Dolci's team was down to three: himself, Carlo, Giovanni. Goffredo was not long out of short trousers.

In any individual yet mass action informed leaders are vital. Without them there can be no self-control.

Dolci telegraphed the authorities, leaving the door open for an eleventh-hour intervention. There was no response. He invited all the trade unions to participate. Two accepted, the middle-of-the-road UIL (Social Democrat) and the Camera del Lavoro. The latter had been kicked out of a moribund state by the refugee-unionist Comparetto who repaid Dolci's hospitality in the hay-loft with interest. Comparetto helped to organise the coming action. In Spine Sante, above the bedlam of street criers and donkeys, details were hammered out over bowls of soup and handout suppers in Dolci's upstairs bunkhouse, which was also the dining-room. Vincenzina served an average of forty people a night. Professor Lucio Lombardo-Radice came to a meeting, and supper, and went away hungry. Friends and journalists were handed a plate of minestrone and a piece of *mortadella* or goat cheese and called into discussions; those who inquired about the flotillas of children coming and going reported that Dolci did not seem to be at all sure which were his. He appeared calm and unsmiling.

Sariddu's idea of 'the Thousand' had blossomed. Monday, 30 January, the anniversary of Gandhi's death, was fixed for a collective peasant hunger strike on Trappeto beach to protest against the continuing fishing abuses. Three days later, if the authorities had not moved, they would return to work on the track again. The fast was a necessary prelude—as much to convince the peasants taking part, as the authorities, that their intentions were honourably peaceful. 'There are to be no troublemakers,' Dolci said. 'Every man must know he's going out to demonstrate in a new spirit; to show that he's got a vast store of riches in his own hands—work.' He added, 'We'll break our bread with our own hands.'

The police were given a week's notice. Posters appeared in Trappeto, Balestrate and Partinico. Manifestoes put up by the UIL and the Camera del Lavoro contained the text of Article IV of the Constitution and an extract from Dolci's writings: 'Not to ensure work for all in accordance with the spirit of the Constitution is to commit murder.'

These words and the plan of campaign were published in *L'Ora* and in Italian newspapers. The word 'murder' had been carefully chosen.

The police reacted exactly as Dolci hoped they would. They banned the demonstrations.

Dolci was called before the police on 29 January and told that the proposed mass fast was illegal. 'Why?' he asked. The carabinieri lieutenant said that starving was allowed, but only individually. Besides, he added, he doubted very much whether it was lawful for large numbers of people to assemble on a beach.

'When I was a youngster,' Dolci said, 'I often went swimming on the crowded beaches at Rimini and the Ligurian Riviera without needing special permission from the police.'

'Perhaps,' the lieutenant observed, 'perhaps there were police among the bathers.'

Dolci said that the people were all in favour of law and order and reiterated the guarantee of work given in the Constitution. The officer replied, paternally: 'My dear Dolci, my dear Dolci—all that's just a Utopia.'

Dolci was formally asked to call off the fast. He refused.

Next morning, the Monday of the fast, it was raining hard. Dolci was woken at three-thirty and told that there were some two hundred police in the Trappeto area, where the fast was to be held. The village was surrounded. He dressed, climbed into the old Lancia and drove to Trappeto. A quick reconnaissance showed that the police had forbidden the boat captains to go without food and were holding up traffic on all the access roads, dispersing new arrivals. A warrant officer, red in the face, was screaming orders at the top of his voice. Outlying peasants arriving on bicycles were being served tickets because their machines were 'out of order'. Because of police concentration Dolci decided it was safest if the fast were held in three different places; he sent a messenger to Balestrate telling the fishermen there to fast in their own village, turned the Lancia round and made back for Partinico. A police car, jammed with uniforms, tailed him. He stopped several times to pick up Partinicans who were already walking out and passed a group of officers standing at the Partinico turn-off. One of them was Chief Inspector Tommaso di Giorgi, sent from the Palermo CID to direct operations. He noted that the police car tailing him had been flagged down by di Giorgi. Dolci drove on up the hill. A mile and a half outside Partinico, by the level crossing, the Lancia ran out of petrol. Everyone jumped out. Dolci ran all the way to the Camera del Lavoro, arriving just in time to prevent the main body of peasants setting out for Trappeto. Meantime the police car had come up behind and discovered the abandoned Lancia. It stopped. There was a hasty conference in the rain. Then the policemen plunged into the fields on either side of the road and began looking for Dolci among the cauliflowers.

At Trappeto the local fishermen had gathered on the rocky beach where the police could not get their Jeeps down. Scores of fishermen stood about, yawning, pondering and smoking in the lee of the boats. Starving to them was normal. From the parapet above their womenfolk watched anxiously. The rain continued. Police swarmed the streets in greatcoats and turned-up collars, patrolled the cliffs, got very wet and waited for something to happen. Nothing did. A northern visitor was approached by a lieutenant. 'What are you doing here?' the officer said. 'I'm a journalist.' 'There's nothing to be seen here.' 'Well, in that case,' the journalist said, 'why are you here?' The lieutenant walked away. By afternoon the carabinieri were reduced to small groups leaning on the houses, banging their boots round smoking embers to get their feet warm, while fellow greatcoats combed the cliffs, hunting forlornly for twigs to keep the fires going.

Hundreds of jobless fasted in the Partinico Camera del Lavoro. They stood pressed together in the bleak room, their eyes fixed on a sheet of paper by the window where Mario Farinella, the *L'Ora* correspondent, sat at a rough table writing. 'They brought me an old typewriter,' he reported. 'I don't know where they got it from. It's rusted up and soaked from the rain. "Here," the peasant said, holding it in his arms, "now you can write your article." It's dark and I can't read their expressions. There's a baby crying. The women in black shawls are sitting down, suckling their children . . .'

In Rome, Gronchi, the Head of State, received a telegram. 'We are not fasting today from desperation, out of despair, but in the hope that we may help Italy to become more civilised . . . Whoever impedes us is an assassin: we do not pay our taxes so that our country, on sea and land, shall become an evil prison-galley in the hands of the powerful. Signed: *one thousand citizens who believe in Article IV of the Constitution.*'

Late that morning the Partinico town council was hastily convened. It was only the second time it had met in thirteen months. Dolci was invited, but on learning that it was intended to distribute soup, declined. 'I did not think that this was the right way to solve the problem of unemployment,' he said later.

More than a thousand men fasted, for 24 hours, in Balestrate, Trappeto and Partinico. The day passed without incident.

The next day, Tuesday, Dolci launched an appeal in the national press. 'Friends of Partinico—The "bandits" of Partinico wish to become Italian citizens, members of a truly civilised society.

'By fasting and meditating together on Monday we have purified ourselves for Thursday's celebration: work. Nobody can stop us from working together in a quiet orderly manner . . .' He called on everyone, regardless of party or belief: 'Let's roll up our sleeves and get out of this abyss of material and spiritual corruption. Unless we pull ourselves out of it, we who are sunk in it and suffer from it, who on earth will do it for us? "If one fails, we all fail".

'We are men of peace,' he said. 'I am certain that nobody will try to hinder us in this sacred task.'

Commenting on Dolci's action, the *Giornale di Sicilia* warned readers of 'an exceedingly strange and anachronistic local phenomenon'.

On the Wednesday the unemployed gathered in the Camera del Lavoro. Salvatore Termini, union secretary and town councillor, spoke. 'Tomorrow let no one ask for money,' he said. 'We're going out to demonstrate that on our part there's a generous will to work.' The cheers were loud.

At the last minute the UIL pulled out.

That night the first police reinforcements reached Partinico. When in the early hours Chief Inspector di Giorgi arrived from Palermo he had four hundred police at his disposal. Shortly before six Dolci and two hundred jobless made their way out to the track. They carried work-tools only. They had left behind even the penknives they normally carried to cut bread. Journalists and photographers were on the track already. The lane fell, muddy and twisting, between caved-in verges to a small stream which cut across it. The men spread out on both sides of the stream and began working. Dolci's group was on the town side. After about twenty minutes seven truckloads of carabinieri arrived. A lieutenant marched down the track and ordered Dolci to stop working. Dolci took no notice. The lieutenant grabbed the shovel and gave him over to three constables. Dolci thought he was under arrest and allowed himself to be led away. Police, seemingly in combat kit, were pouring on to the track, with machine-guns, batons and teargas bombs. 'I hope you won't do these people any harm,' Dolci said to Inspector La Corte, police chief of Partinico, offering his hand. La Corte turned away. Farther on they met Chief Inspector di Giorgi, tall, impeccable in plain clothes and dark glasses. The latter told the policemen to release Dolci. Dolci said he would rejoin the others and promptly doubled back across open country to rejoin the main body beyond the stream. 'Go on working,' he said. The police told him to go away. Dolci grabbed a pick and fell in alongside the men. 'Go on working,' he said. All normal access was now blocked and fresh workers had to arrive across fields and vineyards. Carlo, nearest the stream, was arguing with an officer. Goffredo's group, isolated from the main body, cut over the top and joined in lower down. Puffing, di Giorgi came up to Dolci. He removed his dark glasses and said:

'Mr. Dolci, these men must stop working at once. You must obey the law.'

Dolci said, 'We're not doing anything against it. You've told us to stop working and we've heard you. By the Constitution work isn't only a right—it's a duty of us all.'

The Chief Inspector burst out laughing. 'Mr. Dolci, you mustn't take these things so literally.' Several policemen giggled.

'We've come here to do a job of work,' Dolci said. 'We intend to stay the full eight hours and we don't ask for payment. Whoever prevents us from working is a murderer.'

At the sound of the word 'murderer' di Giorgi stiffened. He gave an order. Five policemen stepped forward to grab Dolci. The latter sat down on the ground cross-legged, arms folded, Gandhi-style. As he was lifted up by his arms and legs his trousers split. 'Go on working, go on digging!' he exhorted the others. He was borne away. The five constables had to carry Dolci across the stream and uphill for the best part of a mile to reach the lorries. Dolci did not resist. Every now and then when they were tired they let him down into the mud.

Dolci was arrested at six-thirty a.m. Termini and five others were arrested a few moments later. In spite of police provocation there was no retaliation from the demonstrators—except for Carlo who, wrangling with his guardians, fell into the stream by mistake. He was re-arrested as he climbed out. 'Poor Carlo,' a colleague said later. 'He's the only one of us with a record. The first time he does something really useful for society he lands himself in jug again.'

The police also arrested a photographer and confiscated his cine-camera. They drew up in a line, sounded the advance on a trumpet and broke up the rest of the demonstration. 'Go home,' the men were told. The men did not go home. They marched down the main street of Partinico in a silent body and when blocked by carabinieri made through the back streets and reassembled at the town hall. There they were promised jobs and were asked to give their names. Those that did so were later charged in court.

Dolci and the six were charged in Partinico on five counts. On the charge sheet Dolci was defined as 'a noted political agitator'.

Goffredo, the student teacher, was arrested next morning. Di Giorgi and another officer questioned him for two hours, a piercing light full in his eyes. Goffredo's work had been mainly with the illiterate. He was jailed for two days. He was then exiled from Partinico by *foglia di via* for having 'no perceptible salary and no fixed residence'.

Two of the six arrested with Dolci were released on bail. Dolci and the other four—Carlo Zanini, Salvatore Termini, the union secretary, Ciccio Abbate, a workman and Ignazio Speciale, a young Communist clerk—were imprisoned in the Ucciardone, Palermo's jail. Dolci was well contented. 'If they arrest us,' he'd said to Vincenzina on leaving the house that morning, 'we're home and dry.'

Sariddu, describing the events to Vincenzina, said: 'What with the plain-clothes man saying to Danilo, "But these men must stop working", and Danilo saying, "But they won't stop working", and Danilo's pants splitting and then the trumpet sounding the attack, *Ma-donna*, it was just like a *festa*!'

Chief Inspector di Giorgi wrote out his report. 'Public order has been restored,' he said.

FOURTEEN

Circus in the House

NEWS of Dolci's arrest was across Europe and the Atlantic in a few hours. In Italy the balloon went up with banner headlines like THEY HAVE ARRESTED DANILO DOLCI (on the Left) and SO-CALLED APOSTLE UNMASKED (on the Right). Liberal intellectuals were indignant at police action; conservatives denounced the intellectuals for daring to be indignant. Reading the newspaper reports, the telegrams and the Acts of Parliament, it is hard to judge which was the greater—the shock of the intellectuals and the Left or the reaction of the reactionaries on the Right.

Dolci, in prison, received thousands of letters and telegrams from friends and cultural leaders all over Europe. Abbé Pierre sent his blessing. La Pira, the militantly Catholic Mayor of Florence, wired the Home Secretary, Tambroni, to release Dolci, precipitating a crisis in the Florence City Council. Influential men of letters—Moravia, Silone, de Martino, Zavattini, de Sica, the former Prime Minister, Parri, among them—held a protest conference in Rome, declaring: 'We consider ourselves in prison with him.' When the Italian Radio reported their opinion—that Dolci was moved by Christian principles—the *Vespri d'Italia* said: 'This is a deliberate attempt to influence the magistrates.' The fascist paper added, 'He is simply immoral.' In the north student groups got out pro-Dolci leaflets. In Palermo Chief Inspector di Giorgi was promoted to Superintendent. In Partinico the union offices were crammed. Demonstrations continued. The mayor told journalists: 'There is nothing abnormal here . . . perhaps a little unemployment'—and was obliged to call in two hundred extra police before he could hold an emergency meeting of the council.

Responsible journalists found themselves in a dilemma. 'To define Dolci is difficult,' *L'Espresso* said. The influential Rome weekly decided he was not a sociologist, not a missionary and not a moralist, concluding rather lamely that he was 'a non-violent man who writes'. Curzio Malaparte, the most pungent journalist of his time, said that Dolci was not a Communist, nor an anarchist nor a subversive; he was an idealist, an apostle of good, a Catholic believer with near-Protestant morals. The American magazine *Time* was more to the point. '*Dolci* v. *Far Niente*,' it said. Most other critics lost themselves, guessing. Dolci did not enlighten them for years. He called himself 'an intellectual with a social conscience' and 'an integrated Christian', which only made the muddle worse.

Government, clerical and neo-fascist organs reacted like small children with guilty consciences who, upbraided for their mis-demeanours, attempt to save face by flinging on their accuser for not attending Sunday School. The clerical journal *Sicilia del Popolo* got bogged in the hygienic system of Borgo di Dio and accused Dolci of running a promiscuous community of free love. Dolci was criticised for driving a 'luxury car'; for refusing the hand of a rich Milanese girl and, in the same breath, for living 'comfortably'; for employing Protestants and for writing books. Christian Democrat politicians reacted as though their virility were at stake. The Government organ *Giornale d'Italia* published three articles by Partinico's senator, Santi Savarino: he attacked Dolci for consorting with Communists, for defaming Partinico, for corrupting the soul of the people and for belonging to 'that intellectual cabal of *useful idiots* which enriches the Italian literary fauna'. He described Parti-nico as 'that fine and generous land where I have the honour to be born'. Senator Savarino lives in Rome.

Conservative governments have never learned how to deal with revolutionaries.

There were strange scenes in the House of Deputies. Opposition members tabled demands for an explanation from Tambroni. The Communists referred to 'the Catholic writer, Danilo Dolci'. The Home Secretary did not reply in person. Instead, in a dry bureau-cratic voice, an under-secretary, Pugliese, read out an official table of 29 statistics. In stony silence he announced to the last halfpenny how much money had been spent in Partinico and said that the num-ber of unemployed men was only 2467·3. Opposition members pointed out that official figures ignored men out of work for six months of the year.

'Please don't read us a list of sums,' the Socialist Musotto said.

The Republican La Malfa observed: 'I understand we're now studying plans to build autostradas in Sicily. They haven't got roads yet.'

'Periodically,' Alicata, for the Communists, said, 'a man is called before us to read out in a monotonous voice documents which offend our intelligence. Hon. Pugliese—doesn't it all seem a little grotesque? Don't you see that in the face of reality all these figures, even if exact, are meaningless?'

The Hon. Pugliese did not see. He was at pains to point out that his figures came from the right source.

'Perhaps,' Santi, a Socialist, said lightly, 'perhaps you asked the Mayor of Partinico for them?'

No, that was not the usual procedure, the under-secretary replied, with a perfectly straight face.

Members tried to define Dolci. They fared no better than the journalists. At one point Musotto produced a copy of *The Outlaws* and read from Norberto Bobbio's preface: 'The moral and religious figure of Danilo Dolci is, above all, that of one who follows a conscientious line of action.' Deputies were baffled.

DEGLI OCHI (Christian Democrat): The Hon. La Malfa said a short while ago that Dolci is backed by Protestants.

PAJETTA (Communist): Could you manage some first-hand information?

DEGLI OCHI: Here the Catholic newspapers say that Danilo Dolci is indeed not a Catholic.

PAJETTA: And is it necessary to put handcuffs on a writer who is not a Catholic?

DEGLI OCHI: Oh no . . . You know very well that I would never dream of consenting to the handcuffing of anyone because he is not a Catholic.

The debate ended in uproar, amid the words of the Christian Democrat Sante: 'As to the protagonist of this deplorable affair, he erupts into Sicily, into a zone where banditry is minimal . . . driven by ideals which have nothing to do with militant Catholicism . . . I would like to profit from this favourable occasion by inviting the press to inquire into what has been written and above all what has been done by this strange apostle in Partinico (*rude words from Opposition members*) . . . with that sense of absolute objectivity of which our journalism is proud . . .'

In the Senate the Government adopted similar ostrich tactics. There was another debate and another under-secretary read out yet another list of sums.

The official Government account presented Dolci as a common criminal, Communist-inspired, who had flagrantly incited the masses with the object of claiming remuneration from the local authorities. He had been arrested 'for abusing and resisting the police who were forced to intervene in order to re-establish public order'. To anyone acquainted with the Mafia client system operating between Sicily and Rome it was a familiar pattern of trumpery.

Dolci might have fared worse. As Malaparte wrote in *L'Europeo*,

Dolci, like Carnevale, had become dangerous to powerful land-owning interests and could count himself lucky to be alive at all.

It is easy to exaggerate the political importance of Dolci's action. But, coming as it did amid a terrible winter, it threw into sharp relief a general situation of unrest in southern Italy. Throughout the south two-fifths of the population was living on one-fifth of the national product and, among the 'working' classes, the average daily wage *per capita* would not have sufficed to pay a Londoner's bus fare from Victoria station to Oxford Circus. The Government was spending tens of millions (pounds, not lire) in the south. Its postwar creation, the *Cassa per il Mezzogiorno* (Fund for the South), was building roads, dams, schools and rehousing settlements from Sassari to the toenail of Italy, and not least in Sicily. But much of the work was wasted. Schools were built without regard for education: absenteeism was rife and hundreds of teachers unemployed. Hospitals were built and never staffed. Rural housing settlements appeared on gaunt hillsides, without water or electricity: the peasants refused to live in them. Dams were planned in areas where rainfall was negligible: when completed they remained empty. Water sluiced through irrigation ducts to benefit only the farms of the privileged. Government prodigality bore no relation to the needs of the people and, in 1956, had scarcely begun to touch the root of southern depression—unemployment. Everywhere, after Venosa, peasants and miners struck, demonstrated, marched behind banners, demanding an end to feudal domination. The Prime Minister, Segni—the protagonist of the sweeping, but dead-letter postwar land reforms—appealed for reason. He tried. But his voice was a reed in the winter winds. Tambroni held the whip hand. The Home Secretary deplored 'these protests'. The police took him at his word. In Calabria and Sardinia there were clashes and many arrests. In Puglia and East Sicily police routed processions with tear gas, cudgelling and machine-gunning labourers to death.

It was all, very largely, the Communist bogey. The ascetic Pius XII gave no lead to a reactionary Church party, and in the key Cardinals of Naples and Palermo—Castaldo and Ruffini—he had two aggressive allies. After eight years of power the Christian Democrats were still suffering from an epidemic of religious McCarthyism which made good Catholic voters think twice about wearing a pink tie, and threatened the fiancées of Left-wing unionists with excommunication if they tried to get as far as the altar. Unemployment was 'upsetting'. Unemployment meant demonstrations, demonstrations meant marches, and at any moment the red hordes would come pouring into St. Peter's Square. That was roughly the pattern of Government thinking.

Dolci's action fitted snugly into this context. It would have been surprising if the Government had *not* claimed it was Communist-inspired. Conversely, it gave tremendous prestige to both Socialists and Communists whose postwar rise was beginning to have a real impact: welcoming Dolci to the cause of social justice it would have been surprising if they had not boasted the 'Catholicism' of their unorthodox ally.

Throughout February Government organs continued their attempts to blacken Dolci's character, thus contributing greatly to the myth of a man they so ardently wished to silence.

In Paris a French journalist heralded '*Le Gandhi de la Sicile*'. The phrase travelled. He did indeed have the Gandhi touch. Just as Gandhi had riled the British administration in India so now Dolci in Italy was driving the Government mad.

Dolci in Jail

IN Palermo jail, the Ucciardone, society's public benefactors—
Dolci and the four—were having trouble with bugs. They were in
a large cell with forty others, visited daily by the young Palermo
lawyer, Nino Sorgi. Sorgi brought the outside news and, about the
middle of February, a message from Donna Topazia Alliata, a progressive Sicilian princess, who had worked briefly at Borgo. 'Ask
Danilo how he is,' Donna Topazia said to Sorgi. 'Ask him if he
needs anything, will you?' Dolci told the lawyer, 'Tell Donna
Topazia the food's quite all right, and I'm kept interested by talking
to the others and listening to their problems. There's only one
thing—it's hard to sleep because of the bugs.' The next time Sorgi
came he took a bottle of DDT from his briefcase. 'From Donna
Topazia,' he said. Dolci returned the bottle. The lawyer reported:
'Danilo says to thank you very much, but he won't accept it, you
know, because there are forty others in his cell and if he doesn't have
enough for all of them he won't use it himself.' Donna Topazia
promptly sent off a consignment of four gallons of DDT, 'hoping
finally that you all may sleep.' When she saw Sorgi again he said,
'Yes, he's using it now—and he's really quite happy about it.'

The Ucciardone is notorious. During one of the exercise breaks
Dolci saw a prisoner grab another and hold him against the wall
while a third beat him viciously over the head with a thorny stick.
Nobody, neither friends nor warders, interfered. In the lugubrious
Bourbon jail on the city's north outskirts many inmates existed in
perpetual fear of retribution, violence and inquisitorial torture—
not from the warders, some of whom were more afraid than the
prisoners, but from the Ucciardone's own internal Mafia. Even
today warders ask to be given heavier guard duty rather than patrol
the lower sections. Hundreds of prisoners each year are attacked;
when questioned about their injuries they invariably say that they
fell downstairs. Sentence is passed by a secret tribunal of 'lifers'
who cow warders by threatening the safety of their families outside,
and if necessary—when a prisoner breaks the law of *omertà* (silence)
—arrange for the latter's execution inside. Not even Pisciotta—
Giuliano's cousin and betrayer—with all his elaborate precautions,

evaded the retributive arm of the Mafia. Pisciotta ate only food prepared by himself or his parents and first tested it on two birds he kept in his cell. He died after drinking a minute cup of his own coffee, dosed with medicine prescribed for a chest complaint which contained enough strychnine to kill a bull.

The grimmest quarter was Section Six. Dolci had scarcely arrived when, from this section, he was sent a plate of bread, olives and cheese.

Dolci and Co. were interrogated on 3 February, and on 5 February in a public statement affirmed that their actions had been entirely pacific. Application for their release on bail was made the next day.

Demands for Dolci's release mounted. Jean-Paul Sartre devoted a special issue of his review *Temps Modernes* to the strike-in-reverse. Northern Italian university students debated the case. The Turin committee rushed up funds, sent workers and opened the first social centre in Partinico. To do this they rented a house in a hurry, not mentioning Dolci's name. Later, the *mafioso* Frank Coppola was heard to remark, proudly: 'What d'you think—in one of my houses I've got a social centre!' Gabriella, the adolescent daughter of Maria Sacchetti-Fermi, begged her mother to be allowed to come to Partinico to help out. Gabriella came. So did Franco, the young mechanic. He was then working a precision machine in a Milan factory. He received a wire from Dolci at six one evening. The following morning Franco's boss found the machine idle, with a note on it, and fired Franco on the spot. Franco was already on the train, three-quarters of the way to Sicily.

Dolci spent his days reading, talking and listening to his companions. One of them had belonged to Giuliano's band. 'If I'd known Danilo ten years ago,' he said, 'I'd never have become a bandit.' In the *aria*, the concrete quad where they were exercised twice daily, he met one of the four *mafiosi* * imprisoned and awaiting trial for the murder of Carnevale. Carnevale had been 'a bit too ambitious', the *mafioso* said. Vincenzina came almost every day, but was able to talk to her husband only through two sets of iron gratings, a four-foot gap between them. Dolci was visited by a delegation of Left-wing deputies. They found him animated and looking forward to an early release. The magistrate set down for the bail hearing was Marcataio, brother of Monsignor Marcataio, an intimate of Cardinal Ruffini. By 18 February, however, after the debate in the House, Dolci apparently was no longer optimistic. He announced:

* Later sentenced to life imprisonment and subsequently, in March 1963, released on appeal, declared 'innocent'.

'From Tuesday next, 21 February—within these walls where our society is now *revenging* itself, and monstrously so, for the evils of everybody, on a few—I will fast, for the time being, for three days.'

Tuesday 21 February was the day set down for the bail hearing. There were five charges: illegal assembly; invading public land and altering its condition; refusal to disperse on the orders of the police; abusing the police and violently resisting arrest; and sedition. The magistrate said he had studied the police reports, the 'gravity of the offences' and the 'criminal intent' of the accused. In his opinion their release from custody might endanger the public peace. In particular, Dr. Marcataio said, Dolci's behaviour, together with his private way of life, gave ample evidence that he was a fellow 'with a marked disposition for delinquency'.

Bail was refused.

Dolci was glad of the extra rest in prison. He was allowed all the books he wanted, and made copious notes of conversations with prisoners in an exercise book which he kept under the bedclothes. The warder in charge of the section knew this and on the nightly cell checks turned a blind eye to Dolci's bunk. 'Why is it you never look under my bunk?' Dolci said to him. The warder grinned and muttered in a gravelly voice: '*Io sacciu che rota gira*'—'I know that a wheel rolls.' Dolci didn't understand. 'In this cell,' the warder explained, 'there was once a man called Parri.' Ferruccio Parri, imprisoned under fascism in the Ucciardone, later became Prime Minister of Italy. The pages of Dolci's notebook were smuggled out every day by Sorgi. The young Palermo lawyer, who was then unknown, gave his services free. In the end he had to sell jewellery and pawn other articles in order to keep his practice going.

Dolci paced the cell, reconstructing and annotating the events on the track, to give a precise account at the coming trial. 'It looks bad, Danilo,' Sorgi said as the days wore on. Piero Calamandrei, the distinguished Florentine lawyer, visited Dolci. He confirmed Sorgi's gloom.

Dolci continued his homework, unperturbed. He wrote every day. His most valuable experience was the encounter with Vincenzo. Vincenzo was a 23-year-old cowherd from the mountains behind Castellammare Bay. He had been brought from the Colombaia, another prison. 'He was short and squat, and stout,' Dolci told me, 'and when he ate he ate like a cow. Thundering noises. And there were other violent noises he made, bodily sounds . . . you know? But there was a lot of likeableness in him. He was a man of four thousand years ago. It's not that he *talked*. There'd be a clot of

'I am a man who desires that his fellow humans enjoy minimum of civilised life'

SPINE SANTE: *Dolci's former neighbour, Sariddu* (upper), *whose suggestions led to the mass fast and strike-in-reverse of 1956. The area* (lower) *where Dolci lived from 1955 to 1960. He was accused of 'living in luxury'. The fountain serves 150 families*

THE TRIAL: (upper) C.
amandrei, on behalf of Do
and the other accused, co
cluding his epic address on t
final day. He was one of fi
lawyers who offered th
services free

Dolci, in handcuffs, await
the opening session; a
later, speaking in his o
defence

EPITAPH—AND AFTER: (*1*) *All that is left of Dolci's 'city' at Ceffarello above Nomadelphia.* (*2*) *An early Dolci clinic at Partinico.* (*3*) *The 'thin sticks' which the Menfi farmers said wouldn't grow.* (*4*) *In a school at one of the Dolci centres.* (*5*) *Children waiting for the centre at Corleone to open*

Pasqualino

Micha

Goffredo

Gerrit

Bianca

Eyvind

...with Dol...

Ilys

Eduard

Corleone 1964. The Hospital: *In 1956 Dr. Michele Navarra, Medical Officer of Health and district Health Inspector, was head of the ancient hospital* (upper). *When the new hospital* (lower) *was built Navarra feared he might not get the directorship. Navarra was also head of the local Mafia. The new building was not opened. In 1958 Navarra was assassinated by a rival* mafioso, *Luciano Liggio, but today the Navarra faction remains pre-eminent in the town. The new hospital has never been opened*

'Mafia: *robber bands operating in Sicily, now considered extinct*'
(Chambers Encyclopædia)

words, and then I'd ask him something, and then half an hour later there'd be another clot of words, and then another clot, and so on. . . . Some of his words were Latin, pure Latin. And he couldn't walk properly, "on shoes", as we say. Shoes with nailed soles, you understand. He was Nature itself, a primitive natural force I'd never known before.'

Clot by clot, Vincenzo's account tumbled out every day for a week:

I always dream of animals—ones out in the fields—because I grew up with animals ever since I was five. I was born with animals all about me . . . not our animals: my father was employed by the year (how many months has a year got?), or by half a year. Either that or they gave him two or three pounds a month. I don't know how many months a year's got. I don't know if I'm seventeen or nineteen. We could get someone to write to the place where they know about those things . . .

When there's no work you eat herbs. Being hungry makes you do queer things. You can't see out of your eyes. You want to kill yourself—all sorts of things. If you've got work you've got everything . . .

What are the stars in the sky? I can tell you. You see, the moon is like the sun. I understand the stars: they come out and I see lots of them. It must be something to do with the smoke, it gets into the sky and at night sometimes you can see the stars and sometimes you can't. The moon is made out of sky, the sky is made out of smoke which is made on earth and then goes up there. And sometimes in the mornings you can see the moon too when the sun arrives. The stars move through the night, they're always moving. When day comes they always go in again; the animals go into their stables, and the stars go into their stalls the same way. What the stars are, that's what us men and animals are . . .

In the world there are different countries—there are the houses. The world's half a pumpkin. In prison I've had all sorts of strange things: a bed with sheets, covers, mattresses, pillows; whenever did I have these before? I know I was born in the country because they told me so, even my father told me that. I saw houses from a distance, from outside, but I never went inside—what on earth would I have done there? I wasn't the owner. When the police came for me they got me when I was grazing the cattle and when I saw them coming I took off . . .

In prison, at the Colombaia, they gave me a bit of school. They showed me an egg—'o' for 'ovo' they said—and that's how I learned to say 'o'. Then they taught me an 'o' with a tiny leg on it, and that was 'a'. Then they went like a cow does, 'Uuu-uu-hh' and that was 'u'. Then 'e'. And then 'i'. And that's all . . .

Of course, there's somebody who rules Italy. Who is it? Mussolini, I think. It's all the lawyers who do us down, all the magistrates have a big conspiracy to keep us under. The wrong-doers, I'd kill the lot of them, I'd set them on fire so you wouldn't even find their ashes afterwards . . .

If I could do what I wanted I'd study and learn to write but I never want to leave my animals. They don't say anything, that's because they haven't got words . . . A cow, though, if I'm good to it, it gives me fruit, it gives me milk: I respect it, and it respects me. But Christians don't give me anything, they only take things from me. I know how to get on with animals, with cows and sheep and goats; but not with Christians, I don't know how to present myself. Animals have always been kinder to me than Christians. Some of the animals come with me wherever I go. I had a kid and a lamb once that used to follow me, everywhere. If I had any bread I always gave some to them. They even used to eat pasta, with sauce on it, that's how friendly they were . . . They were my best friends, that little kid and the lamb. My father was either away at the war or in prison or else they wouldn't let him out of the village, and I hardly ever knew him; however, I know my mother. My mother and my brothers love me all right. But nobody's ever loved me the way that kid and that lamb did, not even God. I saw the kid and the lamb come alive, when they were born, I fed them, they became part of me, I've never forgotten them, they used to come with me everywhere. I fed them by holding them up to the cow's teats, and they used to follow me. They followed me about like puppies . . . Then I sold the kid to buy some food . . . I bought a kilo of bread, a kilo of fish, and ate that. And while I was eating I kept thinking of the kid. Then I didn't eat anything for two days, just thinking about it, and crying. And for the next eight months at work I went on thinking about it, and I still think about it.

In America and Russia there's the same Government as there is here. What's Russia? Russia's a little island. What's China? Is it a sort of grape? I've never heard of it.

Vincenzo was arrested for stealing two bunches of herbs.

. . . They were on horses and they took me off to the barracks. There they threatened me with a knife, they beat me on the back and kicked me with boots, and they wrote everything down I said

—not with a pen though, it was something that went *tin-tin-tin*, who knows what son-of-a-bitching thing it was. Then they made me put a cross on the paper, and they let me go.

Four months later they came back and put me in prison. Then they took me to the Colombaia. Then they tried me and sentenced me to four years and twenty days. They wanted the judge to make it six years. They said, did I want to make an appeal? I was crying so hard I couldn't see through my eyes. And that's why I'm here now, waiting for the appeal, only the landowner whose herbs I took, the one that had me arrested, he never shows up, so I have to go on waiting till he does.

Vincenzo's story in the whole forms a logic of which he alone would have been incapable. On such occasions Dolci, the artist, seeking creation in the expression of shared labour, is at his best. His art is never an abstract thing. More than art, it is his method, his belief and his way. 'Every time we make a discovery like this, a discovery of truth, there's a great joy. And then, in Vincenzo's efforts to express himself, he conquered something himself. And that's what we have to do, not only with the cowherd, but with people.'

The story of Vincenzo the cowherd was to open the book which documented Dolci's trial. The trial was set down for 24 March.

On the eve of the trial two Italian lawyers, Achille Battaglia and Federico Comandini, were at Rome airport waiting to board a plane to fly down in Dolci's defence when they heard that the Rome police had seized a serious review, *Nuovi Argomenti*, containing a sociological account under Dolci's name, and had charged him with 'pornography'. The issue in question had been on sale for months. The intention was obvious. 'This is preposterous!' Battaglia said, in a voice suited to his name. (It means Battle.) His companion nodded, a little sadly. 'Yes, it does seem to be rather well timed, doesn't it?' At that stage there was nothing anyone could do about it.

SIXTEEN

The Trial

THE trial is already a landmark in Italian legal history. It was like something out of Kafka. The police alleged they had been hit, kicked, sworn at and called murderers and attempted to prove that work-tools had been used as weapons. Defence witnesses suggested by Sorgi had either been disallowed or themselves charged. Independent observers had several times to pinch themselves to make sure it was really happening and was not instead some phantasmagoria of the sub-conscious evolving amid the frocks and gavels of a misty totalitarian state.

Fifty lawyers offered their services in defence free, and intellectuals came from all over Italy to speak on Dolci's behalf. The defence had to be cut to six. It consisted of Battaglia, the top Italian penalist, Calamandrei, the most distinguished civil lawyer in the country, Comandini, and the Sicilian lawyers, Varvaro, Taormina and Sorgi.

The trial took place in a room of Palermo's old supreme court, Lo Steri, a fourteenth-century building in Piazza Marina from the roof of which three hundred years before it had been the custom to throw down witches to their death. The building also marked the spot where in 1909 the American criminal investigator, Lieutenant Joseph Petrosino, sent in under an assumed name by the New York Police Department to study the liaison between the Sicilian Mafia and its emigrant child in America, The Black Hand (today ·Cosa Nostra), was assassinated by the Mafia Head, Don Vito Cascio Ferro, a few hours after landing at the port. (After killing Petrosino, Don Vito returned by carriage to an interrupted dinner appointment: he was dining at the time with a Member of Parliament.)

On the opening day of the trial there seemed to be only policemen and poor people. There were two policemen for every three members of the public. Scores were unable to get in. Black-shawled women were jammed round the lawyers' tables, some forced to crouch and peer round policemen's legs in order to maintain a stable position. Journalists had to stand. Visiting lawyers found there were no proper gowns. The presiding judge, Dr. Trainito, flanked by purple-tasselled and white-gloved carabinieri, reached for a bell to call for order, and found there was none. Dolci and Co. arrived in what appeared to be a Red Cross van and were led in between carabinieri, handcuffed and in chains. They were shuffled into place, alongside eighteen other accused, on two benches against a wall. Dolci was squashed on to one end.

'I wish to point out that the defendants are still handcuffed and in chains,' Battaglia said. The public prosecutor, Dr. Lo Torto, said that this was thought necessary for the sake of public order. The presiding judge ordered the handcuffs to be removed.

Dolci, who seemed to have lost a little hair in prison, wore a lapel-less tweed jacket over a habitual white expanse of shirt-front, and no tie. He spoke quietly. 'The Constitution in Italy is the only law of which nobody need be ashamed,' he testified. 'I am no anarchist. I am a man who desires that his fellow humans enjoy a minimum of civilised life.

'In the last two years sixteen murders and suicides have been committed in the Partinico area. You know what winter means to the poor. We didn't want to see people go out to steal or commit crimes. But we were being pressed to find some remedy. What could we do? . . .' He described the arrest in detail and said that 'four or five of them picked me up by my ankles and wrists and carried me face downwards. When they saw they might break something they turned me over on to my back and carried me that way'.

'What do you weigh?' the judge asked.

'Thirteen and a half stone and I am 5 feet 11 inches tall.'

'Did the police tear your trousers?' Battaglia said a little later.

'When they lifted me up my trousers split right down, but I'm sure the police didn't do it on purpose.'

Standing in a tiny, cleared space below the judges' bench, Dolci was seldom interrupted. Occasionally he gestured, nordic brows knitting, his right arm and spatulate fingers spreading out in broad evangelic movements. He admitted that he refused to stop working when ordered and urged the men to go on digging. 'Your Honour, let me explain my state of mind,' he said softly. 'If someone ordered me to kill my father or you yourself . . . I wouldn't do it because my conscience wouldn't let me: because it is criminal. I consider it is equally a crime against the land and against mankind to stop work . . .

'Let's put our cards down. If they stopped us from working we were going to stay there for the full eight hours, sitting down, with our arms folded. We really had in mind turning the track into a sort of effective Labour Exchange.'

'Wouldn't a symbolic half-hour have done as well?' the judge said.

'I didn't say the plan was symbolic. We wanted to do a real job of work . . . I must make it plain that no one took so much as a pen-knife along to cut his bread.'

'No one is accusing you of being in improper possession of arms.'

The judge was mistaken. 'The mass, goaded on by Dolci and the leaders, began to shout in tumult, brandishing their instruments among which were pruning knives,' a police witness stated.

The police tried to insert a scurrilous article by Senator Savarino, published in his own paper, the *Giornale d'Italia*, as part of the case for the prosecution, and while Dolci was testifying two officers, waiting to be called as witnesses, slipped in at the back, and eavesdropped. Sorgi bawled them out for violating court procedure. The officers withdrew sheepishly. Constables said in evidence that when they were carrying Dolci he hit or kicked out. Chief Inspector di Giorgi said that Dolci did not hit or kick out. Inspector La Corte said that Dolci 'even gave notice of the demonstrations in *L'Ora*' and a few minutes later claimed that the demonstrators had attempted to take the police 'by surprise'. One constable, accusing Abbate of violence, offered to identify him: 'I know him because I was the one who escorted him.' Without the court noticing, Speciale quickly changed places with Abbate. The constable promptly identified Speciale. The public roared. The ploy was repeated with another constable who alleged violence. This constable also identified the wrong man. The prosecutor protested at the 'indelicacies': at least the defence might ask the judge's permission before switching defendants, he said. 'In order to test the reliability of police witnesses,' Battaglia replied, 'we will repeat the "indelicacies", if necessary.' By the third day the police case was foundering in a maze of contradictions.

Each night when the accused were handcuffed and taken back to prison a small crowd waited outside to applaud them. Newspapers put out special editions. Foreign journalists multiplied. A group of Italian writers held a press conference in Rome and declared that if Dolci were condemned they would carry on at Partinico in his place. English and Sicilian university students distributing pro-Dolci leaflets were herded into a bar by the Palermo police and the leaflets confiscated.

The defence brought out that there was a film of the entire proceedings which would show there had been no resistance. The photographer in question was unable to help, however. As he was filming the final arrest, he said, 'The police grabbed hold of me, tore the camera from my hands and broke it in three pieces. I was thrown to the ground . . . At the police station, after the film had been extracted, they returned the camera to me—broken, naturally.'

The film was not available in court.

The trial lasted a week. Towards the end a change took place and as, one by one, a gallery of leading Italian intellectuals came forward to testify as character witnesses on Dolci's behalf, the cranky ill-equipped room was transformed into a national tribunal. On one side were the poor and the world of culture and on the other the reactionary forces of law and order, repression and Mafia. Such a collision of forces had never occured in public.

'Men like Danilo—you need lots of them in Sicily,' the novelist Vittorini said. 'An old friend of mine, a monk of the Order of the Servants of Mary, introduced him to me. At first I was uneasy about him. I always mistrust the kind of activity where religion and social reform are mixed together. But once I got to know Danilo my reservations disappeared . . . As for his Indian-type methods which many people find so upsetting, I find them peculiarly suited to Sicily . . . Sicily is very like India. I am Sicilian, Your Honour, I was brought up here. In Sicily you find the same class segregation that exists today in much of India . . . In India there are dozens of men like Danilo who are preparing the way for state reforms, and the Government doesn't obstruct them in the least; indeed it helps them.'

Vittorini was followed by the philosopher Bobbio and the critic Carocci, by Levi, Lombardo-Radice, Tullio Vinay, Maria Sacchetti-Fermi and others. They called Dolci naturally by his Christian name. Once the judge slipped up and said 'Danilo'. Maria Sacchetti-Fermi, a wisp of a woman in a blouse and dark costume, broke down after testifying and embraced Dolci with tears streaming down her face.

'Danilo Dolci's work is the state's work,' Levi said. 'His prime quality . . . is his confidence. It is this confidence which he spreads around him, and which floods his work, which injects hope into the veins of the poor among whom he lives . . .

'Danilo Dolci has been accused of abusing the police with words like, "Whoever stops us from working is an assassin . . ." Dolci has used this phrase before. From memory, it is: "We are living in a world of men condemned to death by us ourselves . . ." Yes— as long as men are excluded from the right to ordinary human existence, we are all of us responsible, we are all of us murderers. *All* of us. I am a murderer, and you, too, Your Honour, you are a murderer, and even Danilo Dolci is a murderer. This is the meaning of the phrase that is the *leitmotif* of his book *The Outlaws of Partinico*— it is one of the noblest phrases a man could utter.'

Ignazio Silone, too ill to attend, sent a message, saying: 'The world of culture is on Danilo's side.' The world of authority, however, was not. Dr. Lo Torto, the prosecutor, asked the court to find the prisoners guilty on all counts. 'This is a perfectly ordinary case,' he said. 'I am not here to deny the right to strike, which indeed is sanctioned by the Constitution. But I must point out that a strike means a withdrawal of labour . . . Are we quite certain that Dolci lives up to his pacifist principles? Or doesn't it appear as if Dolci himself by his behaviour is the one who stirred up all this tension? Finally, you will note that everyone is agreed that he resisted arrest . . . What more do you need to prove Dolci guilty?'

The defence spoke for nearly two days.

On the final day Calamandrei stood up. Piero Calamandrei was a former Rector of the University of Florence—a spare, tall figure who, striding along in overcoat and scarf, might have been mistaken for a British admiral on furlough. 'This isn't an *ordinary* trial at all,' he said. 'It is an exceptional trial, superlatively extraordinary, absurd. This isn't even a trial: it is an *apology*. A trial in which one seeks to condemn honest men . . . men arrested and sent to the dock under the charge of voluntary observance of the law; with the additional guilt of premeditation! . . .

'Looking back, what will appear to the historian its most significant aspects? His eye will be caught above all by the judgment of the magistrate who, refusing the prisoners bail, affirmed, verbatim, the *marked disposition for delinquency of the above-named defendant*: the *above-named defendant*, for those who may not know, is Danilo Dolci . . . Ah well, the phrase has been written: and in fifty years' time the historian will be able to read it and say to himself: "Aha! I'm in luck. Here's an interesting case, the trial of a great delinquent, a typical case of *marked disposition for delinquency*." '

Gazing from behind thick horn-rims with the air of one admonishing small boys, Calamandrei methodically took the police case apart —revealing (with respect) that it was necessary to do so, otherwise the Constitution was a bastard. Several times as he paused, swaying on the points of his shoes, a tense audience crouched at his back seemed about to precipitate him bodily into the arms of the judges. 'Do you remember the immortal words of Socrates in the prison of Athens? He speaks of the laws as of living people . . . In the more perfect European democracies, the people respect the laws because they participate in them and are proud of them: there is no double interpretation, one for the rich and one for the poor! . . . This is the curse of Partinico; but also this has always been the curse of Italy . . . for the weak the laws don't count. To get his dues a poor man has to kotow to some important person—or shout his lungs out. But perhaps not even shouting counts, for if he shouts too loud along comes Chief Inspector di Giorgi and takes him off to prison.

'And so along comes Danilo: "Enough of this curse, enough of this mistrust—and away with violence," Danilo says. "The law is a kind of religion. But before the law can work its wonders, you must first of all believe in it."

'Is he a simpleton? Is he a dreamer?

'Danilo has been compared to Renzo in the famous tavern scene in *The Betrothed*. You remember? "*Bread, plenty, justice.*" Renzo heard it said by Ferrer, who was a prefect of the time. And Renzo believed it: he, too, began to repeat, "Bread, plenty, justice." And he ends up in the hands of the police.

'And so does Danilo. Is he, too, merely a simpleton then? Merely a dreamer? No: Danilo is something more . . .

'No, my dear public prosecutor, this is not a "perfectly ordinary case". This is not the trial of Danilo Dolci. On that bench are exposed other guilts, other injustices, other crimes. We all know what they are, and so do you.

'Danilo is not on trial here; nor is Partinico; nor is Sicily. It is our country which is on trial . . .

'A few days ago I saw in a foreign newspaper this headline: "*In Italy he who has faith in the Constitution is denied bail.*" It isn't true, it isn't true! Your Honours, tell the foreigners that it isn't true! . . . Help us with your judgment, I beseech you, help the dead who have been sacrificed and help the living to uphold this Constitution which sets out to give every single Italian citizen equal justice and equal dignity!'

What followed when Calamandrei sat down is described as pandemonium. Calamandrei was not normally an emotional person. He was a civil lawyer, university don, editor; a severe intellectual. When he had finished speaking he buried his face in his hands. He broke down completely. So did almost the entire courtroom. Policemen flushed, the judge had to turn away, men wept openly. When after some minutes the judge had regained control, first of himself and then of the court, the sound of sobbing could still be heard.

The judges' panel went out just before noon. The public waited, hovering in the courtyard outside. Vincenzina remained sitting, hands crossed in her lap. After nearly six hours, when the jury returned, the room was again full. Dr. Trainito galloped through a preamble sixteen pages long. And then, suddenly, it was over. Dolci and the rest were acquitted on the serious charges, involving illegal assembly, disobeying, resisting and abusing the police; they were found guilty of trespass and inciting to commit an offence and sentenced to fifty days each. They had already served exactly fifty days. They could go home.

On both sides of the Atlantic the verdict was hailed as a victory for Dolci and for non-violence. But not in Sicily. The judgment was appealed against, not only by the defence, but also by the prosecution. In the view of the local authorities, fifty days was too lenient a sentence.

Note: Piero Calamandrei died in 1957.

SEVENTEEN

Dolci Moves On

DOLCI denies lifting his technique of non-violent action from Gandhi. In a similar way Gandhi denied taking the idea of civil resistance from Thoreau's famous 1849 essay, *Civil Disobedience*.

Henry Thoreau was a New England rebel and poet. He fought against Negro slavery. Twenty-four hours in jail for refusing to pay taxes, and thus lend himself to a wrong he condemned, evoked his acute provocative treatise. To be right, Thoreau believed, was more honourable than to be law-abiding.

'As they could not reach me,' Thoreau wrote, 'they had resolved to punish my body . . . I saw that the state was half-witted, that it was timid as a lone woman with her silver spoons, and that it did not know its friends from its foes, and I lost all my remaining respect for it and pitied it.'

Gandhi discovered Thoreau's essay in 1908 when he was (of course) in prison. He cherished the above extract. He read the essay several times. He called it 'masterly'. He began to use the phrase '*civil disobedience*' 'to explain our struggle to the English readers'.

His own code of religious action was *Satyagraha*, which is very close to Christian communism. Gandhi's biographer, Louis Fischer, writes: '*Satyagraha* means truth-force or love-force . . . *Satyagraha* is peaceful . . . The opponent must be "weaned from error by patience and sympathy"; weaned, not crushed; converted, not annihilated. *Satyagraha* is the exact opposite of the policy of an-eye-for-an-eye-for-an-eye-for-an-eye which ends in making everybody blind.' Gandhi called it 'the vindication of truth not by infliction of suffering on the opponent but on one's self'. Gandhi's chief task was to purify India; expulsion of the English would then follow naturally. When in 1921 at Bardoli he called off his first Indian campaign of mass non-co-operation—because of mob violence elsewhere—he said: 'It is better to be charged with cowardice and weakness than to be guilty of denial of our oath and to sin against God. It is a million times better to *appear* untrue before the world than to *be* untrue to ourselves.'

131

Dolci had already adopted this code when he read Gandhi. In 1953 in a pamphlet issued from Borgo di Dio he declared: 'In this world which is an intelligent, organised and often hypocritical school of murder I will never wilfully kill a brother. I shall not live according to my instinct but my spiritual conscience. It is my duty to serve, my place to be with the least, the little ones. I will collaborate with life . . . never with death.' He discovered Gandhi and read his *Autobiography* the following year, finding in him 'confirmation and enlightenment'. More than anything he cherished Gandhi's words, 'I do believe that, where there is a choice between cowardice and violence, I would advise violence . . . But I believe that nonviolence is infinitely superior to violence, forgiveness is more manly than punishment.'

Dolci was influenced by Gandhi much as the latter was influenced by Thoreau. (Dolci has never read Thoreau's essay.) But by the time each had made his discovery—Gandhi of Thoreau, Dolci of Gandhi—each had vindicated, in word and deed, his own private truth. Each was already a champion, in his separate way, of the private conscience against majority expedience. Thoreau and Gandhi got their original idea of passive resistance from the Hindu gospel, the *Bhagavad Gita*. So did Dolci. Thoreau borrowed from ancient India and repaid the debt with interest. Gandhi took from Thoreau and both refined and perfected the strategy of the mass civil disobedience campaign. Gandhi died, assassinated, in 1948. Since then men have developed forms of passive resistance in many countries—Martin Luther King and Bayard Rustin in the American south, Luthuli and Trevor Huddleston in South Africa, Bertrand Russell and Michael Scott in Britain, Aldo Capitini in Italy.

Dolci did not bring the Gandhian torch out of the East. He did not pioneer the reverse strike. But in 1956 he conceived and conducted the first successful mass civil disobedience campaign on Gandhian lines in the West.* He did so from the most violent corner of peacetime Europe.

The fruits of his action purified a local situation. The tortures in Partinico, in the barracks-shed behind the church, stopped; Mancuso and elements of his grafting administration were ousted;

* Students of non-violence may feel that the Norwegian resistance by the clergy and teachers to the occupying Nazis in the last war destroys the claim. But the Norwegian action was anonymous and loose; the thousands who boycotted Nazi decrees responded to their private consciences, they were not led.

Francis Deák's long and successful Gandhi-type resistance in Hungary to the Austrian hegemony (1850–67) does invalidate the claim, if Hungary is considered part of Western Europe.

Inspector La Corte was transferred; in the next elections protest votes against the Christian Democrat régime soared; Senator Savarino was not re-elected. But Dolci's action went farther. It succeeded in welding religious peasants and militant Communists in a non-political protest against social injustice which belittled barriers of class and creed. Partinico's tiny minority voice cried wisdom to the appeal of oppressed masses everywhere. This was the significance.

In putting a spark to Christian communism Dolci lit a lamp on the road to solving a universal dilemma: that of finding a formula for the mental health of nations. He anticipated Pope John's revolutionary *Pacem in Terris* encyclical by seven years.

He was thirty-one.

On Easter Saturday, 1956, the day after the trial ended, Franco Grasso, the writer, was standing in a Palermo suburb holding a copy of *L'Ora*. On the front page was a picture of Dolci leaving prison. 'A woman asked me for the newspaper,' Grasso writes, 'kissed Dolci's image, passionately, over and over again, and then asked me to take her to him to be "recommended for a favour" on behalf of her son. On the same page was a large photograph of Pius XII, giving his [Easter] blessing; it received no part of her effusions . . .'

Dolci came out of prison a bit dishevelled, but clean-shaven, as usual.

In the photograph he is muffled in coat and beret and carries a huge bundle of newspapers, a pair of boots and a kitbag of clothes. He is surrounded by a shoal of well-wishers. He appears bewildered, like a mariner stepping ashore from a wreck.

From prison he went to the quay, saw off Calamandrei and others on the nine o'clock boat, then drove to Partinico where hundreds had waited up in the square and were already fêting the return of Termini, Speciale and Abbate. Carlo Zanini, because of his previous record, was the only one not released immediately. Children presented each with a red carnation. It was after midnight when Dolci, stumbling through the feeble lighting and mud of Spine Sante, regained his family. His two-year-old daughter Libera had put a branch of peach blossom on the table. He sat down to a bowl of soup, and *companaggio*, and presently Vincenzina handed him a bundle of proofs. They were the proofs of all the poems he had kept, including the only poems he had written in Sicilian. While he was in prison a friend, Giuseppe Ricca, had gathered them together for a Milan publisher. (*Poesie*, the collected poems, appeared in April.) Spine Sante neighbours came in and out with a bluster of greetings, and one or two of them said: 'But why on earth did they arrest you, Danilo?'

Dolci had come to a peak of popularity. He did not see himself as a bringer of miracles. 'I'm no magician,' he said. He was a working man, even a plodder. His task was moral as well as practical, to tend seeds of hope already planted, to purify. He went on his detergent way: 'To the press: ... Throughout Italy we are systematically assassins. There is no guarantee of work for all; there is no real freedom of thought, of expression, of action; there is no provision for the invalids and the children of convicts; no education for all. There is talk of reforms, of revolution, of God; yet the maid still waits at table and then goes into the kitchen and eats her meal alone; civil servants still pay taxes towards the upkeep of the brothels; prisoners are treated as if society were waging a vendetta against them. (I shall always remember those convicts serving ten or twenty or thirty years—their pained eager eyes watching intently through the bars two cats copulating in the garden below, while the prison radio blared out a boxing match; and, high on the outside wall, one could read the hypocritical carved words: *Omnia vincit amor*.)

'Better in prison with the victims than out there "free", if privileged. If we're not careful we'll soon see political banishment revived, and then a little later they'll light the faggots again for those who seek the truth, the "heretics", while the prefects look on with candles in their hands . . .'

Yet he did not believe, with Gandhi, that 'we must widen the prison gates and enter them as a bridegroom enters the bride's chambers'. For Gandhi, going to prison was a necessary therapeutic to rousing a nation for liberty. Dolci had no such faith in the medicinal value of Italian prisons. He was prepared to go to prison again himself, but he was not prepared to call for the same sacrifice from a people whose daily life was dominated by the fear of prison. The impact of his campaign did not blind him to the fact that his aims were still mistrusted by the peasants. Another reformer might have capitalised on his success and plunged into a mass civil resistance movement. Politically the moment could not have been riper. Dolci did not believe in short cuts. And he was not for political games. His ideas were unchanged, but evolving. 'Let us multiply and deepen our studies, from below,' he continued, 'realising man's potential and the land's—so that the achievement of an intelligent plan for full employment may be based on sane economics . . . The idea of yeast isn't enough to make the bread rise; you need the yeast itself, and in the flour.

'The tomorrow we long for is coming, even if today it appears only too far off.'

From this a cogent pattern of thought emerges. He feels a responsibility for all—almost on a cosmic scale. He is stirred to action. He remains optimistic. He is impatient to do good. Full employment and moral reform are still the platforms. The tools are love (or truth), non-violence, sacrifice—and courage. The courage to go on denouncing social evil and apathy, go on implanting this idea of resistance to evil in the minds of a suffering people. Terms like 'from below', 'planning for full employment' and 'sane economics' are used together, germinally and clearly, for the first time. His inspiration remains profoundly Christian, universal brotherhood is still the *modus operandi*, but Nomadelphia and Borgo di Dio are far behind.

Dolci put aside cosmic thoughts and came back to reality. In the Ucciardone he had secured from fellow prisoners descriptions of police tortures carried out in Palermo's Papirete Barracks, near the flea market. They are reminiscent of those used by the Nazis or the French in Algiers. Gavin Maxwell, in *The Ten Pains of Death*, was to add to this evidence. The brutalities described are on similar, but more elaborate lines to the *cassetta* treatment used in Partinico: cigarettes ground out on bare flesh, sadistic beatings, electric current applied to men's genitals. These statements he included in the book which grew out of the strike-in-reverse. It was commissioned by the prestige publisher, Einaudi, and appeared that summer as *Article Four on Trial*. The tortures, which were never denied, later stopped.

It was late spring 1956. Dolci looked round him. In Partinico the scum had been whipped off the cesspool, but the waters were still troubled underneath. Dolci's diary records:

9 April: Another young man has been stabbed through the heart in Partinico tonight. He was only seventeen. An old woman, who saw it happen, died on the spot from fright.

23 April: Another woman was murdered in Via della Madonna: she was only nineteen.

5 May: Another man has been murdered, the fourth in a month.

29 May: The body of a youth has been found in an advanced state of decomposition in the water-tank of the house.

7 June: Someone has been shot in the head, but it looks as if he has escaped serious injury.

Opposition had not lessened. Franco went into a tobacconist for some cigarettes. A clerk he knew was chatting to the proprietor. Recognising Franco, the man hurriedly crossed himself and went out.

'There's a lot to be done, Franco,' Dolci said. It was typical of the man that, having put down his pen ostensibly to gather in the threads where he had left off, he should pick it up again almost immediately. Dolci asked his colleagues for their advice—as he always did. They advised him to consolidate the work in Partinico, expand the tiny social centre financed from Turin, press for the dam on the Iato—after all, that was one of the reasons for coming to Partinico, wasn't it? If not, they said, the peasants would be left buoyed up but in limbo, and eventually feel resentment. Dolci listened, and then went his own way—as he always did.

His task, as he saw it, was still to expose. It was not enough to throw a little mud; you had to throw an awful lot, and go on throwing, until some of it stuck.

The question then was not 'What next?', but 'Where next?' In fact, Dolci did not even ask himself the question. He already knew the answer. Palermo.

EIGHTEEN

Inquiry in Palermo

PAUL DE MUSSET, brother of the poet Alfred, describes Palermo as a courtesan whose sultry charms so seduced the Carthaginian, Arab and Saracen invaders that they left her beauty intact. 'The happy city,' he says. Likewise Garibaldi, the last conqueror, fell captive at Palermo's feet: beyond closing the convents and blowing up a few Bourbon arsenals he didn't knock the old lady about very much. Tourists also find the Sicilian capital enticing. There is a fragrance of musk and the Orient. Arab steeds pad the soft black streets. Behind the portrait gargoyles of the Cathedral and the mosaics of the Palatine Chapel, arabesque dirges of hawkers sweep the people's markets, and under wrought-iron balconies young girls, beautiful at thirteen, gaze rapidly before turning their backs on the eye of the intruder. Above the bay where Nelson moored is Mt. Pellegrino, bearing the shrine of St. Rosalia, the only Sicilian saint in the calendar. Goethe called the headland 'the most beautiful promontory in the world'. Below, the city floods the plain, spilling flakes of white farmhouses into a shell of lush green vegetation. The shell rises to an orifice in ochre mountains. Looking back on Palermo from the Norman cathedral of Monreale, the gateway to these mountains, the tourist sighs in the heat, and smells camomile and, gazing on the banded apron at his feet—ochre, green, white and the rainbow blues of the blue-ribbed Tyrrhenian Sea—tends to conclude that Goethe was right, and that sights like the Bay of Naples are vastly overrated.

This is about all the tourist sees. But not far from the broad thoroughfare of Via della Libertà and the chic opulence of Via Ruggiero Settimo, just behind the imposing *palazzi* and the romanesque church fronts, there is another Palermo, a maze of tiny *rioni*, sectors, dank-smelling little *casbahs*, where thousands live in conditions rivalling Asiatic squalor. These are not border slums—they are banked up in the heart of the city, acres of them. If you walk the two or three hundred yards in a straight line from the great Cathedral to the Palace of Justice, you pass through the middle of one of the worst of them, the Capo. They are not like Neapolitan slums—there is something secretive about them, grim and undeclared; after nightfall when the cries of the wandering vendors and the bundles of second-hand American clothing have gone away they wear a curfew look, and the memory of Arab mosques and veils hangs close.

In 1956 more than a hundred thousand people, or a fifth of the city population, were living in these slums. Some were nothing more than holes in the ground, grottoes. About ten thousand people were living in grottoes.

There was no regular work for these people. In Milan half the population was 'active'; in Palermo, a quarter.

In 1860 Garibaldi smelled these zones. He ordered an immediate investigation. Nothing happened. Almost a century later the situation was unchanged—if anything it was worse, because the over-crowding was greater. Cardinal Ruffini's lavish Church aid and Christmas messages had not affected the reality, or the civic conscience. In 1954 the authorities did look at them. The City Council in an official report, said: 'Families at most have one or two rooms without the most elementary benefits of hygiene, without lavatory, kitchen, water and even sometimes artificial light, without air and without sunlight, where humidity, cold, dust and the stink of drains and refuse is appalling. These conditions, plus the overcrowding and the consequent promiscuity, have led to a state of physical and moral degradation which can be described without exaggeration as utterly terrifying.'

The report was unanimously approved by the Sicilian Regional Assembly. Nothing happened. The City Council had a deficit of four million pounds. The Department of Public Works was studying plans to build autostradas.

Dolci saw his task clearly. To leave Trappeto and Partinico with skeleton crews and expose Palermo to the world. The task was greater than it seems. For he chose not the city alone, but the province as well. To do this he first toured the interior in the old Lancia, selecting some of the tragic spots—Alia, Vicari, Bisaquino, San Giuseppe Iato, Villalba. He sent in volunteers, student sociologists and teachers from the north, to sift and document and make the statistical interviews; he did the longer story interviews himself. He worked the city with a man called Gino Orlando.

Gino was an itinerant barber. He is the apotheosis of Dolci's theory that a moral outcast, given work and treated as a human being, is able to pull himself out of the gutter by his own boot-strings. Gino, the illegitimate son of a *spiccia-faccende* (a kind of street copyist) and a municipal clerk, began life as a pickpocket. By the time he was seventeen he had known brothels, the contraband trade and prison; at eighteen, reform school, but he was caught kissing the mayor's daughter behind the bushes and expelled; at twenty he was exiled. Then someone took an interest in him and gave him useful work. He began to follow politics and became a trade unionist, leading peasants in the postwar land reforms to occupy the fiefs in defiance of the Mafia. He did not return to crime. When Dolci met Gino in 1955, he encountered a man who was still living precariously, but who had not been crushed by a nine-year wait at the Labour Exchange for a regular job—a middle-aged man with a limp and an unusual sensibility, a man with a positive attitude to life.

Gino was Dolci's passport to Palermo. He knew every alley and every courtyard, he knew the police and he knew the *ciocolattari*, the narks. He knew where to find a young workman reduced to a paralytic beggar after being flogged by rawhide whips in prison, or an artisan's son who lived as a turkey-raffler doing conjuring tricks at eleven a.m. on Thursdays with a ten-thousand-lire note pinned to his lapel. He knew the 47 'official' activities by which the hungry fifth scraped an existence, and all the unofficial ones. The pair of them worked together fifteen hours a day. With his quick, limping gait Gino covered half the city, from organ-grinders' corner in the Kalsa to the flooded basements of Cortile lo Cicero, Dolci bustling alongside in sandals, open shirt and beret, asking endless questions.

'Work?' Gino said. 'What urge can there be for these people to look for proper work when they know that industry doesn't exist?'

Gino found the subjects and introduced them to Dolci. Dolci, with his flair for gaining a person's confidence and eliciting information, then made the interviews. He wrote everything down in longhand, interviewing each subject two or three times. 'This is *their* inquiry,' he told Gino. From time to time, there were conferences in Partinico when the team came together from the outlying villages. There was no lying up, except on occasional Sundays when they would pile a score of Spine Sante children into the Lancia and take them to the beach; the volunteers went too, as much for their own recuperation as the children's. They worked openly and carefully, and for the most part unmolested. Once when he returned to Palermo from documenting a fief at Tudìa, Turrumé and Arcia, near Villalba—where fifty families lived all the year round in straw shacks—Dolci received word from Sorgi, the lawyer, warning him not to return there. A group of *mafiosi* had called at Sorgi's office to threaten Dolci by proxy. Dolci did go back. Nothing happened. They worked mostly under a psychological strain, the thought of police obstruction nibbling constantly at their minds. The Partinico police watched volunteers carefully, stalking them especially over residence permits. When Lawrence and Maddalena Rayner—he was English, she Italian—came from Rome to help with the inquiry, and filled in their original residence as England, a plain-clothes man asked Dolci to explain.

'Mr. Dolci,' he said, 'I need to know which pass they crossed to enter France from England.' Dolci explained that between England and France there was a channel. 'Look, Mr. Dolci,' the officer said, 'I know very well that you're not one of us. But you must also respect my position—I have to earn my keep. Now will you please tell me *which pass they crossed*?'

The Palermo inquiry lasted the summer. Dolci's workers went round the villages and talked to over five hundred day labourers in the *piazzes*, in the cafés, in the trade union offices. In general these men found work on two days out of seven. The rest of the time they stood about with their hands in their pockets or tried to keep afloat by gathering wild vegetables or snails or breaking up iron crosses taken from the cemeteries in order to sell them. Dolci calculated that 120,000 to 140,000 people in the province lived like this, by work which was not work. For Palermo city the figures were only slightly better.

Dolci's permanent core was Giovanni, Franco, Alberto L'Abbate, a young Florentine sociologist, and Goffredo the student teacher. Goffredo, though banished for his part in the reverse strike, had returned to Partinico just the same and remained, enclosed in Spine Sante, teaching the illiterate. When Dolci proposed—or, as Goffredo says, 'imposed'—the Palermo inquiry, he volunteered to go in first and break the ground, setting up a base from which Dolci might operate later. Dolci chose a quarter bisected by the railroad, a big courtyard a stone's throw from the seat of the Sicilian Regional Parliament. Of it he wrote: '130 families live in 118 rooms, plus five cubbyholes. Only one family has a lavatory. The other families cook, eat, sleep and defecate in their one room.' 'Decent' folk, he added, relieved themselves on the railway line. *Average* number of persons per room: 4·2 'There are five sordid two-storied and three-storied houses in the last stages of dilapidation and a few squalid huts and shacks. The walls sweat with damp and the rooms are live with scorpions, fleas and cockroaches . . .'

This was Cortile Cascino.

Perhaps it wasn't surprising that the Palermitans generally had achieved a certain indifference to the plight of their hungry fifth. A university professor and a Communist member of the City Council said that until Dolci's inquiry was published later he didn't know that Cortile Cascino existed. He lived just round the corner.

Goffredo went in alone. He was eighteen at the time. 'It was a case of going there and doing whatever it was possible to do for these people,' he says. 'I rented a shack for three pounds, ten shillings a month. Danilo had no money. I lived with six pounds a month which Lucio Lombardo-Radice gave me and with whatever the people of the Cortile could spare. I ate with them, every evening a different family. Simple pasta, every night pasta. We ate artichokes in artichoke time and tomatoes the whole summer long. Meat, once in four months.

'Cortile today is pretty bad—then it was a cesspit. There was a kind of lake in the middle where the kids used to play, naked; I can't describe what was in that lake . . . My shed was on the edge of it, alongside the railway line. There wasn't a child above eight who didn't go out to work in a shop or a mechanic's yard or a bakery. Most of them had never seen a school. I taught them to read and write, and also their fathers, from seven in the morning until nearly midnight. It was chaotic. Imprisoned in that shed, people coming and going, the continual racket. I got neurotic; then stomach trouble—I used to slip into Partinico at weekends for treatment.

'Each week there was a frightful row, people got hurt every time. The people were in such despair these strifes broke out over nothing—two kids playing and arguing, the mother of one intervenes, slaps one, screams at the other; the other mother steps in, then her husband, then the husband of the first woman, the neighbours making up the chorus . . . and away it went.

'I was usually called in as peacemaker.

'Living like that though, I got to thinking like them. I learned their *argot* and became one of them. I looked like them, and smelled it. There was one terrible row, half the courtyard swarmed in, and I—I suddenly forgot myself and bored in too. I went berserk. I remember picking up a woman by the hair and swinging her . . .

'The police were too frightened to come near the place. The only time I saw the police that year, they came in a bundle of twelve, at midnight, to arrest one man. It was the only way.

'They planted an informer, a semi-drunkard called Nenne. We all knew him. I used to tell him my movements, to save him trouble. "Hey, Nenne," I'd say, "I'm going to Partinico tomorrow," or, "You know Danilo's coming on Monday?" It was all part of the system.

'My shack was also the first-aid centre. There was a woman giving penicillin injections, the kind where you mix the liquid with the powder, and the poor child she was injecting was yowelling its ears off. The woman was mixing together *nothing*. She was injecting pure powder. I got so angry I grabbed the needle and tried myself. I found I did it much better. From then on I became the nurse. I did two hours' nursing every morning, and then the schooling. I had something like 120 children coming for lessons every day.

'I had no toilet, no water. We washed at the fountain and relieved ourselves on the railroad track. Every time we did that we risked being fined 30s. I had to be thoroughly deloused when I finally left. My father came down once from the north. He scarcely recognised me. He almost ran out of the place. My father's a demolition expert.'

Altogether Goffredo spent two years in Cortile Cascino. He then abandoned teaching and became a qualified social worker; he has just published a study on emigration. He was the first of scores on whom Dolci was to have a positive formative influence.

When Dolci first came to the courtyard the people took him for a priest, because of the beret. They crowded round as if he were a new species. Goffredo told him that to keep alive the boys resorted to stealing, the girls to prostitution. Heterosexual and homosexual prostitution were flourishing. Life expectancy was around thirty-five. Goffredo showed him a room where eight people slept in one bed. 'We sleep four at the top and four at the bottom,' the wife said. 'My uncle, my husband, my sister, myself and four children. We keep the door open to breathe better.'

That summer a baby boy died, the little blood he had being sucked out of him by rats while the mother was at the fountain doing the washing. Dolci knew that when the inquiry was over he would return to fast among these people. •

He worked through autumn on the reports and consigned the book to Einaudi. On 17 December he lay down in Goffredo's shack and initiated a group hunger strike as 'a warning to all'. Fifteen people fasted for eight days—five in Palermo, Dolci and Goffredo in Cortile Cascino, Franco, Alberto and Francesco Lanzaroni in Capo; Mauro Gobbini and Giovanni Mottura at Bisaquino; Grazia Fresca and Carlo Ravasini at Alia; others at Vicari and S. Giuseppe Iato; and a Catholic group from southern France at Partinico. It was a collective protest at the destitution of an entire province, from the feudal terror of Bisaquino and the landslides of Alia to the pollution of the capital, where Mafia continued to strangle living conditions and there was a murder on an average every five days to prove it. By itself the protest achieved nothing, affected nobody, except Goffredo who got cramp and acidosis on the final day and had to be given sugar injections. The authorities saw it as a gigantic bluff. Dolci saw it as a halfway house, a link in a chain of pressurising events, with the eventual goal of 'work—work for all'. 'All' by now was a key word. He was like a machine—he gave himself no rest and he determined that the authorities should have none either. The gadfly was determined not to be swatted.

When the fast was over and he went home for Christmas, he was reasonably satisfied. He already had the material for the next round in his hands—the advance copies of the book which a representative of Einaudi had brought to Cortile Cascino during the fast. In Italy it appeared as *Inchiesta a Palermo* (Inquiry in Palermo); in England as *To Feed the Hungry*.

Somebody compared him to an eagle—watching, swooping, sometimes missing the mark, but always there, hovering. Dolci laughed. 'This isn't an eagle's work,' he said. 'This is the labour of an ox.'

There were visitors to Partinico that Christmas. They were the quiet vegetarian kind. They were a group of French and Italian-born pacifists, all in homespun, from Lanza del Vasto's work-and-prayer colony in the south of France. They had volunteered to join the fast and stayed over for Christmas. Lanza himself is vividly remembered. In height he topped Dolci, a venerable prophet's figure with a lean brown face and a twiney snow-white beard. He wore sandals, carried a staff and kept warm beneath a thick woollen jerkin of unbleached homespun. Even today, at 63, fanaticism has not spoiled him; he remains a gentle, if slightly crazy patriarch, one of the more lovable of Catholic anarchists. On Christmas Eve he handed Dolci a contribution for his work. 'Why don't you give it to the people?' Dolci said. He called Sariddu. Sariddu found himself holding ten crisp ten-thousand-lire notes. 'For the people,' Lanza said. By morning Sariddu, his wife and a few neighbours had prepared food parcels for the forty Spine Sante families most in need, with enough money left over to throw a *festa* for the whole quarter.

A hundred thousand lire (sixty pounds) would have kept a qualified teacher or nurse in Partinico for six months. Dolci badly needed qualified workers. A colleague chided him for his recklessness. 'Get away with you,' Dolci said. 'It's Christmas.'

All the same he knew it was a last fling. The days of charitable gestures were almost over.

NINETEEN

Congress on a Shoestring

To Feed the Hungry was Dolci's Christmas message for 1956. *Figaro Littéraire* hailed it. *The Times Literary Supplement* called it 'not only a literary but also a sociological masterpiece'. Yet when it appeared many good Catholics offered New Year prayers in the hope that the author might be excommunicated. The Partinico archpriest warned his flock to 'beware of the wolf in sheep's clothing' and higher ecclesiastical authorities trusted that the Rome police would not be too long in taking action. The Right retched. Even the Left twitched a bit. 'My word, you've been fly, digging up all that misery,' a Communist deputy said to Dolci. The author was upset. 'I've never denied that the beautiful exists,' he said. 'I merely say that this *also* exists. If you go to a doctor with a bad stomach ulcer it doesn't help your condition to be told what lovely big brown eyes you have.'

The Protestant pastor, Tullio Vinay, said later: 'Why is it that the Food and Agricultural Organisation, which has its world headquarters in Rome, cannot work in Italy? Because the Italian Government continues to shut its eyes to reality, it won't admit it has an underdeveloped zone on its own doorstep. It's this *stupid* sense of patriotism of ours. Italians do not like to hear a diagnosis of their situation.'

The revelation of the lives of the Palermitan poor was a surprise packet all round. Why was this? In 1957 Italy was still, both in the educational and social research fields, in the doldrums; there was yet no School of Sociology. Had Dolci merely catalogued the poor, as professional sociologists did, it would have raised storm enough. But Dolci, the amateur, went farther. Norberto Bobbio says of *The Outlaws*: 'Rather than an inquiry it is a body of witness . . . These people are witnesses who cry scandal.' *To Feed The Hungry* calls up a whole army of witness—peasants and prostitutes, card-sharpers, women fish-curers, leech-doctors, beggars, *mafiosi*, witches, snail-garnerers, cowherds, money-changers and platoons of others. They fall in with their sackcloth morals and bar-alley slang, crying 'work—not charity', and catalogue themselves by request. Dolci spared no details. The book did for the Sicilians what Mayhew, in the 1850s, did for the London poor. Between the lines, *To Feed the Hungry* was also the heaviest indictment of Mafia–Government collusion and of Church apathy-before-the-fact then published. It was a human documentary with the lid off.

It was also a much more homogeneous study than *The Outlaws*. World authorities like the psychologist Erich Fromm and the economist Gunnar Myrdal welcomed it as a valuable contribution to social science. Aldous Huxley, in a preface to the English and American editions, said: 'A new Gandhi, a modern St. Francis needs to be equipped with much more than compassion and seraphic love. He needs a degree in one of the sciences and a nodding acquaintance with a dozen disciplines beyond the pale of his own special field. It is only by making the best of both worlds—the world of the head no less than the world of the heart, that the twentieth-century saint can hope to be effective. Danilo Dolci is one of these modern Franciscans-with-a-degree.' Huxley was wrong about the degree, but his was an accurate interpretation of what an informed public outside Italy thought and felt. Translations were prepared in six languages. *To Feed the Hungry* received a Viareggio Prize, Italy's most coveted literary award. Then the Rome chief of police let fall the charge he had been holding over Dolci's head since the eve of the reverse strike trial in 1956. On 27 June 1957, Dolci appeared in Rome charged with publishing obscene matter.

In the first part of the book, *The Witnesses*, are 31 personal stories. On almost every page Dolci's reportage touched guilty or squeamish consciences:

> Once upon a time the *parrini* (priests) came along on Shanks' pony to beg for charity; nowadays they do their alms-collecting on Lambrettas or in bang up-to-date Fiats.
>
> Some people leave their cars in the street and pay men to sleep in them. It comes cheaper than a garage.
>
> Do we go to mass? 'Course we do—we're all Catholics, every one of us. Religion's going to mass on Sundays and the big Feast Days. Before we begin gutting the fish we always cross ourselves ... Most people vote CD because if they vote CD they're voting for Our Lord.
>
> Since I've been to prison I've let my beard grow. When I come out I shan't be able to hawk materials—I can't pay back the money I borrowed, so I've no cash for a permit. I shall have to go on practising magic ...
>
> 'If He's really up there, why doesn't He send us work?' I say to myself.
>
> What's the Mafia got to do with coffins? Coffin-making's one

of the very few industries there are in Palermo; it may not be large, but it's very profitable and the competition's fierce. This year four or five coffin-makers were murdered. The industry's controlled by the Mafia of the wholesale markets . . . The cigarettes (contraband) are often hidden in coffins . . .

If we haven't enough leeches we send for the barber who opens a vein in the sick person's wrist and lets out a stream of blood. We hardly ever call in the doctor; it costs too much.

Every morning we relieve ourselves on the railway lines. (It's been the custom as long as I can remember, my father did it and his father did too.) Sometimes if we're caught doing it we're fined 30s. for committing a nuisance. It costs us a hell of a lot to shit.

The police had singled out the story of Gino Orlando. They objected to a pungent factual six-line description of Gino's visit to a licensed brothel, with three other youngsters, at the age of twelve. Dolci was charged, not with Einaudi, the publisher of the book, but with Carocci, the publisher of *Nuovi Argomenti*, the serious review in which Gino's account first appeared.

Once again eminent lawyers came to Dolci's defence. A book wasn't dirty in itself, it had no smell, Dolci said. 'The aim was not to work scandal. The aim was to give a voice to those who offered— and were denied—their useful labour; and to pose a problem.' Dolci claimed that the work was a scientific study which only scientifically qualified men could judge; and that the harsh realism was dictated by the needs of the argument and the whole tenor of the investigation.

A large public was turned away. The entire case was held in camera. The judges refused to hear evidence from men of letters and from sociologists and other experts. Dolci's plea was rejected. The passage was alleged to be injurious to public decency and, with Carocci, he was sentenced to two months' imprisonment.

They did not go to jail. An appeal, and bail, were allowed and a year later the judgment was reversed and they were exonerated. It did not matter. The original sentence stuck in the Italian mind.

From 'habitual delinquent' in 1956 Dolci thus graduated to 'pornographer' in 1957. He was thoroughly branded.

'The obscenity laws in Italy are pretty strict in theory,' *The Observer* commented, 'but in practice passages like these get by so long as they are written by nice safe novelists without social consciences.'

The Official Mind is fairly porous. The effect of Dolci's fact-finding brought out leaks in the strangest places. When a year or so later Stephen Peet made a documentary television film in western Sicily, based on the conditions Dolci had revealed, and the BBC transmitted it, the Italian television authorities had a fit. Peet made the film as a tourist, using a 16-mm. camera—and smuggled it out in his assistant's underwear. The explosion occurred at a European Broadcasting Meeting at Cannes, when the Comptroller of Italian Television, in the words of an eye-witness, 'went nearly apoplectic with rage that the BBC had had the gumption to put this thing out'. About the same time, in London, Peet was asked to call at an address in Victoria. It turned out to be a branch of the Italian State Tourist Department. It was late one afternoon. The manager and his secretary, both Italians, were sitting at their desks. Peet introduced himself. The manager looked up and said, 'Did *you* make the film about Sicily?' Peet admitted it. 'What would you think if an Italian came over here and made that kind of film about England?' Peet said nothing. The manager continued in a loud voice: 'Would that be right? Would it? Eh? EH?' Peet let him get it off his chest. When he had finished the manager got up, put on his coat and bade the secretary goodnight. At the door he grabbed Peet by the hand and shook it hard. 'Well done!' he said. 'May God go with you. There should be a film like that made about Italy every week.' With that he departed.

Dolci is a man of ideas. He takes them seriously. Words and thoughts and ideas are the stuffing of his work. He has no time for small talk; in fact, he has none. Sometimes ideas obsess him. It can be frightening or it can be embarrassing. Chatting with him, I have thrown an idea up, banteringly, and been horrified to find it immediately seized on, like gold dust, and examined under the weighing glass of those inscrutable rimless spectacles; and then when I explained it was in jest he was momentarily offended. So it was, during a recess in the Rome trial, when a friend suggested he should organise a meeting of experts to discuss the implications of his various inquiries: he seized on the idea and made it his own, and began immediately to put it into operation. Dolci is a big man, and he likes big ideas. He did not organise a *riunione*, a meeting. 'We'll have a *convegno*,' a congress, he said. And thus a few months later in Palermo there came about the Congress for Full Employment.

'Really, we think that Italy and in particular Sicily have already had a stomachful of study conferences,' the *Cittadino Siciliano* said; 'but Danilo apparently hasn't noticed this.' It was quite a friendly comment for the neo-fascist press. The congress was to be a form of inquiry, of pressure and resolution, by experts. There was the usual pre-inquiry dust-up in Partinico among the group, some of whom thought Dolci was becoming 'study mad'. But Dolci by now had hold of his idea, like a mastiff. The critics had to bow before the grip, or depart. Before long some of them departed, Giovanni and Goffredo among them. Others, with visions of the workhouse looming, mentioned that a congress would cost money. What would they live on afterwards? 'Never mind,' Dolci said. 'Something will turn up.' In the moments of fiscal stress which have occurred throughout his life, rather more commonly than the seasons, he has usually said this. He has usually been right.

He announced the congress in July 1957, months in advance. 'The problem of full employment will never be solved if it is never posed,' he said. 'In Italy £360 million are spent each year on the police and the army, all carefully thought out and planned in advance. Yet in Italy there does not exist one single study centre for full employment.' He warned that if an awareness of the problem had not registered on the public conscience by the end of the congress, three days later he and Franco would begin a fast, and go on fasting until public opinion was thoroughly roused. What was the man up to with his Utopia of '*full* employment'? people wondered. In fact, the term was practically unknown in Italy. Italians had never got past a dream of *maximum* employment.

The congress was preceded by four months' work. It was organised from Spine Sante, in the bedroom-cum-night-school-cum-writing-room halfway up the stairs where Dolci worked and slept, and in the communal bunkroom upstairs where almost everyone else slept, and it took place in one of Palermo's more grandiose *palazzi*. It was floated on the art of Carlo Levi, the Viareggio Prize, the Lancia, a few pawned articles, the patronage of public figures and statesmen like the former Prime Minister, Parri, and the goodwill of a considerable body of international experts from Scandinavia to Brazil who sent messages of support. Levi (painter as well as writer) did the posters, and the Lancia—bought for £150, sold for £30—paid for their production. The Viareggio Prize, worth £600, paid for the congress. It took place on the first three days of November and was attended by leading Italian sociologists, economists and town-planners.

By the end of 1954, the Socialist Giolitti told the gathering, the national economy had lifted itself out of the depths of the war, beaten inflation and taken on new life. Meantime a Parliamentary Commission had revealed that a million and a half southerners were completely out of work and a further four million able to find jobs for only six months of the year, a fourth of the southern population was living in real poverty and a sixth was illiterate. Then, he said,

Government experts had presented the Vanoni Plan which, it was stated, would resolve *everything*. But the plan had never been used, 'except by the ruling classes for their Sunday speeches'. If anything the situation in 1957 was worse than in 1954 when the Vanoni Plan was presented. A message from the Swedish economist Gunnar Myrdal said: 'Full employment is essentially a matter of organisation.' But the congress found that in Italy the problem had first to do with a Government's faculty of hearing. After digesting and deliberating fifteen papers presented by specialists, and a basinful of facts collected by Dolci's team in ten communes, it found that the people themselves were not aware of their problems, did not know how they could be solved—nor did the planners. 'The politicians don't know,' roared the chairman, Bruno Zevi, a lively Rome architect, 'because they don't *want* to know!' It found that official projects failed in practice because there was no interaction between the planners at the top and the people at the bottom. They were completely out of gear.

The congress restated fundamentals. It called for experts to band together and study a flexible co-ordinated policy which would make full use of the resources of the people. It urged research groups in the towns and in the villages. It brought the term's *full employment* and the new-fangled *pianificazione*—'planning for the planners', someone called it—into common usage and gave them a sharp new dimension. It posed a gigantic problem.

If the Government was aware of the need to tackle the problem, it gave no sign. All the principal authorities were invited to the congress. None came.

Three days after the conference ended, on the evening of 6 November, Dolci and Franco kept their promise and stopped eating. They fasted in Cortile Cascino, in a grey, stagnant room that was never deserted, in a cardboard-cut-out shack papered on the inside with Levi's posters and on the outside with the perennial criss-cross of poor people's washing. On 14 November, the eighth day, a Sicilian journalist wrote: 'The children of the Cortile have made friends with this huge hungering man who speaks their own language . . . Yesterday morning scores came to see a comic film of Charlot, the first film of their life. As soon as it gets dark the men come. It is a ritual. They can't all get in at once, and wait their turn, standing outside until late.' The fast spoke directly to the people. Through them Dolci asked the authorities the simple ancient question, 'Why do you spend money on that which is not bread?' There was no reply. After ten days, friends began to fear for their health. Franco, lacking oxygen, had just enough strength to get up and open the window.

He thought he was going to die. On the following day, Sunday 17 November, Levi and the German political historian, Robert Jungk, visited them and told them it was time to stop the fast. It had already stirred sluggish consciences, they said. Dolci said he had received no such official assurances. That night, still fasting, the pair were taken by car to Palermo's vast hall of oratory, the Politeama, where an audience of thousands heard Levi make an appeal for liberty and equality worthy of John Stuart Mill. Ever since the publication of *Christ Stopped at Eboli* Levi has had a fabled reputation with a big section of the Italian public. With the Sicilian veteran, Girolamo Li Causi, he represents that very special brand of Italian Communist, born of the Resistance, who is no more Communist than George Orwell was; in his unbending socialism and his sensitivity to the gerrymandering products of fascism Levi is, in fact, about the nearest equivalent to an Italian Orwell. His appeal to a Sicilian audience, despite a rather shaggy exterior and a front line of yellowed teeth, eaten away by Tuscan cigars, is strong. He understands low-keyed oratory and when he stood up in the Politeama and accused the authorities point-blank he was given an ovation. He talked, not of slums, but of 'concentration camps of misery'. On unemployment he said: 'This army of jobless is the fruit of all the deficiencies, the mistakes, the favouritisms of our nation's history. It's natural that the authorities don't want to dirty their hands over it, that they have but a single reaction to the pressure of facts: silence. This silence is the essential stock-in-trade of that archaic organisation which you all know well, the silence of the Mafia.'

After the speech the silence, from the official press, continued. Dolci and Franco returned to Cortile Cascino and went on fasting. They refused to take anything more than the juice of half an orange, squeezed into a tumbler of water daily, which the doctor ordered. They were both exhausted. They broke the fast on 19 November, at noon on the thirteenth day, when Dolci was finally persuaded that there had been a sufficient impact on the public conscience. The long protest was rewarded. A few days later the Palermo authorities announced a thirty-million-pound plan for slum clearance. The plan included the tearing down of Cortile Cascino and a neighbouring slum in rather worse repair called Hole of Death, and the rehousing of the twelve hundred inhabitants in new low-rent flats.

It was, people said, a complete capitulation; a victory for the poor. The long chain reaction, which had begun with an inquiry in Palermo eighteen months before, was over.

Dolci did not think so. A programme of public works, as far as he was concerned, had nothing to do with a policy for full employment. Slum reform had nothing to do with a reform in slum-thinking. The problem that the congress had posed was still there. He talked it over with a reduced band of tired helpers. There was that let-down feeling which comes after giving birth to something you don't quite expect, and which remains there, sitting up gawkily and leering at you. Dolci was in a quandary. In his mind he turned over the litter of his six years in Sicily: three major inquiries, four books, two trials, one stretch in jail, six fasts. He had come full circle, the 'triangle of hunger' was complete—Trappeto–Partinico–Palermo; probing–exposing–starving; inquiry–book–fast. He had done it three times. He had performed a kind of sociological hat-trick. For what?

At Trappeto he had founded a white elephant and spent three thousand pounds of Government money on a 'People's University' which was now empty. A kindergarten was functioning, the town had got a face-lift, but the Mafia still ran the seas and every month more fishermen went away to the north for work. In Partinico the authorities were seeing to the drains; in Palermo, to the slums—or so they said. But unemployment? Everything as before. He was convinced of one thing: of the need to remain in Partinico—because of the dam. Partinico was the nerve-centre for the whole scheme.

But it was all too chancy, too unco-ordinated. There was a need to put things 'under expert management', as the TV advertisements said. Everything pointed ultimately to the overwhelming need for experts to plan *with the people*; and everything pointed, immediately, away from the Government being the agency to do it. 'Research groups', the conference had said . . .

Dolci is one of those people, like Shelley, for whom the miseries of the world remain miseries, and will not let them rest. I do not know if the thought sequence I have described went on quite in this way. Nobody does. As one of the team says, 'Danilo disappeared for three days.' For the third time in his life Dolci went into a kind of coma, muttering to himself, thinking aloud, talking to nobody, staring at meals. He came out of it in rather poorer shape than he had emerged from the fast, but he came out of it resolved. The Government obviously had no intention of tackling the problem of full employment. In that case, he would. Simply that.

He was no longer fighting a lone spiritual battle; technological as well as cultural aid was assured—the conference had indicated that. The conference had also said 'organisation', 'planning', 'study groups'. Very well. He would provide the study groups. He would become an organiser *and* a planner.

'There is something un-Italian about this selfless reckless

champion of the underdog,' *The Observer* noted in a profile earlier that year. Reckless was the word.

Dolci had no money. The conference had taken everything, including some of the Turin committee's grant intended for the social centre. Funds were so low that workers were reduced to cutting the wires in their house to save the electricity bill. To found even a skeleton study scheme he needed about fifteen million lire.

'Something will turn up,' he had said. It was December 1957. He told the others of his decision. There was no charity from Via Iannello that Christmas, dinner was sackcloth and hashes. Dolci put out no Christmas message. He seemed weighed down, hunched into himself, like a shepherd in a snowdrift waiting to take his flock over the mountains in search of new pastures, peering bleakly at the lowering ridges for a passage that might carry them safely through.

New Year came, and the clouds lifted. On 1 January 1958 Radio Moscow announced that 'peace partisan' Dolci had won the Lenin (formerly Stalin) Peace Prize. It praised the 'incisive vigour' with which he had depicted the conditions in Sicily and invited him to Russia to receive the prize. The announcer added that it was worth about sixteen million lire.

Dolci heard the news on the radio, like everyone else. He took off his spectacles, blinked and said, 'Good—it will be very useful.'

He was quite unprepared for the fresh storm it unleashed. The Communists exulted, claiming him for their own. Friends, however, told him he could not possibly accept. The voice of the Social Democrats, *La Giustizia*, called on him to reject an award which 'comes from the executioners of the workers in Hungary'.

Dolci didn't even hesitate. The prize had no conditions attached. 'I'll always accept from anywhere gifts that help my mission of good works,' he said. He accepted the £9,500 prize gratefully, and promptly announced his plan to found a chain of study centres for full employment in western Sicily.

It was the third and most momentous turning-point in his life. He marched boldly into the mountains.

From time to time, plotting a path across the salient peaks of Dolci's career, I have had recourse to the singular document mentioned in the preface, which a colleague has sub-titled 'Gullible's Troubles, a Guide for Innocents'. This is the confidential police report on Dolci presented to me by the offices of Cardinal Ruffini. Page three deals with the Congress for Full Employment. In the opinion of the police and, evidently, of Cardinal Ruffini, the congress was a 'complete flop' and changed nothing. They are wrong. The congress did change something. It changed Dolci.

PART III

*Often there are those moments, dark, dark, when you work . . .
alone with God; those moments when everybody betrays.
Those are the dark painful times. Those are the times when
life is carried forward.*

—Danilo Dolci

TWENTY

Prizewinner without a Passport

THE change that came over Dolci after the Lenin Prize was that he made the sacrifice of not living with the people any longer. He withdrew, into an office. Inevitably this led to misunderstanding and bitterness, especially among the saint-worshippers.

Dolci is a man whose normal, natural way is that of listening, encouraging, imparting, the way of individual charity. But it is equally important for him to do things. In order to do the things he now wished to do he began to pull round himself a mantle of bureaucracy which he asked for but really did not want. This did not happen immediately. When it did, it all but stifled him. A man, born essentially to be a free agent, found himself constricted by the beast of his own creation. He became more detached, to the point where it appeared he had forgotten the peasant. Yet, given his temperament, which is basically incompatible with any organisation, the wonder is not that he became more detached in these years, but that he survived them at all. Any normal man would have been broken before the end of 1959. Between 1958 and 1961 Dolci went to court twice, wrote two more books and dozens of pamphlets, held a congress which rocked Italy, attended hundreds of meetings, worked a minimum of fourteen hours a day and, when available, gave Vincenzina two more children. He also visited three continents, and lectured and presented papers all over Europe. ('I often wonder,' Kathleen Nott said to me recently, 'why it is that reformers like Tolstoy and Gandhi and Dolci have such perfectly bloody home lives.' *That* is why. It would be strange if Dolci's abnormal 'doing' did not make for unorthodoxy in his home life.)

It is easy to apportion blame in these years; but more realistic to see them in perspective as experimentally necessary to Dolci's inner education and to try to imagine the cumulative effect of Government repression on the mind of a man forced to live on the bleak comfort of his own wits.

On 16 January 1958, after the news of the Lenin Prize, Dolci made a speech in Palermo in which he said: 'I am not a Communist. I accept this prize and am profoundly thankful. Some people will say, "Here's another useful idiot playing the Communist game." On all sides I've been asked for an explanation. I really believe in the need for peace—that is, in the non-violent struggle and revolution, clean in method and without compromise. I've seen that you can murder people by shooting them, but also by neglecting them. I've decided to choose, not to follow any particular trends, even if they've been suggested to me as a virtue or a necessary discipline. I know this new way might be dangerous, that there's a risk of presumptuousness or isolation. But I also know this: an apple, when it matures, becomes ripe either for eating or for wasting away until from the seeds are brought forth fresh fruit; if you sow apples you can't expect to reap carrots, if someone has pneumonia you don't cure him by beating him. I know many people say, "Oh, he's ingenuous, a dreamer, he doesn't understand that what really counts in the end is force." *I'd* say that he who hasn't yet understood that the discovery of truth is the strongest force of all, he's the ingenuous one, he's the dreamer. I believe that men will collaborate better as their thoughts, with the help of scientific analysis, are shorn of all rhetoric, superstition, complexes, dogmas of all kinds. Reality is complex. To understand it men have tried Christianity, liberalism, Gandhism, socialism. There's some truth in all these solutions. We're all mendicants of truth.'

He told Sasha Moorsom, of the BBC: 'I'll take money from the Devil or the Pope. I'm not fussy where it comes from.'

Criticism of him did not diminish. Socialists who had previously supported him were incensed. (In 1957 Nenni, head of the Socialist party, had refused to accept the same prize, because of Budapest.) Old friends were bitterly upset, especially the novelist Ignazio Silone.

Dolci said he would go to Moscow to receive the prize and make a speech there on non-violence, 'if they will give me the passport'. He was not allowed to go to Moscow. He travelled none the less. He went out and asked questions. He went to Italy, Switzerland, France, England, Scandinavia. The headings of a series of newspaper articles he published on return give the tone of his inquiries: '*How Sweden Seeks to give Work to All.*' '*In Norway Unemployment rather than Unknown is Inconceivable.*' '*A Century of English Initiative towards Conquering Unemployment.*' He noted that the Swedish wore their well-being uneasily and that the English were worried by the American recession; and wondered if overdeveloped countries like these did not perhaps suffer from a worse moral evil than did Sicily.

He lectured. He put Sicily's case squarely. In England he told of trained Sicilian teachers 'in plenty' and of absenteeism from schools of well over fifty per cent; and was misreported as describing a town of sixteen thousand people attended by a single agricultural expert who had difficulty in getting petrol for his car and by 237 armed police (he cited 97 police). In France he met Abbé Pierre, Pastor Trocmé, Sartre and others, and told journalists, when asked what the local churches and the Mafia did to help: 'It is very likely in the backward areas that the Government authority, the religious authority, the judicial authority and the Mafia are one and the same thing.' Jean Steinmann,* a young Catholic theologian, of Notre Dame, who had met Dolci before, said: 'The man no longer hesitates'; the Paris weekly *L'Express* compared him to 'a surgeon operating in emergency'. In Stockholm Dolci was reported to have said that 'the Italian Government offers Sicily the single contribution of the police force' and, according to *Aftonbladet*, that 'In Palermo the tourists walk the main streets whereas the police forbid the slum inhabitants to do so . . . When an epidemic breaks out the police isolate these quarters and allow people to die in misery.' Italy, he said, was too proud to accept foreign experts for its underdeveloped south and the foreign aid it did receive it often squandered. If there was so much misery then in the south, he was asked, 'Why does Italy spend so many millions each year buying foreign soccer stars?' Dolci said he didn't know.

He spoke fearlessly and with some restraint. He exaggerated about freedom of circulation in Palermo, but otherwise told the basic truth. He was not always accurately reported.

Everywhere he appealed for experts to come to his aid.

He returned to Partinico towards the end of April. He had just time to write the series of articles and to prepare his case in time for the appeal against the 1956 reverse strike sentence. The appeal was set down in Palermo for 2 May.

On 30 April a police officer called at his house in Spine Sante and asked to see his passport. The officer said he wanted to inspect the visa entries. Dolci handed him the passport. The officer put it in his pocket and walked away. The next day, 1 May—the eve of the appeal—the Italian Home Secretary, Tambroni, announced that he had withdrawn Dolci's passport because 'he has defamed Italy abroad'.

It was the second time the Government had attempted to prejudice Dolci in the eyes of a jury immediately before a court case.

Tambroni was deluged with telegrams of protest. Leading foreign newspapers criticised his action heavily. At this time the 1958

* Author of *Pour ou Contre Danilo Dolci* (Cerf, 1959).

national elections were under way and Left-wing parties were increasing in favour. *The Guardian* commented: 'The action of Signor Tambroni in withdrawing the passport suggests that the strain of the electoral campaign is beginning to wear down the Government's nerves.'

In the words of the influential Milan weekly, *Corriere della Sera*, Tambroni 'came a cropper'. But having fallen down, the Home Secretary made no move to adjust his position. He was backed up at once by the Siena police who charged Dolci with insulting public institutions and spreading false reports likely to disturb public order. Dolci had addressed students in Siena on 22 April.

Sixty French writers, editors and poets wrote to the Italian press, calling on Tambroni to restore the passport—among them Cocteau, Sartre, Mauriac, Daniélou, Lacroix and Gabriel Marcel. The protest of so many noted Frenchmen, many of them fervent Catholics, shook the Italian Catholic press. According to the Jesuit *Civiltà Cattolica*, the quasi-official Vatican periodical, the appeal was 'astounding'. Another Catholic journal, *Il Quotidiano*, said the French writers were 'out of touch', because they had obviously not read the things the Vatican mouthpiece, *L'Osservatore Romano*, had said about Dolci.

Dolci offered documentary proof, published in book form, that what he had exposed was true; and said that in common with Gandhi he believed there was strength in truthful reports. He challenged the Home Secretary to refute his facts by expert opinion. Tambroni did not respond.

In court Dolci's counsel, Battaglia and Comandini, refused to proceed with the reverse strike appeal until the matter of the passport was settled. The presiding judge, Dr. Francesco Re, a rickety old man with sleepy eyes, half closed behind myopic spectacles, said he did not think the court could consider the request, as the authorities had allowed, by this stage, only another half-hour before the next case came on.

'What?' Battaglia interrupted. 'With eighteen defence lawyers yet to speak?'

Altogether, two hours had been allowed for the appeal, involving Dolci and the twenty-two others convicted of lawless occupation of Government land and sedition, the time normally taken (in a Sicilian court) to dispatch a common case of chicken theft. The sitting took place in Palermo's new Palace of Justice, a speckled structure in marbled blocks and vast colonnades, built at a cost of one million pounds and sited imposingly between the slums of the Capo and the spires of the Cathedral. International correspondents heard

Battaglia and Comandini, who again gave their services free, press their plea:

BATTAGLIA: We can't accept this—this unjust and infamous accusation.

COMANDINI: Dolci has the right to defend himself.

CROWN PROSECUTOR: The passport has nothing to do with it.

COMANDINI: This concerns an official statement of the Minister.

CROWN PROSECUTOR: But we came here to try Dolci, not the Home Secretary.

COMANDINI: I demand the right to produce documentary evidence to show that the Home Secretary (*turning to the other lawyers*) . . . how shall I put it? (*the lawyers smile*)—Yes, that the Home Secretary is a liar.

The court was in a quandary. Unwittingly, the prosecutor gave it a piece of sound advice. 'We must not allow a tiny incident in Partinico to develop into a national episode,' he said. The court, after several adjournments and hesitations, took the hint. The appeal was postponed until the autumn—well after the elections.

The appeal was eventually heard in November 1958. This time Dolci was sentenced to eight months' imprisonment. But an amnesty and another appeal—to Cassation, the highest court—were allowed. The eight months' sentence was not quashed for another four years. In the meantime the court reserved the right to enforce it at any time.

The Siena police let the charge of insult drop.

Dolci walked out from the abortive appeal in May 1958 with no passport and wondering who the enemy was—the Law, the Internal Affairs, the Police or the Mafia. According to at least two newspapers, Dolci's arch enemy was now none of these, but one man—Cardinal Ruffini, Archbishop of Palermo.

Tambroni's action in withdrawing the passport was taken on the advice of Cardinal Ruffini. Telling me this quite voluntarily, His Eminence's secretary, Monsignor Longhi, added with relish: 'And the Government was right to punish Dolci!'

TWENTY-ONE

Crops and Failures

IN some ways Tambroni's was a fortuitous blunder. It acted as a clarion call to philanthropists and informed observers all over Europe. In Switzerland two emigré sons of rich Sicilian landowners began a subscription effort. Elsewhere friends sought recruits. Danilo Dolci Committees were formed. These foreign committees, which became the human and financial cornerstone of many of his new activities, took some time to shake down. And as they had to keep pace with a man called Dolci, and as everything Dolci did was both urgent and unorthodox, it is not surprising that some of them came about in a similar way.

In 1958 a Dutch languages student, Bianca Dony, and a 25-year-old French journalist, Alain Godon, were in Paris working with Abbé Pierre, the French worker-priest, when they heard of the passport seizure and decided, over a cigarette, to visit Dolci in Partinico. They hitch-hiked down. Dolci explained the area, the study centres he had begun to set up, arranged accommodation, took them round. Godon went back to France. Bianca went home to the Hague. There she decided to send Dolci a contribution. She thought of sending a hundred pounds. To get the money she wrote a newspaper article and asked two journalist-friends to do the same. She says: 'The articles appeared. And seven hundred pounds arrived, like that. Then my trouble started. I thought: "Never send money, not this much money, to an Italian—not even a northern Italian." So I kept it. And every day, another journalist came and asked for an interview. "How is it down there?" And, "What are they doing to this man?" And so on. More articles. And in a short time this seven hundred pounds had doubled. I was upset. I didn't want to get involved, I was too busy with my own studies. These journalists asked, "What are you doing with this money? Is there a committee? Has it a bank account?" And, of course, I must have said yes. Yes, yes, I said. It was getting beyond me. And then—I ask you. There it was in all the papers: committee, bank account, secretary, Sicilian Gandhi and all.'

At that stage there was a girl of nineteen, holding an 'account' (a suitcase, stuffed with cheques and guilders, under her bed) for a man who knew nothing whatever about it. Thus the Dutch Danilo Dolci Committee was founded.

Bianca eventually called in friends qualified to form a regular committee and became the secretary. Godon, who returned to Sicily, was the first of several workers it supported.

By 1959 there were Dolci Committees in England, France, Holland, Switzerland (two committees), Norway, Sweden and North Italy (various). Germany and Belgium followed later. Most were founded or actively supported by men with international reputations in the humanist sciences—Waller and Kuenstler in England, Friedmann and Rochefort in France, Trocmé in Switzerland, Myrdal in Sweden, Jungk in Germany, Van Lier in Holland. In Italy Dolci continued to be supported by intellectual groups and occasional Catholic rebels, like the 'saintly' Mayor of Florence, La Pira. But no official body recognised him. No Dolci Committee was founded in Sicily. Even Italian Communists were becoming wary of the reformer who was making such good friends of the capitalists abroad. Dolci had previously been asked, three times, to go into Parliament —once by the Socialists and twice by the Communists. 'Thanks,' he said, 'but our work is different.' In 1958 the Sicilian regional secretary of the Communist party said, while praising his humanitarian outlook: 'We do not agree with Dolci's vision of the world.'

Dolci had become an irretrievable rebel on a limb, held up entirely by voluntary groups outside Sicily. His 'vision' had not yet become clear. It was submerged beneath an onrush of volunteers.

They were agro-technicians, teachers, social workers, nurses and an assortment of students on vacation and ex-journalists. The more enthusiastic ones didn't bother to apply through the committees. They simply bought train tickets for the thousand-mile-plus journey to Partinico and arrived. Some hitch-hiked. One bicycled. Later, 'a young Englishman arrived, wearing a Scottish kilt and without any money'. After a week he was lent the necessary ten thousand lire for his journey home.

Dolci moved, reluctantly, from his base in Spine Sante to a bigger ramshackle building at the other end of town. It was known as the Centre. It stood at the end of a blunt alley, Via Capua, in the wine-sellers' quarter and from its gloomy second storey looked on to open country towards the hills of Montelepre. Rather, it would have looked on to open country had not an ancient ecclesiastical decree forbidden the tenants to use the only windows which commanded a view. Until the Lenin Prize was cashed, they couldn't afford even a duplicator. Led by Pasquale Malpede, a former rural mayor in

L   161

Salerno province and the first administrator, the recruits marched in bearing planks, bricks, old light-bulbs and hundredweights of blank paper. Office equipment included two typewriters, one of them rusty, a rubber stamp and an instrument for punching holes which someone had acquired in the Palermo flea market. A small band of farmers and artisans—Ciccio the peasant, Peppino the cart-wrecker, Giuseppe the wine-seller, Pino the mechanic, Salvatore and Dionisio the potters—promptly opened a bank of unlimited credit to all Dolci workers, procured furniture at bedrock prices, enlisted errand boys, presented wine, *objets d'art* and other home comforts at no price at all.

Franco had now returned, for good, and became Dolci's general factotum and secretary. He was followed by a handsome blond German in his forties, Eduard Wätjen. Eduard was Dolci's first mature adviser. He wore khaki and corduroys and was a philosopher of the celestial kind. He was not always practical, but he gave everybody courage. Eduard had been a key man in the German underground. After helping to organise the *putsch* against Hitler he had escaped execution, smuggled himself out and ended the war as vice-consul in Basel. He went to America, observed the growth of the materialist image, and left again in horror. Back in West Germany he was asked to stand for the new Federal Parliament, decided against politics, returned to Switzerland and devoted himself to abstract painting and the young Karl Marx. He became interested in philosophy as an aid to science and development work in the corners of Europe, came to Partinico and, realising the potential significance of Dolci's work for southern Europe, stayed. Like everybody else at Partinico he did several jobs. He advised, arbitrated, translated, worked on the expansion programme and unscrambled the workers' private problems. He is still the Centre's soul-doctor.

Apart from Eduard and one or two others, Dolci did not quite get the élite, the experts he wanted. Nor could he go out again and look for them. The Home Secretary still had his passport. Following his old maxim, 'There's good in everybody', he tended to take on almost anyone. Many recruits were guided more by inspiration than experience and the committees who sent them, most of whom had no idea of real conditions, can hardly be blamed for sometimes sending unsuitable material.

Dolci told newcomers they were going out to work in unyielding ground, amid a peculiarly introspective mass misery where no spirit of co-operative enterprise existed and where 'it is almost an article of faith that a man must keep himself to himself at any cost'.

They would each be in one of five zones, into which he had divided a big slice of West Sicily—an area of 430,000 inhabitants, containing only four people with degrees in agriculture, no competent authority on education or sociology, and with an average of a murder every five days. Each worker would be a 'moral reference point'. Each centre, built round an agro-technician and a welfare group, would try to stimulate local employment, to encourage a consciousness towards self-help rather than provide an outside stimulus which would cease if the centre should close. This was the basic dogma. Political propaganda of any kind was banned. Charity was out. Violence was to be disowned, also 'falsehood, opportunism, fanaticism, dogmatism and above all waste'. He outlined a series of projects, 'in no sense intended to replace or oppose existing public services, but rather to inspire them to work with greater efficiency'. His main advice was, 'Go slow.'

To those who realised the importance of proceeding quietly, it made sense. But to the majority it was all rather woolly, like a tactical commando exercise over unmapped territory in the dark. It was going to be rough, on typist's wages. Many were short-term volunteers and, like Dolci himself when he came to Trappeto, anxious to get things *done*. It was going to be difficult to 'go slow'. It was also going to be lonely.

After a shake-down in Partinico the workers were deposited in the field.

Dolci had selected three villages fairly close together—Trappeto (Italian-financed), Roccamena (Swedish) and Corleone (Swiss)—ringing Partinico; and two farther afield—Menfi (British) and Cammarata (Dutch and Norwegian), both in Agrigento province. These were the guinea-pig centres, the spokes of a radial plan to study full employment for the west of the island.

The workers settled in openly and conspicuously—it was impossible, amid police interrogation and folksy peasant curiosity, any other way. Roccamena centre was two tumbledown rooms and an irresponsible lavatory. Menfi, a villa. In Cammarata a young Dutchwoman, an animal specialist, worked alone from above a butcher's shop. Roccamena, where the peasants traditionally burned manure rather than use it to fertilise a barren soil, had been chosen for its extreme backwardness. Corleone, because of an unbelievable rate of death by violence and because of the extent of *omertà*, the code of silence which surrounds any Mafia crime. Cammarata, the most remote centre, because of a history of landslides and pagan superstition—a third of one sample of peasants interviewed said that soil

erosion and landfalls were due to 'magic spells'. Menfi was chosen
as a classic example of water wastage.

Dolci had sited his centres carefully, but few will ever thank him
for selecting Corleone. It happened apparently by accident. Michele
Mandiello, an enterprising agronomist, was with Dolci at the time
and recalls: 'It was to be either Bisaquino or Corleone. We drove
into Bisaquino and went into the *trattoria*. They said we could eat
there. We were both starving. "What've you got?" Danilo asked.
"What've you *brought*?" the proprietor shouted back. Danilo looked
at me, strangely, and we got back into the car and drove on to
Corleone.' Corleone at least had a kind of restaurant. (In the eating-
houses of the interior it is still normal for patrons to take along their
own food to be cooked.)

Corleone (population, sixteen thousand) is probably the most
violent and sinister town in the peacetime world. It is a living
graveyard. The town is dominated by a shaggy spectacular rock, on
top of which sits the jail, and a hundred yards or so due east by the
church which is as big as a cathedral. These two edifices, the jail
and the church, glower at each other across the heights; in between
are the houses, bunkered hovels, clustered greyly about a maze of
serpentine alleys. The people wear the habit of mourning, perpetu-
ally, and in the soul of this habit repose the essence and the apotheosis of *omertà*. Mafia draws strength from *omertà*. *Omertà* means
manliness or self-control, and the idea of keeping oneself strictly to
oneself in every circumstance; it implies refusal to help established
authority and is native to the Sicilian's character by the time he is
ten years old. Thus, surrounding any Mafia crime, there is a blank
wall of silence. A policeman's job becomes impossible. Eye-wit-
nesses who are persuaded to give evidence invariably state they were
looking the other way when the shot was fired; neighbours of the
criminal, that they saw him peaceably sunning himself on his
balcony when the crime was committed. Since 1944 more men have
died unnatural deaths in Corleone (153 of them between 1944 and
1948) than the number of Corleonesi killed at the front in both world
wars. Despite the presence of 97 police, hardly any of these crimes
have been solved. The social reformer similarly finds himself
surrounded by a conspiracy of silence. Many people have been
asked to work in Corleone for Dolci, and declined, myself included.
Among the first to volunteer were young women—Swiss, French,
German—and it is the women who have stuck. The men, the
agrarians and the teachers, have continued to change rapidly.

All the centres were in Mafia communities, all sick with chronic
unemployment. Of the five, including Trappeto, only two had a

cinema, one a sports paddock, and in no case did the church show an active interest in anything but souls.

The secretary of the Swedish Committee, Ingrid Reiñius Larsson, visited Roccamena in 1959. She called on the priest to pay her respects and asked how many children went to school or received various kinds of help. The answer was, 'These are questions for my conscience and God alone.'

It is hard to communicate the experience of working in a Mafia community. It is beyond frustration. After the first unqualified reception, cordial, homely, overwhelmingly hospitable, you become intangibly sorted into a dozen different compartments, all of them wrong, and the object of sinuous tugging opinion—a curiosity amid an intensely curious people. The villagers remain childlike, helpful and amazingly unreliable; acceptance is possible, but only on their terms; normal values of truth and justice, normal sensitivities vanish. The conventions are *other*. The chief conventions are apathy and mistrust. They are not hidden conventions; they are stated. For anyone trying to accomplish anything even remotely connected with 'change', no matter how busy he may keep himself, they make for an intensely lonely existence. To this day, the feeling no Dolci worker in the field has been able to overcome is the feeling of deep isolation.

Volunteers lived almost exclusively on a basic diet of raw onions, tomatoes, bread—sometimes soaked in oil—and pasta. The work consumed them and rarely did they last as long as six months.

Teams began discussion groups, sewing classes, courses for illiterates, theatre activities—anything to break down the wall and get close to the people. Dolci's *doposcuole* (after-school) came into being. These *doposcuole* were free-expression classes for children of all ages, and became so popular that in three centres enrolling had to be restricted until more teachers were available. (Today more than five hundred children, normally denied a reasonable education, benefit from them.) Nurses had to combat not only antediluvian cures imposed by quacks, but ostracism by the local doctors themselves. Agronomists encouraged the use of new methods and fertilisers, sowed demonstration plots, planned model farms, liaised with local authorities and studied extension projects. Aurelio Finelli, a Neapolitan technician who worked for a time at Cammarata, describes the terrain: 'It takes courage—it can be actually dangerous—to go off into the countryside after heavy rains. I've seen with my own eyes peasants transporting sacks of grain get as far as they can with the mule and then off load the stuff on to their own backs and stagger on for a mile and a half, knee-deep in the mud.' In Palermo a sociologist continued Goffredo's work in Cortile Cascino and began a rag co-operative. Dolci's old writing-room in Spine Sante became a dispensary. Within a fortnight of its conversion it was clinic, first-aid station, crèche and maternity post, and two nurses were worked off their feet. Sometimes peasants brought along their mules for an injection.

Considering the language barrier (most workers had only a smattering of Italian on arrival), the enervating heat, the diet, the ill health (tummy bugs, plus complications—almost everyone was affected), the fact that no reliable doctor was on hand, that escape to a relaxed atmosphere was impossible, given the inevitable clash of temperament (the technicians, who were paid, tended to look down on the volunteers, who were not) and the fact that nobody *quite* had Dolci's combination of God-given confidence, unquench-able enthusiasm and ox-like constitution—it was a brave start.

Dolci visited and encouraged; at Partinico he collated, advised, chaired endless meetings, took VIPs round, lamented the lack of interpreters, drew up schedule after programme schedule and—a big bone of contention—diverted workers to collect data for his sixth book in Italian, *Waste*. He worried about the dam for the Iato River. Unemployment had eased only slightly, and for the wrong reason—emigration. Every week more jobless men asked his workers to help them fill in labour permit forms for North Italy, Germany, Switzerland, Belgium, France. Everywhere the men were emigrating in a neurosis of despair. He feared that planning for the dam had got bogged down, but could do little about it. He, too, was becoming bogged down—by the bureaucracy of his Centre. Almost every weekend there were meetings. They became increas-ingly theoretical. Capitini speaks of Dolci's 'passionate thirst for order'. Newcomers discovered that his favourite word was 'exact-ness' and that besides orderliness he was a stickler for punctuality, annotating, scheduling and measuring. It marked his interview technique with peasants—no phrase was ever omitted—and it marked his administrative method: no detail was too small, no fact too insignificant for consideration. He was not helped by an admini-stration, trying hard in five languages, which was devotedly ineffi-cient. Pasquale did his best, but he was really a soil specialist. Thousands of facts and graphs and analyses piled up on reject doors which had become tables and on long planks laid on bricks which had become bookshelves. Peasants who entered timorously through the cardboard doors, seeking advice perhaps for foot-rot or mule-dishing or bovine gestation, thought they had stumbled into a paper factory by mistake. Workers, reporting for these general meetings, found they had an odd poetic flavour; they seemed to bear no relation to the immediate problems they were facing in their villages. Arriving tired and sometimes irritable they were asked to comment on schedules labelled 'method of approach' and 'nature of action', which they did, only to find that their advice was seldom heeded. They were puzzled. All they wanted was a bath.

The tendency to introspection is an occupational hazard of shoe-string humanitarianism. Dolci's expanding Centre, which had a four-year teething period, was not an exception. After a time workers found the meetings had a languorous therapeutic value. No other escape from isolation being possible, they came to accept them almost with relief.

Introspection is also part of outcast living. Paradoxically, it is one of the cogs which keeps renegade group machinery going. And it now became conditioned by factors outside anybody's control. It was a time when the Italian political Right was beginning to shiver. Rumblings everywhere foretold a coming swing leftward. Prime Minister Segni's Internal Affairs Department was unnaturally testy about social experiments such as those which Dolci's guinea pigs were now implanting.

Tambroni's war began quietly enough. On 20 July 1958 a press release from Sicily stated:

> The Italian authorities refused to allow a Swedish economist to speak yesterday in the small farming community of Rocca-mena, some thirty miles inland. The economist, Gunnar Adler-Karlsson, who has a scholarship from the Swedish Royal Academy of Science, was invited by friends to talk on 'Aspects of Social Life in Sweden' after showing some U.S. Information Service films. At first the authorities claimed that this was not the moment for such a talk, because of the 'international tension' in the Middle East. Later, the police commissioner in Palermo explained that 'being a tourist Mr. Adler-Karlsson did not have the right to address either public or private gatherings . . .' According to the commissioner, 'A tourist may only be a tourist, and may not study or participate in any other cultural activity whatsoever without special permission.'

There was no lasting objection to Mr. Adler-Karlsson showing the American films.

Mr. Adler-Karlsson had been conducting an economic survey for Dolci in Roccamena.

Foreigners are required in Italy to take out a residence permit after three days. It is normally renewed every three months. For some reason the police insist on inscribing all visitors as 'tourist', whether they are on holiday or not.

The police had begun making small difficulties for the workers, chafing them with long harangues, pistols evident and, occasionally, veiled threats. In Sardinia a group of university lecturers, including Capitini, came under individual police scrutiny when they announced active support of Dolci's programme. Mention of the name Dolci, Capitini says, was now enough to give policemen 'the trots', while in Rome the Home Secretary's dossier, 'Danilo Dolci Movement', was full to bursting. An enlightened Englishwoman, Daphne Phelps, who ran her villa at Taormina as a guest-house for friends, entered Tambroni's black book after Dolci had stayed there a night. 'Miss Phelps, you don't know,' a policeman said to her, 'but that man is dangerous!'

In Roccamena a peasant who attended the centre's weekly agrarian meetings, was invited to the police station and asked: 'What are they doing at these farmers' discussions? Are they spies?' Offered payment, for information, the peasant said, 'I am not a rat,' and left.

At the end of 1958 Dolci had some thirty workers, engaged on as many minor projects. In Roccamena the locals were coming to see them—nurses like the Swiss-German girl, Meta Berchtold, and the French journalist-teacher, Alain Godon—as good capable people. Literacy classes, house-to-house visits, practical agricultural advice, had started to instil a little hope.

But this was too much progress for one small farming community of 3,371 souls.

Meta's permit was due to expire in the summer of 1959. On 6 February it was cancelled and she was told to leave Italy within two days. Godon, applying to renew his permit, was given a week to get out. He refused to go. He was asked to sign a statement that he was 'undesirable'. He refused to sign and went to Rome. From there he was expelled, abusively, by *foglia di via* (the device had been officially annulled two years before). Inquiring about the expulsions, the lawyer Nino Sorgi was told they were by order of the Home Secretary.

Two Swiss welfare workers, laden with equipment for Partinico, were stopped in a train at the Italian border, arrested and locked in a room at Bardonecchia. Their passports were in order. After three hours they were put on another train and turned back.

In the Senate a spokesman for Tambroni said the expulsions were necessary because Dolci was a defamer and an undesirable, and

168

'It is almost an article of faith that a man must keep himself to himself at all costs'

'Even if we make a just remark it's always wrong because we haven't any money'

'This land is like one of the many beautiful little girls you see in the alleys of its townships. The beauty is often there beneath the scabs, the raving hair, the wild and tattered rags . . .'

therefore anyone coming to Italy to work for him was in the same category. Pressed, he said: 'They didn't have the right papers.'

At this time the BBC transmitted a sixty-minute radio documentary, championing Dolci and his work, prepared by Gavin Maxwell and Sasha Moorsom. It was outspoken, but truthful. The Italian Government protested hotly to the Foreign Office for the 'false and tendentious accusations'. In the programme Aldous Huxley compared the slums of Palermo to those of Cairo or Calcutta and described Dolci as 'the ideal twentieth-century saint'. The Rome political weekly *Il Mondo* said that in all probability Mr. Huxley had now entered Tambroni's black list.

In a paper later delivered at Basel, Dolci wrote: 'It takes great wisdom to give the best of oneself in creative work (to give without loss, to grasp the flame without coming to harm—but oh, how difficult!).'

Other short-term volunteers went home, some were recalled by worried parents. Dolci was left with mostly Italians. He was boxed in, his source of supply cut. Even consignments of powdered milk arriving for his clinics were held up by Customs.

In London the British Committee, advertising for a social assistant for Menfi, was besieged with requests. But all the committees could send was sympathy.

Dolci continued to rise at four, with the peasants, pull on an old cream sweater, walk through the darkened streets from Spine Sante to Via Capua and work through the dawn hours on the chapters of *Waste*. He wrote: 'This land is like one of the many beautiful little girls you see in the alleys of its townships. The beauty is often there beneath the scabs, the raving hair, the wild and tattered rags: and already you can picture what an appearance of graphic and noble intelligence a good upbringing would give to those features . . .' By the time Franco arrived at eight-thirty he would have done three to four hours work and, after a sortie to the corner-bar by the baker's for breakfast—a glass of milk and a roll—be ready to start his normal activity dedicated to that upbringing.

Some relief did appear. It came in the form of two houses and a person.

The first house was Daphne Phelps' spacious villa, high on Taormina cliff. Miss Phelps is an English woman and the island's least-known benefactor. She is sometimes referred to as the Squire of Sicily. She inherited the house from her uncle Robert Kitson, a painter, and has been living in Sicily rather longer than Dolci. She, too, is somewhat embattled, being a natural target, as a friend put it, for 'lots of little dark men on the make'; she is constantly being defrauded by the local gigolos, the local Mafia and the local tax-collector who periodically rides up to see her, fully armed, on a mule. To escape the taxes, which promised bankruptcy, she turned the place into a lodging-house (select, friends only) and, hearing of Dolci's plight, offered his workers a week's rest, free, in time of need. The care and attention she and her cook lavished on the early volunteers averted more breakdowns than the committees will ever know.

The second house was a nest of bedrooms, laid end to end, above Giuseppe's wineshop and almost alongside the Partinico Centre. It was baptised the House of Volunteers and served as shake-down for new recruits, discussion centre, mash-house and general visitors' club. Sometimes visiting professors were installed there. Among other things it had been the local brothel. It is said that the first visitor was an English journalist. He had just drawn the shutters and turned the lights on when a man banged loudly on the door below. The journalist opened his window, leaned out and said, in his best Italian, 'What d'you want?' There was a pause, and then a Sicilian voice said: 'Holy Mother—men!' and vanished. It was not a delightful place, but it was an improvement on the only hotel, which *was* a brothel. It had a bathroom which—besides affording a useful view of the police barracks—had a bath. When Giuseppe remembered to turn on the water pump, the bath worked. A cook was engaged. Giuseppe's cloudy wine was elevenpence a litre, meals a shilling, and a bed was five shillings a month, the price of laundering the sheets. It was a haven.

The person was Pasqualino (Pasquale Marchese). He was Sicilian. He was essentially a bringer of light and laughter, a morale booster, at a time when the Centre's run-down body, blocked in most channels, was in dire need of a laxative. He was a little man who smoked Alpha cigarettes, who could never be found and yet who achieved a prodigious amount of work. He burst on the scene in the spring of 1959, bearing his dearest possession, a duplicating machine, and with it proceeded to churn out thousands of words monthly to Dolci subscribers all over Europe. He was an expert on Sicilian language, unscrambled the difficult dialectic interviews for *Waste* and worked for an initial wage of three pounds a month. When off-duty he compiled a Sicilian dictionary, a volume of popular peasant poetry and, in odd corners of his two-room dwelling, enough pieces of traditional wood carving—from dismantled mule barrows—to rebuild an entire cart. His intense love of Sicily, his chaotic cheerfulness, and his table, endeared him to all the foreigners, especially the English, and he worked tirelessly for Dolci for three and a half years. His talent had flowered shortly before, in his early twenties, when he became the youngest newspaper editor on the island. At Sciacca he wrote, edited, proof-read, accounted, distributed and sold his own paper, probably the first—and last—independent newspaper south of Rome. It was known for a remarkable horoscope. Pasqualino composed his horoscope with care from the horoscope of another paper, a well-known national journal, which he cut into pieces and shuffled together again more or less blindly, according to whim. Readers swore that Pasqualino's horoscope was infallible. He was a Genuine. He was intellectual, poet, antiquarian, raconteur, historian. Like many others he was under-valued, and spent most of his time at the Centre turning the handle of the duplicating machine. When he left, in rather sad circumstances, it was a double loss, for he took his duplicating machine with him.

The year 1959 ended in a flurry of question-marks. The Rome Government called for tenders for the Iato dam. It got none. A policeman called at Spine Sante and returned Dolci his passport. No explanation. Dolci had been invited to present a paper at the 14th Rencontres Internationales in Geneva, a world forum for science, humanism and sociology. He was now able to go. Open police persecution of Dolci's band now ceased. The change in official attitude was due, it is reliably stated, to intervention by the Italian Prime Minister; Segni found that the unfavourable reaction created abroad was damaging Italy's international reputation.

Troubles continued none the less.

Dolci had managed to attract a new group of Italian social workers, to compensate earlier losses, led by a woman-consultant, Gisella di Iuvalta. While he was in Geneva she closed down two centres and recalled the social workers to Partinico; on his return Dolci was presented with an ultimatum. The ultimatum was discussed at a seminar at Trappeto lasting, it is said, 28 days. He was told that his way of combining social and agrarian work in separate centres was wrong and that documentary inquiries raised false hopes among the people; he was asked to concentrate the welfare services in Partinico and cede a measure of policy control or Gisella and friends would leave. They left. Among others who went with them were Goffredo Fofi and the sociologist Alberto L'Abbate, the two veterans of Cortile Cascino. The Dutch Committee also withdrew its workers and closed down at Cammarata. The schism had a sequel. Goffredo, Gisella, Alberto and others sabotaged funds from one of the north Italian committees and, with the money, began doing social work in Calabria—in opposition, as it were, to Dolci.

Nowadays Goffredo, one of the leaders of the coup, tells the story against themselves and admits that most of the muddle they campaigned against at Partinico is well overcome.

Dolci had lost the Cammarata centre and a base in Palermo, a committee, most of his social workers and agronomists, and two other centres were closed. His regular team was down to five—Franco, Eduard, Pasqualino and two agriculturalists, Pasquale and Michele. Dolci has summed up his empirical philosophy in this way: 'It is to extract the truth from my own experience.' Experience now told him it was time to stop patchwork volunteering.

He was not deterred. He needed long-term specialists. He would go out and get them. Luckily, now that the ban on foreigners was lifted, some were already on the way.

In a few months things were back to normal. In spring 1960 subscribers abroad learned, in *Notes for Friends*, that

at Roccamena

The peasants' meetings continue weekly . . . The main topic of discussion has been the construction of a dam on the River Bruca . . . (Andrea Ferretti.)

at Corleone

At first little Francesco used to work with a dour, closed expression, never asking questions. Now he arrives looking confident, grinning from ear to ear. (Cécile Goy.)

Enthusiasm for the [dressmaking] class has grown so that every day more mothers bring their daughters along to see if they might join. One woman brought her own chair to make quite sure that her daughter was accepted. (Verena Wolfensberger.)

at Menfi

. . . 39 experimental plots are now sown . . . about a rood each on an average, enough to enable us to successfully demonstrate new crops and different techniques of cultivation to smallholders who know absolutely nothing about them . . . (Michele Mandiello.)

at Trappeto and Partinico

William and Pino have been doing the cropping chart; Hans has nearly finished the playground; Annie is supervising a group of girls who are sewing dresses and making puppets for the theatre which Hans and the boys are building from old crates . . .

Gianfranco, Franco and Pino are making final revisions to the book [*Waste*] . . . Elaine is looking after the youngsters, advising on hygiene and giving injections. Gerrit has taken on the film showings and, with Pasquale, is trying to convince the peasants about the importance of the dam. Elsa does house visits and also the cooking. . . . (Anna Alasia.)

A course has been started for illiterate boys, aged from 10 to 15 . . . They work as cowherds and day-labourers. Several are getting on well and can already write their own names. (Lorenzo and Paola Barbera.)

There was also an item about Silvio who was making notes on parasites and preparing for a conference to be held at a town called Palma di Montechiaro.

TWENTY-TWO

The Great Smell

IN February–March 1960 Dolci lectured in Switzerland, France, Sweden and England. He was troubled by a heart complaint and mentioned it privately. Publicly he said he was 'not tired, just a little weary'.

He told audiences of a Sicilian girl who had become engaged to a young man of a well-endowed family. They became intimate. Then, after pressure from his parents, he left her. Before long the girl's friends, relatives and neighbours approached her, one by one, saying: 'How is it you haven't killed him? Here you are, your reputation's done for, and yet you haven't killed him?' It was the girl's father who bought her the revolver. After a month or so of this advice she shot the young man three times in the heart and killed him.

It was not an isolated instance, he explained. Nor was the girl anti-social. She had been compelled to kill in order to remain accepted, within the social framework of her village.

'Our work is complex,' he said, 'and irrational. The problem is not one of money, but of men. Experts are needed who can see the problem objectively and precisely. Its solution lies in an awareness and an exactness of action. It's as if a crane were trying to lift a very heavy weight. If a button has to be pressed in a certain spot, it's pointless to press here—or there; it must be pressed *here*, and only then can the crane lift the load. If you put even the greatest pressure on the wrong spot nothing happens.'

The tour was a big success. In Paris he was fêted. In London one meeting drew fifteen hundred, and in Oxford so many turned up to a lecture chamber in the town hall that the meeting had to be moved to the main hall. The sixteen-stone reformer with the 48-inch waist, who travelled second-class with no luggage drew crowds everywhere. His careful social inquiries sometimes led officials to consider him naïve and innocent, and a Lancashire employment officer said: 'I shouldn't think things will work out as he hopes, but things will nevertheless work out a lot better than they would without him.'

On Dolci's last day in Britain Stephen Peet's documentary, *Murder by Neglect*, showing Dolci's work, was screened on BBC television. Audiences who knew the island through a Byronic haze of temples, Taormina and *tarantelle* danced amid orange blossom, were disturbed—among other things by the sight of a twelve-year-old boy searching for his unemployed father until he discovered, accidentally, that his father had been arrested a week before for stealing to feed the family; and by the sight of a family of eleven, living with their mule, in one room in a town called Palma di Montechiaro.

On tour Dolci, a serious man, without noticeable sense of humour, is dogged by tragi-comedy. The one hitch on this tour was the seat of his trousers, which split, while he was lunching near Tottenham Court Road. He was due to speak that night and had brought no spare pair. Peet, who was there at the time, scoured London for a pair of ready-made dark trousers, waist 48 inch. Shopkeepers laughed at the thought. Desperate, Peet rang Moss Bros. 'Yes, sir,' a voice said, 'how many pairs would you like?' The English Committee bought the trousers, and the coat to match. It was the first suit Dolci had owned since leaving home in 1949.

In Partinico some of the experts he needed were already settling in. Dolci arrived back in his new Moss Bros. suit, but instead of getting down to work with them, he made a characteristic swerve. For three weeks he was lost in a maze of consultation, statistics, and sorties by car, far and near, in the company of a thin, bespectacled doctor named Silvio Pampiglione. Then he collected statistics, colleagues, and all the motor transport available and bundled them all off to the distant town of Palma di Montechiaro for a congress.

Today at a distance of four years the value of this gathering is still hotly disputed. Many who were there cannot remember where they lodged or how any work at all was accomplished. It was that sort of congress.

Palma di Montechiaro is a seaside town of little more than twenty thousand inhabitants. It lies on the Mediterranean coast between Agrigento and Licata and faces, or more properly leans towards, Africa. It is the town of *The Leopard*, Lampedusa's masterpiece about the Sicilian aristocracy taken at the point of decline. Lampedusa does not describe what Dr. Pampiglione found there.

Pampiglione is a Roman doctor, with a scientific bias for vermin. He is lecturer of parasitology at the University of Rome. In 1959 he offered his services to Dolci and the latter suggested Palma. Pampiglione spent some months in Palma and made a remarkable report. He asked for a congress. Dolci, who had other things on his mind, shelved the idea. He felt it wrong to scatter his resources any farther afield; the admonishments of the Trappeto seminar had taught him that conferences were apt to leave villagers high and dry and, unless followed up by practical social work, greatly disgruntled. He went abroad. Returning, he found that in the meantime Pampiglione had been promised considerable backing for a conference, and changed his mind. He threw his weight behind the idea and on 27 April 1960, supported by pressmen, regional deputies and half the Italian sociological and cultural world, drove down to take the unsuspecting town by storm.

Until that day Palma had never seen foreigners at close quarters. Sicilian motorists pass through the village rapidly, if possible with their eyes closed. It does not have the quaint wedding-cake bulge of the typical poor southern village. Its poverty is spectacular. The cavernous streets are scored by serpentines of black faeces and other matter and a veil of chalky dust pollutes the air. From the main road the whole plaster town tilts downwards, as though arrested in a macabre lunge towards the sea. Once I drove through with a woman companion. She looked once, and screamed. She did not speak again until we were some distance outside the township.

Kathleen Nott, the critic and writer, arrived for the opening of the congress. It was a hot spring morning. She says: 'My first impression was a frightful smell about a mile up the road which nearly killed us [Daphne Phelps and an English accountant were with her]. A smell of non-drains. We'd hardly stepped down when the people began climbing all over us like flies—"Send us a suit of clothes?" or, "Please, a box of toys for little Giannina?" They thought we were Americans. They can't tell the difference anyway. I got stranded alone and was flat on my back beneath people most of the time. The only place I know of at all comparable is Calcutta.

'It was meant to be a sort of Dotheboy's Hall situation—"cleen windows", you know. We were told that 84 per cent of the population had no lavs and then to go out and smell for ourselves. I thought I'd be driven completely out of my mind. I couldn't stand more than a morning first of all, and escaped to Agrigento. Most of us thought it was a great mistake to hold the conference *there*. And yet it was a brilliant idea, even if it was madly distracting.'

Mistake or not, it lasted three days.

The congress was held in the cinema, second only to the cathedral in status. It was opened by the President of the Regional Government and blessed by the Archbishop of Agrigento. The President arrived two hours late—he had been spending this time, it was said, praying with the archbishop. The cinema was jammed with Palma folk who rushed it in droves the moment the doors opened. Perhaps fifty per cent understood what it was all about. Many were old women in black headshawls, bent nearly double. They sat there, bowed and silent. They thought it was a kind of vaudeville. Those who could not get in massed in the square and listened to the discussions over loud speakers. Proceedings were broadcast all over the town by a public address system which did not break down, so that passing motorists carried reports up the coast of a freak election contest. The neo-fascists had put it round that the visitors would distribute twenty million lire. Delegates emerging from the cinema for air were pounded on, pawed, grabbed, begged from and followed wherever they went.

Yet the congress succeeded.

Simultaneous translation was contrived in three languages. Sufficient carabinieri were rallied as a bodyguard to impress the President. And appetites were satisfied by a small body of nuns who prepared meals in a nearby convent. 'Curious, this congress,' the Sicilian writer Sciascia notes, after breakfasting on coffee and spiced almond cakes in the refectory, in company with priests, cardiganed students, regional deputies, armed policemen and white fluttering nuns, unobtrusively but actively hawking their handicraft on the side.

Chaos distresses most people. It inspires Dolci. The miracle of his last-minute tactical improvisation was such that the congress itself never got out of hand. Overall it produced exactly the effect of horrific revulsion on the thinking outside population that he desired. It was perfectly consistent with his expressionistic way of rousing people's consciences.

Palma was splashed across every major newspaper in Italy.

Visitors did not enjoy Palma. They felt it was terrible. But they have never forgotten it. Nor have the Sicilian authorities who for the first time, and to their credit, sat down alongside Dolci at a congress from which they themselves could emerge only as scapegoats. (They have never sat down at a public table with him since.) For the first time Dolci was seen in a responsible scientific *cadre* by his opponents.

The speakers appeared on a stark platform, casting long scalloped shadows. Pampiglione stood up, lean, square-jawed, wearing black-rimmed hexagonal spectacles. He carried a black satchel. In it was the report. Even today in cold print it has an air of crisis. It is the only statistical report I know which is at once repellent and compassionate. With Dolci's first book, *Act Quickly and Well*, it should be compulsory reading in all western schools.

It told the conference that conditions had not materially altered since 1639, when the first census was taken; that 90 per cent of the houses were without water and 86 per cent without lavatories; that from 267 children examined three-quarters had tapeworms, and

from 235 people of all ages almost 50 per cent had dwarf tapeworms
or other varieties; that the *average* was five people to a room; that in
the heart of the town 3,404 people shared their rooms with 5,085
animals—mules, donkeys, horses, goats, cows, calves, dogs, cats,
ferrets and backyard animals 'of all descriptions'—and eight
varieties of bugs and insects. The report added that:

illiteracy was 64 per cent;
only one house, of 600 seen, was free of rats and mice;
of 100 women taken at random little more than half their total
    births (827 pregnancies) had survived;
infectious diseases were rampant;
there had been a hospital—in 1666.

Pampiglione had studied 600 families, person by person. 'However,' he said, 'there is no reason to suppose, from official figures
available, that conditions in Palma di Montechiaro . . . differ greatly
from those existing in other west Sicilian communities.'

The mayor, the prefect, the local bishop, the archbishop, the
Sicilian President and other officials, listened to it all, and were
moved. The same, many of them, who a few years before had denounced Dolci for daring to suggest that Sicilian villages were
destitute.

Dolci and Pampiglione, in contrast to everybody else, made quiet,
controlled speeches. 'Nobody could have doubted which was Dolci,'
Kathleen Nott says, writing in *Commentary*. 'An exceptionally tall,
big-boned, youngish man with a round, pale, mild countenance and
dressed in what looked like a black soutane . . . I did not really take
in his clothing; it was like some rather abstract stage direction to
express a dedicated, even a consecrated personality.'

It was, in fact, the Moss Bros. suit.

He spoke about waste, his perennial theme, and explained what
he was trying to do at Partinico and the other centres. For Palma
he proposed nothing. He merely stated. Afterwards people came
up and asked what he intended *doing* about Palma. He replied, 'Go
and look at this place.' The evasion infuriated many people, and,
prodded by a situation which she felt to be a direct incitement to
violence, Miss Nott was moved to say, in her frank, hearty way:
'What would you do if you landed yourself in a revolutionary situation where non-violence was impractical?' Dolci said he didn't understand. Daphne Phelps, whose Italian was fluent, repeated the
question. He said he still didn't understand. Miss Nott demurred.
Finally, Dolci said, 'Go and look at this place yourself.' 'I now see,'
she writes, 'that Dolci could not have answered me in any other way.

To have given an answer one way or the other about the future, as it might be determined by his opponents, would be doing a kind of violence to that present which he is trying to initiate. Though to outsiders Dolci can appear somewhat mysterious, I believe myself that this is only because he is so obvious, so naïvely honest and so consistent.'

In the light of the gerrymandering excuses which have been made for Palma, and places like it, it is revealing to compare Dolci's sincere humanism with a fairly typical Italian political attitude. Girolamo Li Causi, the father-figure of Sicilian Communism, later said to me: 'We Communists should be ashamed. We once had Palma in our hands, but we did nothing to rid it of its misery.'

Dolci has always believed that if you solve people's economic problems for them you don't solve all their problems; and that it is just as important that fifty men should get together and lay their own drain as it is that they should enjoy the benefits of sewerage.

He hoped the Sicilians would do something about Palma themselves. This they are now doing—after some delay, naturally.

Nobody expected that anything would really happen during the congress. Surprisingly, on the last day, something did. A cable arrived from Holland offering six thousand pounds a year for five years. It was addressed to a Dutch Franciscan delegate, Father Salvinus Duynstee. Duynstee, a sociologist-priest, announced he would begin social work in Palma immediately. After the congress he set up a busy welfare centre.

Dolci also received offers of money, from Germany and northern Italy.

He returned to Partinico and incorporated Pampiglione's report, worm for worm, in the last section of *Waste*. The book is a scientific, humane and deeply moving account of mass exploitation. With the Mexican studies of Oscar Lewis, it gives a new dimension to the art of social documentary and makes most other sociological studies seem museum pieces by comparison. Pampiglione's report is a terrifying chapter, like all the rest.

Dolci left Palma as he found it. For some time he had to live down the mutterings of newly acquired colleagues, on Lampedusa's theme of 'change everything in order to change nothing'. (*The Leopard* is self-prescribed reading for Dolci recruits.) In this period, until 1962, nearly all Dolci's new chillun got wings. They wanted him to fly in many different directions; whether he went, or not, it still provoked criticism. His simple stubbornness caused him to back very few of their ideas. Pampiglione's was an exception. Dolci says: 'I once made a list of all the things people wanted me to do with the Centre—historical studies, chicken-raising experiments, folk high schools . . . by the time I reached thirty, I gave up. If I'd listened to them where would I be now?'

After Palma, Sicilians coined their most unloving label for him, '*il professionista della miseria*'. Dolci seldom replies to these taunts.

By accident *The Times Literary Supplement* demolishes this one for him. It notes that the Palma *exposé* puts Lampedusa's 'wonderful elegy on the old Sicilian nobility . . . into some perspective'.

It is worth adding that Lampedusa's words, 'change everything in order to change nothing', are really the maxim of Church and Mafia in Palma di Montechiaro—as Visconti discovered when he attempted, without success, to film *The Leopard* there in 1962, and as Father Duynstee was soon to discover when he began his welfare centre, to his sadness and eventual exile in 1963.

Dolci wished the Dutch priest well and turned resolutely to his more complex, more durable ideas of change. He had some difficulty in communicating these ideas, clearly and forcibly, to his new specialists. But they made an immediate impression on one woman who had arrived a month or so before.

TWENTY-THREE

A Place by the Sea

'FOR years we've been searching for community development officers and adult educationalists for Western Sicily,' Dolci told a peace conference in Basel later in 1960. 'In Italy these people don't exist. I don't believe there are any in Germany, nor have we managed to find any in Switzerland or France. In England we have found one person; and she is working down there now, submerged beneath the tens of thousands of people.'

The person was Ilys Booker, a Canadian woman from Winnipeg. She came to England in 1954, on holiday, joined the Council of Social Service in London as a development officer on the new housing estates and never went back to Canada. She came to Menfi for the British Committee in February 1960. She was forty.

Explaining Dolci's work to *Guardian* readers, Professor Waller had written, almost apologetically: 'The British have undertaken to do what they can in a place by the sea, Menfi, between Selinunte and Agrigento.' Nobody expected that Ilys, a single woman, would be able to do very much. Ilys is a modest, quiet-toned woman with her hair, greying a little, tied in a bun. She has a wry Canadian accent and a man-sized chuckle, neither of which prevents her from merging unobtrusively into her surroundings. When she came to Sicily she spoke no Italian, had never worked in an underdeveloped area and knew little of Sicilian values. But she did know that Dolci's slow way towards self-help was the only permanent, the only valid approach to the Sicilian problem.

Menfi was the least backward centre, a small flat town of thirteen thousand inhabitants, gridded into squares and straight alleys, neat and almost sewered, with globules of colour from flower-pots over courtyards and gleaming pans visible in the kitchens of houses which did not appear to be on the verge of collapse. The houses wore paint, the streets a little bitumen. The centre was closed up when she arrived. There was only Michele, the southern Italian technician, and a lively social worker, Gianfranco, who left a week later against his will. Gianfranco was removed by a posse of two friends, his father, mother, and two uncles, to the safety of North Italy, on the strength of a doctor's certificate stating he was 'mental'.

For money, Ilys discovered, you could get a Sicilian doctor to agree to anything.

Waller gave her a similar insight. (Ross Waller is Professor of Adult Education at Manchester University and was one of the first to proclaim Dolci's importance to the English-speaking world. He is chairman of the Dolci Trust in Britain.) He wrote to Ilys: 'We were at Partinico at New Year with all the volunteers. I expounded with fervour the principles of self-help and local development and finished with the question, "Now, are we to believe that the Sicilians won't help themselves?" Silence. Then a serious-looking man I didn't know said thoughtfully, "Yes, I think they will, if they are paid just a little bit for doing it."'

Ilys did not reopen the previous centre, a terraced villa near the carabinieri barracks. None of the early volunteers had understood the need to go in quietly; people had stopped sending their children to its *doposcuola* when workers appeared with questionnaires for *Waste* ('We were afraid of all these questions,' the melon man told her); Menfi had been scandalised by mixed sleeping, terrace parties and an Englishwoman who spent part of her time leaning over the balcony blowing kisses to the carabinieri. 'One feels a bit guilty that we sent you out there,' Robin Dixon, the trust secretary, wrote. Ilys replied: 'My method is one of slow, slow, slow contact.' She refused to impose.

She took rooms in the Street of All Goodness on the other side of town, quietly opened a small centre in yet another quarter, Via Mazzini, and went there every day with Michele's niece, Aurora. For weeks she did nothing but go there with Aurora, absorb the language and the customs and talk to a few women. Later, when they said, 'Are you going to have a *doposcuola*?' she began helping the children with their homework: on the first day seven children came; on the second, 26; on the third, 35; on the fourth, 43 . . . Then the mothers said, 'You must teach us to sew.' Ilys pretended to. In the first half-hour the women realised they sewed much better than she did, but they never accepted the fact, on the traditional assumption that the foreigner is always more capable. 'It becomes apparent,' she noted, 'that there is a deeply rooted habit of thinking enthusiastically, going hand-in-hand with a fantastic resignation and absolute belief in their own powerlessness.'

In her small house she did her own chores, never went out at night, slowed her pace to the timeless rhythm of her neighbours. She wrote endlessly to Waller and Dixon. 'An unmarried woman, without her family, living alone in the town is considered immoral just on the strength of combined circumstances,' she wrote. It was three months before the quarter round All Goodness Street accepted the fact that she was not a dangerous, loose woman. People took her automatically to be an Evangelist and she wondered, as she walked about that first spring, why the mothers—all of whom knew her— suddenly began to snatch their children out of her path. Then she heard that the archpriest's sermon had included the passage: 'Don't let your children fall under the shadow of the foreigners.'

'It is inconceivable to the Sicilian that anyone would work without political or religious motives,' she reported.

She also observed: 'In an agricultural economy eggs are imported from Israel, potatoes, onions, beans and milk from Italy, meat from Yugoslavia and Holland . . . Large numbers of unemployed men stand about day in and out, waiting to be called for work. They give the impression it is a holiday, as indeed it is, an almost perpetual holiday.'

Ilys received a Swiss social assistant, and rejected Partinico's offer of 'a nice young Englishman' who would be glad to help for two months. 'And when I asked what he could do, they said he was handy at all sorts of things, and could unblock drains.' All through she had one hand tied to the erratic apron-strings of Partinico, where for the first time amid the *bêtises* and petty rivalries which commonly bedevil community development work, Dolci was beginning to wince. As Partinico's growing pains mounted, Ilys felt as much for Dolci as anyone. 'I feel that poor Danilo gets dragged hither and yon by all those enthusiastic workers . . . and he tries to be agreeable to all until the force of their will gets to be too much for him and he closes down transmission and it's not possible to communicate.' Waller wrote back, in April 1960: 'He is a truly great man. That doesn't mean he is a good organiser or administrator; that he isn't and never will be. But his spirit matters a lot.' 'Part of the trouble is his own damnable modesty,' Ilys replied. 'He refuses to "give orders".'

Most of Partinico's problems, in miniature, came her way. She had to conciliate Michele, who was beset by irrigation worries. Some years before, the Government had built a dam, but neglected to tell the peasants how it worked. As a result three-quarters of the water flowed straight into the sea. Michele laboured amid the illogical spectacle of the rich man's fields profiting by a system intended to water the poor man's dead soil; and when he began to explain the meaning of secondary and tertiary channels some farmers actually complained that the modern canal system *ran across their land*. One or two progressive peasants deliberately misled the ignorant over irrigating experimental crops. Michele encouraged soil conservation and gave away poplar saplings. The peasants didn't believe 'those long thin sticks' were really trees and were surprised when they later produced leaves. They grew cereals only on land flogged bare by centuries of misuse. But as they saw the miracle of irrigation flower on Michele's 61 demonstration plots, they began to experiment; with each new crop a little mistrust vanished.

Ilys took on three young British teacher-social workers, John Ogden, Philip Reidford and Janet Rees. She put them through the same apprenticeship she had undergone herself. Janet lived with Ilys, the boys elsewhere. They ate at her house and left every evening before nine. It was months before either Janet or Ilys was able to walk the town with the boys without causing raised eyebrows. Partinico chafed Ilys' excessive caution. 'I preferred to err this way,' she says. Once she and John took Nina, the first Sicilian teacher to help, to buy some books in Palermo. Nina was seen by a Menfi lawyer sitting in the railway station bar with John—Ilys was at the news-stand twenty yards away. The lawyer thought they were on a *scappata* (weekend spree, sex implied) and reported to Nina's father. 'Half the town jumped to the same conclusion as the lawyer.'

The boys moved about the town, chatting, listening, assessing problems, drinking endless cups of black coffee, and filled in the four-months-long summer break with creative activities for the children who normally ran the streets wild. John listed thirteen major problems in Menfi. One was sex taboos. Inevitably he was involved in an almost daily conversation with peasants which went like this: 'In London how d'you enjoy yourself?' 'Oh, take a girl out—a meal, a film, go to a concert.' 'Then what d'you do?' 'Usually take her home, eat something, you know, talk——' 'Then what d'you do?' 'I usually go home.' 'You never *do* her?' 'No.' 'Why not?' 'We're not married.' 'And you call that enjoying yourself?'

Ilys tried several times to meet the archpriest. He avoided an encounter. Requests to use church stages for dramatic activities for the children were refused. A progressive young priest conceded Janet an interview for an hour. She explained Dolci's story and aims carefully. He said: 'But even though the Church might agree you are doing good work it must condemn you because this work comes under the aegis of one who has moved away from the skirt of the mother.'

Some three hundred school-aged children had not had a day's education and half of Menfi's 85 qualified teachers were unemployed. From its hobby-like beginnings Ilys built up a thriving *doposcuola*. But the local schools director would not co-operate. He told her it was against the law to start a completely free after-school schoolroom, and local teachers, aching for jobs, were afraid to join her in case they were penalised. 'It's naïve in the extreme for people to think that if we make friendly visits to the priest and so on . . . that they will smile and let us get on with things,' she wrote.

Summer was the real enemy. Sicilian heat is not unlike African. It hangs about the streets like a vapour. Summer meant occasional relief at Porto Palo beach, but it also meant flies and a flow of visitors from Partinico. Only some committees appreciated that the Partinico headquarters was not a travel agency—'Last week we counted twenty unexpected arrivals in four days,' the normally placid administrator, Eyvind Hytten, told the English committee. 'Every one represents, in addition to the trouble of finding rooms, at least some half-hour of explanation of the work, and at times several hours . . . Please tell your friends . . . to eliminate persons who come here in order to look with awe at Danilo, and who back out with disgust when they learn he does not sit the day long half-naked on a carpet, distributing bread and nice words to starving children.' About half the hero-worshippers got dysentery, and the English-speaking ones, imagining Menfi-by-the-sea as a kind of recuperative Butlin's, filtered down to Ilys' doorstep. Most were of the pestiferous kind. Cranks, beards, women artists, dilettantes, photographers, philanthropists and incompatible vegetarians in outrageous dress. Several fell sick on her. She fed them all—in August 1961 she cooked two hundred meals above normal—all, that is, except an Englishman in his seventies who came on a bicycle and, against advice, braved the local restaurant. He used sign language to order a cup of tea and a poached egg. The waiter brought the tea and an egg in its shell. 'Poached,' the old man said, imitating the action of cracking the egg. Whereupon the waiter cracked it straight into the cup of tea.

Ilys circularised Partinico and points abroad: 'Women, please do not wear shorts or slacks and please do not wear bikinis on Porto Palo; men, please do not wear shorts.'

She was made occasional chairman of the Partinico meetings, fretted at their drawn-out wastage, and told Waller: 'I'd give a lot to be a Cheshire cat and just disappear and leave my smile behind . . .'

Menfi's saving grace was its semi-autonomy. It was the only centre responsible directly to its committee abroad and paid directly by it. Other centres had their money channelled through Partinico. Menfi workers were thus envied—their salaries arrived regularly. Even so budgeting was painful. Ilys reported: 'Phil brought a list the other day—"Monthly: stamps 19s., coffees 16s., stationery 1s. 2d., toothpaste 2s. 4d., soap 1s. 2½d., razor blades 3s. 6d., haircut 1s. 9d., cigarettes and matches £3 2s. 4d. Total, £5 7s. 3½d." He asks if it is possible to have a little more than the £3 10s. a month.' The *doposcuola* went on growing. Two Sicilian teachers joined it—they were paid just a little bit for doing so. For a long time it was a school for manners, an uphill battle in a society which encouraged children to yell all day long, tear toys limb from limb, capture lame birds in order to strangle or torture them, while adults stood and laughed. Ilys and the three all got dysentery. Philip got jaundice. The doctor came and without getting out of his car said Philip was to eat nothing. He drove off, saying he was going hunting and would be back later.

Gradually they became accepted. Adults asked for English lessons. People began to ask for help of all kinds. John found it difficult not to sympathise with their fatalism. A family he knew well called him in—the father, unemployed for two years; six children—a fourteen-year-old shepherd, a girl of eleven, children of eight, six, three and a babe-in-arms; the mother, ill with pulmonary trouble; the girl of eleven ran the house, the eight-year-old had not been to school because there was no money for books, the six-year-old wanted to go but couldn't because of a head infection.

'You know there's ECA (the municipal social security office),' John told the father.

'Yes, I've been there.'

'What did they do?'

'They gave me ten pounds of pasta.'

John secured chits from ECA for medical aid, explained countless forms to the family and, after long delay, ended up with medicine for the mother, books for the boy, treatment for the child's head infection and shoes for one of the other children.

When I called on Ilys in January 1961 there were 110 children attending the *doposcuola*, many queuing for up to an hour before the doors were opened, and five exhausted teachers sweating out two shifts daily. 'At first they couldn't fathom our quiet methods, our willingness to explain, couldn't understand why we didn't beat them,' John said. 'Now kids who used to truant are brought along every day by their parents.'

'After fifteen months,' Ilys wrote, 'the women are becoming more friendly, but it will take many more months before we could embark on community centre activities; fifteen months serve only to make people more accustomed to foreigners. It doesn't compel them to take action . . . The *doposcuola* seems to have a much more profound influence than the elementary school. It "awakens" the children, people say to us. This supports what I have always believed, that if one works towards developing awareness, people see it and feel it, and after a year they are now expressing it . . .'

Ilys went on as she had begun, quietly, keeping her team together, mustering goodwill, plugging away at the silent saboteurs—ignorance, apathy, suspicion, fatalism. Then, because she was also working closely with Partinico, factors outside her control intervened. Sicily is the original European home of intrigue and it was perhaps natural that, with a dozen high-powered individualists on his staff, including two or three anarchists, some of it should rub off on to Dolci's organisation at Partinico. Workers flared up—a series of minor suppurating schisms—and the insidious unnamable quality which tinges the Sicilian atmosphere began to sap everyone's will, including Ilys'. In May 1961 she told London, 'Whoever comes to Menfi should be aware that odd situations develop in a sense outside Danilo himself.' In June she took to her bed, exhausted. 'I'm no good at intrigue,' she said. In August she left, a tired but not a despairing woman. 'I have high hopes for Menfi—five years of continuous slow work would change a lot.'

When Ilys left Menfi after eighteen months she reported 'no practical or visible results'. She left, however, something more. 'Our business as educators,' Dolci had said, 'is to get people to recognise their own problems; by raising questions we cause these problems to exist for the people so they may begin to seek ways of solving them . . . We prepare the ground for change.'

Her tedious preparatory approach laid the basis not for a social agency, but for a pilot community development project. As a result, durable changes of attitude are now taking place in Menfi. 'Dolci' and 'progress' are no longer synonymous with 'subversion'. Local body hindrances are of the past, even the church is vaguely co-operative. The *doposcuola* is officially recognised and has a staff of nine teachers, all Sicilian. Peasants who in 1960 would not use manure because 'it dirties the land' are now producing tobacco. Farmers who once said 'we were born to be wretched' and 'the Government has abandoned us', and whose ideas of solving their problems were either 'emigrate to Venezuela' or 'leave them to God', have formed a two-hundred-plus-member co-operative to stimulate production and marketing of new crops. The measure of confidence Ilys' successors, Harry and Winnie Jamieson, were able to instil is directly related to the calm unflappable policy of the woman before them. Ilys improved on Dolci's maxim, 'go slow', and went slower than anyone.

In its diminutive way Menfi is as good a piece of extra-colonial development as the British have achieved anywhere for many a long day.

TWENTY-FOUR

In Daniloland

DOLCI'S Centre at Partinico was never really planned. It grew
through a maze of debits and devoted servants, both godless and
god-given, by check and by hazard and by expedience, by the
frailty of indecisions and the strength of mistakes forgotten, and
above all by the sublimation of an enormous will to serve. It is
really an extension of Dolci's personality. There have been casualties
all along the way. But in the lonely world of the reformer it is not
unknown that the qualities which make him great in battle—self-
confidence, courage, refusal to compromise—are the very ones to
balk him in times of lull.

I first met Dolci after Palma, in the winter of 1960. It was a time
for Italy of industrial boom and of strikes in every trade and profession, of a victory against neo-fascism in the north and a harden-
ing of ecclesiastical arteries in the south, of mounting pressure from
the Left and half-baked Government reforms at the centre. The
tourist budget was jolly. In Sicily anti-Mafia propaganda was rising
and the tourist rate was starting to slump, urban poor were mortgag-
ing themselves into the grave with television on hire purchase and
peasants were abandoning the land. The Centre was expanding.

Dolci was preparing for a trip to America and about to embark
on a series of tape-recorded conversations with peasants, the theme
of *Conversations*, his next book. I was curious to meet a man who
was only then becoming controversial in a European sense. I had
to wait a few minutes to see him. The Centre had a frayed look.
Police needling was by no means ended, and a continuing series of
Mafia murders in Borgetto, a mile up the road, did not make for
relaxation. Until recently Dolci had refused any salary or personal
expenses and specialists were told, 'I hope we shall manage to keep
you living in these months.' The building was draughty and
smelled of grain, must and rat poison. It was thin and angular, and
whenever a lorry went down the main street it wobbled. A scene of
humanitarian chaos hit you the moment you came up the stairs.
The walls and every inch of flat space were covered with files,
papers, maps, graphs and charts. People came and went from a
series of partitioned cubbyholes. The men wore old clothes, the

women seemed not to have known make-up for weeks. There was a buzz of tense conversation, a feel of improvisation and a strong emphasis on manual labour. One felt instantly an unseen driving force. Amid a catharsis of foreign tongues and tension one felt strangely welcome. A door opened and I caught sight of a blond man in khaki and a skull-cap poring over notes and muttering to himself in German. Later, over lunch, when he expounded to a new female recruit the folly of wearing trousers, even by dark, in a Sicilian community, I knew it must be Eduard. A thin, silk-voiced Italian introduced himself as Teresio the demographer. He had a bundle of maps under one arm and a roll of loose spaghetti under the other and invited me to supper. He said Dolci was with a Dutch photographer from Milan. He introduced Marius Hammer, a Swiss economist, and Birgitta, a Swedish girl, who was sorting leaflets. She was preparing a musical programme for the *doposcuola*, she said, and had been asked to teach English to Sicilian adults, but was having difficulty learning Italian. She mentioned that Vicky had tripped over a body on the way to work the day before. Vicky was Josephine Bawtree, from Oxfordshire, who had given up a £22-a-week job with United Nations to become liaison officer. A hand appeared from behind a door and hung a notice on a nail. The notice said, 'Duplicating. Go Away. Pasqualino.' A nuggety peasant wandered in and said he was Ciccio; he had a message for Eyvind, he said, about the well. He was followed up the stairs by a lean Australian journalist called Lonnie. She took orders for lunch, and said if I wanted sheets to see Piero. I explained that I was not the new volunteer. Lonnie said the Centre was invigorating after the BBC, but that Partinico was hell for a single woman. If I was going back to England, she said, would I please send her a bottle of Jeyes fluid. 'There are two things in Sicily you never understand,' she said lightly. 'One is the Mafia, and the other is the Centre.' Later, when I became involved in it, I realised that the confusion was more apparent than real; and also that a certain amount was necessary to Dolci.

A door opened and Dolci stood there. He blocked the door-frame. He was wearing the milky homespun sweater Lanza del Vasto had given him. One cuff was frayed and a button missing from the neckline. There was a friendly bear-like confidence in his greeting, and when he sat down, spreading his massive arms on the desk like tree-trunks, he spoke with a gentle authority. It was a serene, groomed presence—the close-clipped fingernails, the impeccably shaven oval features, the precise notes he made of all my questions—in almost clinical contrast to his unruly surroundings. The room had a minimum of comfort, the only concession to the twentieth century being a tiny watch which he disinterred from a mass of papers and consulted before sitting down. Workers slipped in and out, urgently, as we talked. He spoke in gusts, calm, equable statements, and the current of his personality came across the desk in minor shock-waves. We talked, as I remember, mostly about folk-music; in fifteen minutes he gave me more valuable information about peasant life than I would have got from a month in Palermo. Once, when I asked about his beliefs, he jumped up and charged down the corridor to show me Einstein's declaration on human rights—it placarded a whole wall. 'That,' he said, 'is my religion.' Several things he did indicated that he was not altogether at ease amid the encroaching civilisation of his Centre; that he was not really a desk man. And yet, paradoxically, he was the groomed one— it was the wild thing. Or so it seemed. I remember he said, almost formally: 'Everywhere you'll see poverty, suffering, ignorance. We're engaged, we're committed, and therefore we have to take account of the political means by which these evils can be remedied. We belong to the world of politics, but not to the world of party politics. Nevertheless, we believe the mass of people needs in its own interests to move Left, that is towards social and economic progress.'

My main impression was of extreme gentleness and of a man utterly in control of his emotions.

That night there was a gathering at his home. Dolci had moved from Spine Sante to a modest apartment on the Corso, by Nightingale Street. A talented staff stood about, pressed into the small dining-room, drank wine, discussed the various studies, sang spirituals and, when Gerrit, the bearded co-operativist, presented a Dutch version of 'Old Macdonald had a Farm', sat on the floor with Dolci's children and clapped vociferously for more. Dolci's safety-valve was a lean-to, upright piano on which he played Bach and Schumann's *Scenes from Childhood* with a subdued pensive touch. Everybody went home early.

Partinico by now accepted foreigners, almost gratefully, yet commented thoughtfully on almost everything they did. Partinicans never quite believed, for example, that Elsa was Gerrit's wife: they said the couple *couldn't* be married, because they went on picnics together. Some lived in the House of Volunteers, the rest in solitary rooms over muddied streets. Michael Faber, the English economist, converted an empty flour-mill for his family. A Norwegian professor of moral philosophy, Eyvind Hytten, who had given up a teaching post at Stockholm University to become the new administrator, lived with his wife Kerstin and two children in an abandoned farmhouse. It was reached by gumboots and sticky cart tracks. Kerstin drew all her water from a well. I visited Eyvind often, and later worked with him. His frail, candid features seemed incongruous amid the devious runnels of a high-powered action group. 'It's like walking on eggs,' he said. 'There are more snags inherent in the work than you'd think possible. People say our whole system of financing the work by voluntary aid is irresponsible—but then the whole damn organisation is irresponsible in a certain way. There are always hangers-on. Many come in search—not because they've found—and with different talents. Most have different ideas. Naturally many go away again. We're bound to experiment. And it would be ingenuous to pretend that an initiative like ours must develop automatically, without obstacles and times of stagnation.' Eyvind accepted the task cheerfully. His boyish appearance masked a shrewd nordic maturity and loyalty which were to temper despair and keep the whole organisation from sliding over a cliff.

Soon the Centre had moved uptown to an even bigger building, a rambling white arsenal with walls a yard thick towards the Alcamo end of the Corso where Garibaldi had marched in. In May 1961 Dolci had a total staff of sixty-one.

The most valuable work done at this time was a socio-economic study by Faber, Doglio and others. Michael Faber was a young Oxford economist who had been forced to leave a university teaching post in Southern Rhodesia after opposing the Government's racial policy. Carlo Doglio was an urbanistic consultant responsible for the Olivetti community development project at Ivrea. They typified an élite of gifted, sometimes brilliant planners the Centre attracted at this time. There were also men like the Sicilian Giuseppe Ganduscio, a former union leader in Ribera who had been forced to leave Sicily because of threats from the Mafia. He sold up his factory in Florence and returned to work for Dolci, only to fall victim to cancer from which he died in 1963. Vincenzo Borruso, the Sicilian student who had worked at Borgo in 1954, returned to become the Centre's permanent doctor. A Canadian vet, Frank Manolson, arrived unexpectedly from Paris in a T-shirt and a battered Volkswagen and began a rabbit-breeding experiment to raise the meat consumption of peasant families whose average intake was less than a third that of the national average. The scheme is financed today by Oxfam.

The year began with the eternal worry over money—there were no funds to pay half the salaries. By May the monthly debt was £1,200 and rising. By July the Centre was receiving only a third of the money it said it was spending each month. Dolci does not waste money; he uses it. Pre-1962, his cavalier attitude to it infected Centre policy, though he was doubtless encouraged by the lack of a qualified treasurer. Even today the Centre hasn't *quite* discovered the need for one. The Centre is unique.

It was a strange world. You worked too long and ate too little, and the water at Ciammarita beach was not refreshing because there was too much salt in it. You had no privacy, worked to no discipline, save what you imposed yourself, you had no criteria because the conditions were new and apart from Dolci's figures, which were accurate but limited, no statistics worth counting on. You found yourself swinging between exhilaration and despair, and wondered how much *longer* the local Sicilians would go on feeling abandoned, because Dolci no longer distributed old clothes in the weekends. You swore often, drank too much heavy wine and were comforted by the thought that if you fell seriously ill the nearest good hospital was in Rome. You witnessed more quarrels, heard more screams, saw more mawkishness in a week than you had known in a lifetime. You began to lose your sense of humour. Perhaps you were becoming insensitive too. You created small frictions, unknowingly, among friends, and you tried to relax. But you couldn't relax, because of the noise, and because that sharp shouting Sicilian dialect was starting to annoy you. In six months you aged six years. A sort of blankness descended and you found yourself funnelled into a vortex of town double-talk and compromise which you never accepted, but never wholly rejected either because compromise often saved time and time, somehow, seemed important. Sometimes you found yourself believing, along with Gandhi, that it was the reformer and not society who was anxious for the reforms. Gradually you found yourself becoming involved in a love–hate relationship with the place, and knew that when you left there would be deep nostalgia for this curious organisation and these smelly streets. You wondered how in hell you had become embroiled in what was really a pacifist outfit, and then you remembered that behind it all was the inspiration of this plodding, moon-faced man who had such an unshakeable belief in the basic goodness of human beings. You supposed that that was what kept him going. He neither smoked nor swore, and seldom drank, and worked harder than any three of you together. You waited for him to crack but he never did. He seemed to grow younger with the days. When you arrived you quickly recovered from his habit of calling you instantly by your Christian name; attunement to his use of the royal 'we' and his habit of ignoring your private world and occasional love affairs took a little longer.

Above all, you realised in the summer of 1961, there were now too many individualists at the Centre, when there was really room for only one, and that was Dolci, and sooner or later someone would have to go. But Dolci had a curious habit of retiring from open conflict and you were not quite certain how it would come about.

Thurber, in an autobiographical sketch, tells of an English tutor he suffered called Miss Groby. Miss Groby had a fetish for 'the Container for the Thing Contained'. It nearly drove James Thurber mad. Dolci has a comparable weakness—he invests some words with a quality of magic which the words alone do not possess—and in that summer of 1961 this had much the same effect on his team. It has to do with authoritarianism. Dolci dislikes discipline. Most pacifists do. Dolci dislikes the word and the act. He has always rebelled against authority, whether that of his father, of Don Zeno, the Church or the State. He talks most of his father's 'heavy hand'. I have the impression that Dolci the reformer was born deep in youth, with the beatings he received from his father. When he pulled a cumbersome organisation round his shoulders and lined it with ideas and personalities he realised that, to work in a group, discipline was necessary; but he shied at using the word. Instead of 'discipline' he preferred 'co-ordinate' (his title is Co-ordinator), instead of 'control', 'verify' . . . words which did not have the ring of regimentation or fascism. He imposed the words but neglected to impose the actions they represented. In routine matters this is not serious, it is merely confusing. A volunteer, for example, told the Centre would 'contribute towards expenses' was never sure if this meant he would have his train fare refunded or merely enable him to get his shoes repaired free. But, as policy in time of internal stress, it evades a very real problem. For while you may easily verify a clan of unruly guests in your house, it doesn't necessarily follow that you have effectively controlled them or set your house in order.

It was the paralysing effect of this Indian word-magic which split the Centre.

While Dolci was in America early in 1961 a splinter group, Italian, vaguely anarchical and Communist-aligned, grew up within the organisation and consolidated itself on his return. It had a name and held its own meetings. Its influence proliferated, Faber's study was impeded, tempers became frayed. Instead of taking disciplinary action Dolci attempted to 'co-ordinate'. 'Danilo is quite aware of a difficult situation,' Ilys wrote, 'but he won't order anyone off the premises . . . He's in a proper bloody mess.' Meetings grew taut, outside pressure groups were involved, in the end nobody knew who was allied to what. Dolci appeared preoccupied. He seemed, in Ilys' words, 'to be going round some curious bend'. Part of the trouble was the insidious atmosphere of Partinico itself; almost everybody had become a little Sicilianised by it. Eventually Dolci, with the help of Eyvind and Eduard, shrugged the group off, but not before the various side-effects had undermined loyalties. The Communist clique left, but the wound healed slowly. A procession of leave-takers followed over the next months—Ilys, Gerrit, Michael, Marius, Frank, Pasqualino. Some would have gone anyway, but at least three losses were conditioned by Dolci's ambivalence and his peculiar numbness in the face of the original crisis. 'He will not impose himself on other people's personalities and activities—it is a disabling and not uncommon aspect of the pacifist complex,' Waller had written prophetically in February 1960, eighteen months before.

Several times in conversation, remembering people who had served him, Dolci told me he had failed to 'valorise them properly'. By valorise he meant extract the best and channel it thriftily. He remembered them sharply, poignantly, little bits of guilt appearing out of the subconscious. He did not own to wastage. The one time I taxed him on it he said: 'If I hadn't had the will to go on serving the area—I'm stubborn, you know—I'd have been all over the place. I know, I've been accused of being false. How many times! Because I tried not to destroy relationships with people, not send them away, and at the same time remain true to the needs of the zone and that which convinced me.'

In that same summer of discontent Dolci announced his intention of going to Russia in the autumn. The trip was to be largely at the Soviet Government's expense. But coming on top of a trip to America—where prospects of a new committee and more funds were bright—it was likely to jeopardise the American feeling and his colleagues advised him to postpone the visit to Russia. 'But I'm not a Communist,' Dolci said. 'We know that, Danilo,' they said, 'but the Americans don't.' They pressed him hard. He would not be budged. He went to Russia in the autumn.

If these things show an extraordinary *naïveté*, they also reveal a deep simplicity.

It is one of his greatest strengths. Dolci is a very simple man. He has made some extraordinary mistakes. Mistakes become stepping-stones. He casts off trouble like a skin and carries on. 'I think this is one of the secrets why he has gone on for such a long time,'

Eyvind says. 'He has this ability to just wipe out the past, just go on. This fantastic ability to forget, to forget good things and also bad things, to have neither bad conscience for what he did not achieve nor pride for what he actually did achieve.'

Dolci also has the ability to draw people from the ends of the earth, use them, exploit them to the full, even exhaust them; he may tread on them, disillusion them, even forget their existence; but in the end the extraordinary leavening effect he exerts on the Italian intellectual world works its changes on them too. In the end he does change them. And usually they remain grateful to him. Many of those who left during the troubles of 1961–2 have written to tell me this.

Lamberto Borghi, an outstanding Italian educationalist and one of Dolci's first colleagues, has said: 'Danilo is a man of power, there is a great original energy in what he has done and it is greatly worth while to be associated with him, frustrating as it may sometimes seem . . .'

Years before, at Trappeto, he had written a poem in Sicilian in which he said: 'I must be that which I have never been.' He had wanted to be a planner, an organiser, and was not. But if the rupture of 1961 showed he was not a planner it also showed, more significantly, that he was not a politician. More and more, I believe, as the world wears on and into the Orwell era, what it will need most are simple men, not politicians. Saints, if you like—but the human kind.

TWENTY-FIVE

Prelude to a Fast

DOLCI has a daemon in him. It is irrational and instinctive, and capable of lying dormant for long periods. When it is roused it has the voice of authority. People listen.

All the same it goes about its task methodically.

Dolci emerged from the rupture unscathed, his beliefs unimpaired, his passion for energising and doing things undimmed. It is fairly clear that by 1962 he felt he was becoming chained to a desk. It irked him, administrative decisions bored him. Like Spartacus, the Thracian revolutionary, he was more acted upon than acting, and not always convincing. He was losing touch with the people.

A main reason for his coming to Partinico was the projected dam for the Iato River. It was the hinge of his plan for full employment —the project Faber and Co., and now Doglio, were studying. This depended on a chain of three irrigation dams, in areas where Dolci had sited his centres. One of these dams, on the Carboi River near Menfi, was built and in Mafia hands—hence the wastage and Michele's daily educational battle at Menfi. Proposals for the other two, the Iato and the Bruca, were mysteriously blocked.

In 1961 the Iato had been just another source of disagreement at the Centre. One group declared the project technically unsound. Dolci barely listened. He had not invented the dam. Technically it was out of his grip. He was concerned with the moral issue. He had been morally involved for a long time.

Suddenly the issue came sharply into focus. Dolci decided to fast.

Once again there was division in the ranks. He was told his decision was badly timed, was undiplomatic.

Dolci has always believed that truth and acts of faith carry with them the seeds of their own best propaganda. Against the advice of his colleagues he carried on. He was convinced that he was right.

Had the thousands of acres of woods which once covered Sicily been spared by the early invaders, artificial lakes might not have become a matter of life and death to Sicilian agriculture. Water is a basic problem of all Italian life. In Sicily, the peasants say, 'Water is another God.'

Water is also important to the Mafia. It is a traditional lifeline. In 1962 Mafia controlled water supplies, selling the precious liquid by the hour at rates no peasant or share-cropper could afford. It controlled its 'right' by syndicates, and defended it when necessary by force. Something as large as a six-million-pound irrigation dam threatened to take control right out of Mafia hands and struck at the very core of one of its most ancient monopolies.

This partly explained the history of Iato.

Iato went back to 1948 when the Italian Government voted money for an irrigation project in Partinico. Dolci did not know this when he came to Trappeto in 1952 and broached a modest scheme using a forty horsepower pump. His scheme had grown to a £32,000 irrigation plan by the time he discovered, at Regional offices in Palermo, that preliminary plans for a full-scale dam already existed. He moved to Partinico, began an educational campaign and, on frequent trips to the capital, was assured plans were 'progressing'. At the end of 1955, when two-thirds of the male population was out of work and there was still no executive plan, he fasted; 1,500 peasants signed an appeal asking for speedy action. Few understood then what a dam would mean. In 1956 the Region set aside £1·2 million for initial surveys. Rome sent reassurances. 'I was ingenuous enough then to accept the Minister's promises,' Dolci says, 'and for eighteen months or so I let things slide.' 'Slide' is typically Dolcian. In these eighteen months or so he went to prison, wrote two books, fasted twice and held a congress.

A word is needed to explain what happens to public works in Sicily. Many are called for. Few serve—in any efficient sense. Since 1948 Sicily has had political and fiscal autonomy; but Regional public works agencies, like ERAS, the land-reform branch, are responsible ultimately to a parent finance body in Rome, the *Cassa per il Mezzogiorno* (Fund for the South), for special tasks. Dams enter this category. Usually the chain of command is such that between ERAS and the *Cassa* there is scope for deep incomprehension. No one can say accurately how much corruption devours public works departments in Palermo; but recently a regional deputy gave a fair guide. 'They offered me public works,' the deputy related. ' "No thanks," I said. "If I go there one of two things happens: I either become *mafioso* or I become a corpse." ' By 1955 the Mafia had influential friends lodged in all the furrows of public administration in Palermo. Government contracts were a prime source of profit—it could lift them or bury them, more or less at leisure.

In 1956 Dolci's correspondence on the dam weighed more than 40 lb. The following year the executive plans were finished, and

FIRE UNDER THE ASHES

finally, in 1959, the *Cassa* called for construction tenders. No Sicilian firm tendered. The *Cassa* called for tenders twice. There was no response in Sicily. The Mafia had let it be known it considered the dam 'a bad thing'. At this stage Dolci began to re-awaken the fag-ends of hope among the peasants—those who had not emigrated—and sent in his own technicians to check the surveys. Where technical advice failed, the bearded charm of Gerrit the Dutchman helped to conquer. But it was a tedious peasant-to-peasant drag. Then in 1960 a big Roman firm, Vianini, took up the contract. At this time nearly all major industry in Sicily was concentrated on the east of the island, away from Mafia intimidation.

The Mafia had two weapons at its disposal, fear and violence. It chose the former—fear of non-compensation. Peasants whose land would be flooded had a very real and justifiable fear of being paid 'late and badly', as experience at Menfi showed. Menfi farmers, whose land had been expropriated for the Carboi reservoir, were not only still awaiting compensation but actually paying taxes on land and houses which had been under water for five years. The Mafia so indoctrinated the Partinico farmers that all ERAS' efforts at negotiation failed.

The dam was bigger than anything existing in West Sicily. It would flood a wide valley of vineyards five miles south of Partinico, ironically the best land in the area, but irrigate 25,000 acres of barren plains. Dolci's men calculated that it would increase agricultural fertility by 225 per cent, create between three and four thousand new jobs, raise income entering the zone by half a million pounds a year and encourage small-scale industry and processing factories, then non-existent. Ten communes would benefit.

It was now 1961. In Partinico Mafia interests were controlled by a syndicate of big landowners, headed by a man called Centineo. It had its own technicians and its own lawyers. Its headquarters were a stone's throw from the Centre. Dolci, unaware of the depth of Mafia infiltration, was in correspondence with Giulio Pastore, the Minister in charge of the *Cassa*. Dolci exhorted urgency. Pastore said there would be no further delays. Vianini sent down its top technicians.

A game of cat-and-mouse began, with four groups of specialists in the area—the ERAS technicians, Dolci's, the Mafia's and Vianini's.

Left-wing unionists began campaigning for the dam. Dolci intensified his campaign. Construction materials arrived at Palermo harbour and airport. All seemed well.

Newspapers carried reports that work had begun.

In July Dolci announced his visit to Russia.

In August the Mafia produced its second weapon and opened fire.

At this time a series of water projects ringed Palermo province. The Mafia first attacked a dam on the Scansano River behind Palermo, being built to provide drinking water for the capital, causing damages of half a million pounds in a night. Elsewhere workers' yards and quarters were destroyed. Engineers were frightened off. One had his car burned. A tugboat was damaged.

It then set its sights on Iato. On 12 August the house of a popular dam supporter and leading Socialist, Fiorino, was razed by fire, and his vines and fruit trees destroyed. Fiorino's land adjoined a property of Centineo's. Dolci warned Pastore of the explosive local situation. There were rallies, mass protests, investigations, assurances from the Regional President. A six-hundred-ton vessel which had arrived from France to drain the mouth of the Iato was damaged by a plastic bomb. Five watchmen were needed at all times to guard major equipment at Palermo. Intimidations, anonymous letters, threats, continued.

The war of nerves had the desired effect. Quietly, ERAS and Vianini withdrew their personnel. Concessionary contractors withdrew men and materials. Vianini later said they had found it 'too difficult to continue'.

By spring 1962, when the dam should have been half built, all activity had ceased. Not a pick had been lifted, not a stone turned.

Dolci was then in a Swiss clinic, on doctor's orders. He was overweight and bothered by recurring heart trouble.

In April 1962 the Italian Senate, after years of prevarication, agreed to set up a Commission of Inquiry into the Mafia, and the Home Secretary, Taviani, made history by becoming the first Cabinet Minister to deplore publicly the secret society. Previously it had rarely been mentioned by Government benchers, let alone discussed. However, having said that Mafia was a bad thing, Taviani then did about the Commission exactly what Pastore was doing about the news that his six-million-pound dam had been muzzled—nothing.

Incredible as it seems, at the beginning of August 1962, fifteen years after it was first projected, only a handful of people had any idea what had become of the dam for the River Iato. Cataldo, the Mayor of Partinico, for example, told journalists he thought it was 'well under way'. The Mafia and politicians with vested interests knew. The firm of Vianini knew. ERAS and the *Cassa* knew. Presumably Pastore also knew, as Vianini were claiming £240,000 damages.

In a statement made about this time Pastore says there was 'some delay'. This was due, he explained, to a 'unilateral modification in the agreements already taken as regards expropriation'. It was, as Eyvind said, 'an exquisitely political problem'. One suspects that Pastore, who is a reasonable but not an inspired man, was in a delicate situation.

Dolci discovered it was a total Mafia situation in June. Returning from Switzerland he called at the *Cassa* and was told privately (not by Pastore) that the Mafia had threatened to throw bombs if Vianini's technicians even attempted to lay the foundations. He decided then to act, but kept his counsel for two months. In this period he appeared at the Court of Cassation, where the reverse strike sentence was finally quashed—though he was not completely exonerated: he was ordered to pay considerable costs resulting from the original trial. So far he has refused to pay any costs. He went to India, delivered a paper to an anti-nuclear-arms convention, and returned to cope with eve-of-publication alterations to a new book, *Conversations*, and a backlog of correspondence, meetings, VIPs to show round and the usual flow of summer visitors, most of whom wanted to present, personally, a small cheque towards the work. One Sunday he took Vincenzina and the children to the beach. A visitor commented that he was working too hard. 'No, no, it's quite normal,' Franco said. 'In the old days you'd never catch him taking Sunday off.' Dolci then left for a world peace congress in Moscow (he completed his speech on the plane) and was away nine days. Immediately on his return from Moscow he announced he would fast for ten days in September. He had not fasted for five years. To Pastore, he called it 'a protest and a warning', but it amounted to a non-violent ultimatum to the Mafia. It was then the end of July.

Gaspare Centineo, president of the partinico syndicate formed ostensibly to protect the interests of the farmers whose land would be flooded, was a wholesale merchant in fruit and vegetables. He was 37, Dolci's age, tallish for a Sicilian, elegantly dressed, with an overbearing manner and a bulking aggressive stare. Partinicans regarded him as Santo Fleres' probable successor, and referred to him as *'uno che sa scacciare le mosche'*—one who has a way of removing opposition.

When Dolci and Franco called to see Centineo on the night of 26 July at his warehouse, the syndicate headquarters, they noticed on the walls photographic maps of the flooding zone, prepared by ERAS, the same maps which the Centre had tried repeatedly to obtain without avail; and a letter from the *Cassa* to a CD deputy in

Rome, Calogero Volpe, reassuring him that the interests of the syndicate would be protected. (Volpe was a friend of the late Mafia Head, Don Calò Vizzini.)

All that Dolci knew, from his technicians, was that ERAS had offered £225 an acre for first-class vineyards and then more than trebled the offer; that the syndicate had demanded eight times the original figure, without consulting the majority of farmers involved, who were ignorant of the latest ERAS offer and many of whom were prepared to sell at £225.

Centineo arrived late, from the country, and was shortly joined by another man. 'There's a lot of confusion,' Dolci said. 'We'd like to get the facts straight.' Centineo replied heartily that to be against the dam would be 'uncivilised'; their technician had made a report, consulted with ERAS—'We don't know any more,' he said. Dolci probed patiently. 'Could we see this report?'

'No, it isn't here. We haven't got the keys.'

'Could we meet your technician? Where does he live?'

'I don't know. At Palermo.'

'It could be important, this meeting,' Dolci said. 'Are you sure? You don't know where your own technician lives?' He appeared to smile.

'Look, Mr. Dolci, it's useless to smile. I've told you to be against the dam is uncivilised. But I tell you something else—this land of ours is priceless. You say we don't want to reach an agreement——'

'No, I don't say that exactly. I say that from what you've just said, or haven't said, I'm not convinced you do want the dam built.' There is something deadly about Dolci's quiet insistence. 'I'm quite sure you want to reach an agreement, Mr. Centineo. But it won't come if your prices are unreasonable.'

'You've no right to come here and insult us. Who sent you?'

'Look, let's be frank. At the *Cassa* I've been told that bombs might be thrown. At Palermo the police persuaded ERAS to call off valuation surveys because of the threat to public order.'

'We haven't said we'll throw bombs. We've said they'll have to walk over our bodies first to get on to the land.' A moment later Centineo added, 'We're organised.'

'Well then,' Dolci concluded, taking out a small Biro and writing: 'You say—one, "We are not against the dam"; two, "We want just prices for our land"; three, "At present we don't know how much we want for our land." '

The man alongside Centineo sat silent and glaring throughout.

Reading a report of the meeting in Franco's typewriter next

morning, I saw that Franco had added a postscript: 'This sort of person is capable of anything.'

A few days later Dolci received through a third person a warning from the syndicate. 'Stop meddling,' it said.

The Centre was sharply divided. The critics counselled less haste and a less overtly dramatic form of protest than fasting. Old friends like Senator Parri were also sceptical. 'This dam business is a typical tilt, Italian-style,' Parri wrote. 'Be consoled it isn't the only one. Bureaucracy and *camorra* run the whole of Italy today. Sadly, the most glaring examples seem to come your way. I don't agree with the fast. Not even the atom bomb impresses people these days unless it bursts in their own backyard. I would advise mass meetings . . .'

'Dearest Danilo,' a letter said, '. . . I can't imagine why you stubbornly go on using a method which might have been effective thirty or forty years ago but not today when, so it seems, life is no longer considered a precious gift from God, to be preserved with the greatest care, but is thrown away with the greatest ease. Frankly, I consider your gesture an attempt at suicide. How easy it is to fall into heresy, even though one wants to do good, when one loses sight of Christ . . . With tender affection, Aunt Agnes.'

Eduard, away lecturing and raising funds in Germany, wrote to say the fast was 'ill timed', and told Dolci he feared it would only antagonise the Government planners. Most of us feared for Dolci's health. Franco feared for his life. Franco, his warm-hearted primitive shadow, became nervous and intense. Only Dolci seemed cheerful, at times to the point of intoxication. He went about with his sleeves rolled up, and one day came along in white ducks.

'If the dam fails our work in the area becomes useless,' he told me during a long conversation. It was early morning, barely six o'clock and already hot. We were sitting on the concrete steps outside his office. A few feet away eight big Red Burgundy rabbits—the nucleus of Frank's breeding experiment—crinkled fretfully against the netting of their cages, waiting for Angelo, a Sicilian poet who came twice daily on a bicycle to feed them. The bump of mule-carts and the shouts of the cowherds, milking their animals from door to door, rang clearly in the white morning.

'The greatest lack here,' Dolci was saying, 'is a lack of faith in progress. Each man is alone. This is the cause of the greatest depression. The Sicilian is a man like any other who generalises from his own experience. A man whose experience has always been of a static society makes the generalisation that progress never occurs;

he remains immersed in an ancient culture in which the distinction between power and truth is not yet made. But it's enough to show this man that progress is possible . . .

'Our aim—we're not creating a pastoral idyll—our aim is to be a complex of pilot services of quality, to encourage the greatest possible development and to be assimilated by local initiative.'

'You may be overtaken by industry first,' I suggested.

'It's possible. But there's a problem of quality and a problem of acceleration and they have to be seen together. A new economy would naturally favour the development of a new (non-Mafia) culture. But this *isn't enough*. It's necessary to live and work in a direction that opens the way for new moral standards. You see, this is why a dam is so important. These people who are used to looking on the summer as an enemy that burns the earth, will find that the summer, with water, brings new life; what was dry, yellow, will become green. The water is important for their *hope*. If the dam doesn't come it means for these people groping in the dark for years, for decades of years to come, and this would be senseless.'

'You're *convinced* about fasting again?'

'You tell me a better way to act so that everyone shoulders his responsibilities. Words, speeches, don't convince. But people who've known hunger, they understand—they feel compelled to take up a stand, as men, a position "of courage". And then the thing deepens and spreads——'

He gave me the best part of two hours. He spoke without rhetoric, and chuckled once when he said: 'I'm not looking forward to fasting again, I can tell you.' It was impossible to tell then that he was really frightened, but later it showed: he began to drop things, started when the telephone rang and moved everywhere quickly.

I mentioned the fast to a mechanic I knew. He was underneath a lorry at the time. He stuck an oily head out and said, 'How long for?' 'Ten days,' I said. 'Ten days?' he reflected. 'Ten days—without *living*?' His eyes radiated an expression of intense pity.

At that moment I understood. Others became convinced in much the same way. As the humanising effect of Dolci's conviction spread through the Centre, all scepticism vanished.

It was then 2 August. Dolci would stop eating on 7 September. He had barely five weeks.

Five weeks is not a lot of time to organise a campaign; not if you have to recharge from a cold start all the static particles of Partinico and district, then Palermo and then Rome, and at the end have only ten days flat on your back in which to alienate a vicious pressure group unconcerned with rules, so that all the various other bits fuse and create action. Simply, on 2 August the beacon of hope was thoroughly doused; there were five weeks in which to gather kindling and fire it; and ten days to fan it into a roaring blaze. This was Dolci's task.

He had a team of ten. Altogether he had 54 workers. But 44 of these were engaged on other essential tasks. He made do with Franco, three social workers, two technicians, two part-time office girls, a mailboy and a liaison officer. Only Franco could type faster than 25 words a minute. He had one weapon: publicity. He used it.

Correspondence on the dam, covering nine years, now weighed some 60 lb. In four weeks this doubled.

Thousand of letters, telegrams, phone calls, declarations went out to committees, newspapers, politicians, university and cultural bodies all over Europe. The declarations were cyclostyled. The letters Dolci wrote by hand early in the morning, while the others slept. As the incoming mail bulged, stray visitors to the Centre, those with a gift for languages, were pressed into temporary service. 'Would you mind translating this?' Dolci would say, piloting them to the nearest table. 'I'll be back in a minute.' He would reappear half an hour later, having attended a meeting, made several phone calls, seen the mayor and trotted down to a bar in the Corso for a glass of milk. In this way he gained an extra liaison officer, a New Zealand schoolteacher on holiday, Diana Fussell, who came for the afternoon and stayed three months. He sent out four scanners, on foot and by car. They were told to sound Mafia intimidation, clarify the compensation muddle and marshal support. There were about seventy organisations to canvass.

Most of the landowners were scared. It was thought that only a few hundred were involved. It turned out that there were more than a thousand, many of whom, owners and part-owners of three- and four-acre strips, were illiterate and could not prove their land titles. And as Pippo, the Sicilian technician, discovered, how can you be sure you have won over a peasant anyway when, in one breath, he says enthusiastically: 'Of course we want the dam—water's so short we dole it out to the kids like medicine, a spoonful at a time'—and, in the next: 'We say round here that those countries which have water all the year round have a different God'? Encounters had a tantalising poetic flavour. At one gathering of peasants the following exchange took place:

'The dam will never be made, never, never. If all the Mafia at Partinico die, then perhaps it will be made.'

'Water in Sicily controls man most, not Christ.'

'What's the use of one man fasting?'

'Look—if there are a hundred sheep and there's no shepherd, what d'you do?'

'What a lot of rot. What d'you mean?'

'He's talking in riddles.'

'No, he's not, he's talking about the sheep and no shepherd.'

'But there *is* a shepherd.'

'Who?'

'Yes, who?'

'Ah-h-hhh—you mean Danilo?'

Sometimes there were as many as seven meetings in a day. They began any time from six a.m. on, and involved every political, municipal and student body within a radius of thirty miles. Dolci went to every one.

Encounters, however slight, were summarised, typed in triplicate and discussed. These impromptu digestions took place with Dolci wherever he happened to be—in the corridor, at home, on the beach, in cars, cafés, news-stands and barbers' shops.

He relaxed sometimes, driving to the meetings, and did not seem worried by the fact that the country roads over which he drove almost daily were visited by masked hold-ups which occurred regularly throughout the summer. He drove slowly, for an Italian, expressed a morbid fascination for prisons in passing villages, ate vast quantities of fruit which he bought from roadside vendors and discussed tonal gradations in the landscape at every opportunity. Everything was scheduled to the minute. He allowed himself one luxury outing. This was an early morning drive to Scopello, a secluded tunny-fishing inlet beyond Castellammare Bay, a mile-long swim, a hill-climb to admire the view, followed by breakfast at seven-thirty—fresh bread, soaked in oil, salami, figs and lemonade. Dolci managed a loaf by himself. He led his companions on an architectural tour of a Saracen tower and ended up with his back against a boathouse, a beaming human ladder, while the others clambered one by one on to his shoulders, so they might peer down at the ark-like craft within. He changed on the roadside and drove thirty miles to Alcamo, arriving at nine-twenty-nine, a minute before the meeting was due to start. When it was over he drove straight to another meeting at Partinico.

Frequently he arrived back at the Centre to find a coach-load of visitors waiting. Once there were forty German boy scouts sitting patiently in the courtyard. He would give more time to youth groups than important visitors. If the VIPS were also pressed, he would take them along to the next meeting and chat en route.

Almost every meeting began late, at least three mayors failed to show up to appointments. Lack of punctuality was the only thing that riled him. 'And yet,' he would say, more in sadness than anger, bustling along the street, 'how can you expect these people to conceive of the value of time when they don't yet know the value of human life?'

A meeting at Montelepre was arranged with the town councillors and unionists. He arrived punctually and was told: 'It's the *festa*. They've gone to the races.' Sighing, he walked up to the square and spoke to some men outside the café. A crowd gathered. He held his meeting impromptu. After a little he said: 'What would you think of a demonstration to urge that the problem of water be resolved in the whole area?'

'If there were plenty of people the Monteleprans might join in,' a peasant said. 'If they could split up, lose themselves.'

'*Lose* themselves?'

'Yes. The syndicate's got "friends" here too—in the council, everywhere.'

'But aren't the people concerned about water?'

'Yes, they're concerned,' a student said. 'When there's no water the women stand outside their doors and start praying, saying the rosary. But then, we know our people here. They wouldn't join a demonstration.'

'What about students?'

'There are only three of us. I'm one. There's—but he's no good, his father's *in* the syndicate. I'll see if I can talk to the other one . . .'

I saw Dolci give way to frustration only once. He became withdrawn, hunched into himself, almost tearful. He was trying at the time to get in touch with Lord Russell in Wales. He had booked a call via the fish-shop, which was also Partinico's telephone exchange. The operators were two matronly fish-vendors whose talents lay in that direction. It was difficult for either of them to believe that anyone in Partinico really wanted to converse with a philosopher named Russell, telephone number unknown, at a place called Plas Penrhyn Penrhyndeudraeth. The call was kept in for three nights and cancelled in despair.

Cables and letters of support were pouring in daily.

The temperature rose steadily. For three days it hovered round 137 degrees in the street. Villagers walked the squares at night, unable to sleep. Hillsides of vineyards ignited spontaneously. The earth turned a sickly brown. Twenty of the rabbits died one noon, cooked alive in their cages.

There was no respite. While Italy went on holiday, discussions continued at the Centre behind closed windows. To open them let in the *sirocco* which fanned the air like a furnace blast and made you want to faint. A vinegary smell, from a waterless lavatory and too much disinfectant, pervaded every room.

Dolci's occasional habit was to bound into the passage, seize you by the arm and whisk you into his room, where you would be handed a summary of the latest meeting and asked for an immediate comment. For this reason it became rash to visit the toilet—it faced his office which lay three steps beyond. He worked facing the open door, his white shirt-front filling the frame, his head bowed over mounds of paper and a spray of small blue-black ballpoints which he steadily wore out, one by one.

Eduard wrote from Switzerland, advising closer contact with Rome. Eyvind replied: ' . . . a hundred different things are happening at one time . . . Danilo doesn't do anything else but keep in touch with such people, La Malfa, Pastore, etc. Yesterday he saw Gatto in the morning, Dragone was here in the evening, Gassman wrote a long letter and I don't know how many phone calls went through. Now we go to the meeting in the town hall. In the afternoon a meeting to inform all the collaborators of the situation; tomorrow morning the monthly general meeting as usual . . .'

Dolci was on a heart diet, but this—heavy on greens, light on sugar and salt—was about the opposite of a recommended pre-fast diet. He would disappear for sudden bursts of physical exercise and on Sundays appear briefly at the beach and plunge into the buoyant Tyrrhenian Sea, his tremendous flailing stroke outdistancing the other swimmers until he was almost out of sight. He would hurl quoits around violently and then lift one of the children on to his neck and meander away to the end of the bedraggled foreshore.

Gradually the whole Centre was drawn in, subservient to his will. If the atmosphere at a meeting was cold he broke it down by getting the peasants to sing. Vincenzina seemed pensive. 'Do you have any say in all this?' I asked one night over supper. She smiled good-naturedly. 'Beh-h . . .' she said. 'If I did it wouldn't change him, would it?'

Dolci informed Pastore of his plans, step by step. 'If it is now understood in Rome that this work is in the public interest let construction start without delay,' he wrote early in August. '. . . If the *Cassa's* authority be insufficient to deal with a small but powerful pressure group, let the Home Secretary intervene. As everybody knows the police force is the only thing in the area which is not underdeveloped . . .' He added that popular pressure would be brought to bear, coincidentally with the hunger strike.

On 11 August Pastore sent six lines in reply. He asked Dolci to be 'reasonable'. Apparently it was hot in Rome too.

Dolci invited Pastore to the demonstrations.

September began with no further word from Pastore. *L'Ora* remarked: 'The *Cassa* hesitates. While the Regional Government has, for some time past, been sleeping profoundly.'

About half the provincial organisations canvassed pledged support. From the promises everything, or nothing, was predictable. Dolci had two elements in his favour. One was the recent rise of a centre-left Government in Rome, tentatively pledged to social reform and representing the best change in Italian politics since Mussolini was shot. Diehard Christian Democrat Ministers were still in office, but the coalition contained two influential allies in Ugo La Malfa (Republican), the passionate Minister of Finance and Planning, and, ex-officio, a dynamic architect, Bruno Zevi, a member of the new commission for national economic planning. The other factor was the continuing heat. Water was short from the Po Valley to Puglia, and what had become the most punishing summer in twenty years promised to heighten Partinico's thirsty appeal.

On 4 September Dolci went home early and rested. Next day he had a light fever. On 6 September, the eve of the fast, he had a light supper of minestrone, salami, cheese and olives. He ate fruit, drank water and retired at ten-thirty. He slept well.

TWENTY-SIX

Fast for a Dam

Via Iannello is a crabbed and broken street 50 yards long and about 9 feet wide in the heart of Spine Sante. Number Six is a one-roomed hovel streaked with blue paint, a reminder of the Moors, like all the rest. When Dolci left Spine Sante in 1960 he installed a television set here for the quarter and kept the room for meetings and conversations with the peasants. It is here that he fasted. In the evenings the street is so cluttered with the poor and the contagion of the poor that a stranger might be forgiven for thinking he had stumbled on a desiccated reincarnation of a scene by Brueghel the Elder dating from the sixteenth century. Figures sit out amid hen-coops and mule carts, eating, shouting, gesticulating, dozing, and every so often one will dart forward and scoop a yowling child out of the mud and, until the light reflecting off the blue-wash walls turns indigo and it is too dark to see, pick the day's lice from its hair. It is a street of inertia. Occasionally a resident is removed to or discharged from prison; this causes no surprise. On the corner of the next street, Via Giannola, is a fountain which serves 150 families. At night the families bolt themselves in behind enormous wooden doors. But for the light burning over the Madonna and the leaden gleam of pasta pots impaled on the stone walls these rooms might be dungeons.

Dolci came down to begin fasting at six a.m. on 7 September with Cielo, his eight-year-old son, and lay on a crumpled bed facing the door. The neighbours cried out that only the dead lay with their feet pointing that way, but Dolci said he wasn't superstitious and asked Franco to bring some DDT. Cielo fetched a bottle of water from the fountain and shortly Osvaldo, the mail-boy, brought along a pile of telegrams which he put on the table by the bed and some of which Donna Filippa later mopped up when she cleaned out the room. There was a table, a partitioned hole-in-the-ground, a couple of posters including Einstein's declaration, a pocket mirror by the door where Dolci shaved at five-thirty every morning, and another bed where Franco slept; this bed was always covered with press clippings and bodies, so that until ten o'clock when the door was shut (the only way to get the visitors out) Franco became a sort of homeless lamp-post, ministering dazedly to the wants of all, but especially to Dolci whom he cared for as a mother. Their mutual understanding, joyous and intimate, evoked memories of older days when there were just the two of them, no Centre, riding out together on a painted motor-scooter, sharing the bloom of discovered stories in the wild virgin places. Vincenzina came every day with the children, but usually stayed in the background, shyly, as if not wishing to intrude. The room normally held ten, in comfort. When I arrived that first evening the only uninhabited part was the hay-loft above Dolci's bed where in 1955 he had hidden the unionist, Salvatore Comparetto. After that there were never less than seventy people in the room, ten and twelve hours a day. The stifling heat continued. There were always flies and television cameras with flood lamps full on the bed, and it seemed rather pointless when on the third day Franco entered triumphantly with a fan, 5 inches across, to blow the air round. '*Macchè!*' an Italian journalist gasped, after two minutes in the room—'*What* air?' I saw Dolci grow impatient once, when a photographer's lamp blinded him, and he cried out sharply.

My view is necessarily one-eyed, because I saw events almost entirely from within, living between the fasting-room, the post office and an improvised base at Number Ten, Dolci's old house. What follows is the result of daily conversations with Dolci, in diary form, because it happened that way:

FIRST DAY Dolci is violently attacked by Government Party organ, *Il Popolo*, in Rome. ('This Danilo Dolci who fasts—or pretends to; who in fact checks on him night and day?—is flanked by national and international communism . . . The dam will be delayed just the same . . .') This angers some of the mayor's local Christian Democrats, but Palermo CD headquarters dissuade them from retaliating. Hereafter no official or Right-wing paper mentions the fast.

I suppose about two hundred came today. One was a Communist regional deputy. Most of the seventy deputies in Palermo know our work, but—even on the Left—there's still diffidence. The mayor came. He heard on the radio that the Regional President and ERAS were behind the dam—not the fast, of course. I'd like a Government representative here for the demonstrations on Sunday: at Rome they say it's the Region's responsibility, and the Region says Rome is responsible. I'd just like them all to get together and say things very clearly.

I'm more relaxed. It's Franco and the others who do the work now. I'm curious to know what people think about the fast. Vincenzina is—she's resigned to these things. She didn't eat all day. I saw she was pale and then I asked one of the children and she didn't want him to answer me. There used to be a picture here, a Chinese picture. Ask Franco to look for it, would you? There's a vine with a leaf, and on the leaf are eight characters. I'm told they mean: 'If you look ahead ten years you plant trees; if you look ahead a hundred years you plant men.' It's very dear to me . . .

I wrote to my father three weeks ago, just saying things were going badly and that 'a rather strong intervention' would probably be necessary. (*Smiles.*) He'll have already understood what's happening . . .

SECOND DAY Dolci discusses the demonstrations for tomorrow. Saragat and Russell send messages. Sicilian news bulletin announces the fast, the first authorised mention by state radio of Dolci's activities in ten years. He drinks two litres of water daily and is rigorously controlled by a Sicilian doctor.

There's something hard, something angular about Russell, but he's a man without vanity, with tremendous capacity for looking ahead, almost prophetic. This is what persuades you. Abbé Pierre is another who has this limpid vision.

A few key farmers came—none of the big landowners. (*Chuckles.*) I don't think they've any intention of showing the slightest solidarity.

This isn't like the other fasts. I feel a transition—from private to public action. Let me explain better. *If* we'd managed to work more profoundly there would have been no need for this fast because the political forces would have carried the work forward by normal means. But we haven't been able to make this happen. And so now it's become necessary to do violence—non-violent violence.

My head's spinning a bit. It makes you ill when there are a lot of people. Evenings are worst. Franco's a rock. I found him in a night school—I told you. He was like a younger brother then; now, we're just brothers.

Some say this is theatrical—photographers, journalists, publicity for my books, so on. Often it's not the moments of publicity that are the best. Often there are those moments, dark, dark, when you work —as the mystics say—alone with God; those moments when everybody betrays. Those are the dark painful times. Those are the times when life is carried forward. Once I believed in 'silence'—I didn't give enough importance to publicity. I'd taken up an attitude of direct contact with God, that is, with Truth, if you like. But then I came to understand that it wasn't authentic if it didn't come through men . . . The important things for humanity are two or three. Once you've understood these, it would be stupid to go on thinking about them, you have to *do* them. And there's no need to say what they are. We know them ourselves. Why is it necessary to do these things? Because the moment they start to preen themselves they become almost sacrilegious . . .

About publicity: if more people read my books because of the fast I'm pleased. We don't write a book to amuse ourselves—we write it because it becomes an instrument for action. For me it's always an instrument. There's a need to clarify a situation, an argument, and a book is born. When a book comes out I keep it on my desk, it pleases me, but after a month I put it behind me. Personal attacks don't matter. They can spit in my face or say bravo. The important thing is that they should get together and get the dam built. Things like that article in *Popolo*, they make me sort of smile. And then I think that things which are *so* mistaken can provoke a reaction, and from this reaction other things take fire.

It's when there are friends who don't understand—then it's really painful. Yes, this time it's happening too. I don't know why it should be like that. Perhaps it's a form of conflict between a part of us—I don't know. I must think about it . . . No, publicity doesn't give me that inner joy. The deep joy comes when I see things being transformed.

A late wire: 'Tomorrow is the vigil of the nativity of Mary. May this anniversary bring concrete and visible hope to the people of Partinico and of all Sicily—Giorgio La Pira, Mayor of Florence.'

THIRD DAY—SUNDAY Bruno Zevi chairs press conference attended by all political parties and national correspondents. Mafia plants claque and shouts down mayor who is also disowned by his own party for visiting the fasting room. Eduard, back from Switzerland, brings the news:

Marvellous! Now I really am *for* the fast, Danilo. It was very funny. They all began by attacking you and then got annoyed with each other. When they isolated the mayor all the journalists, even those of the Right, got so angry they issued a statement in your defence. Then the whole atmosphere changed—they forgot the fast and began crusading for the dam, which is exactly what we wanted. When I left they were all fighting to climb on the bandwagon . . .

Afternoon: meetings, marches, speeches in Piazza Garibaldi from neo-classic marble dais, symbol of waste in Umbertine Italy.

Regional Secretary for Agriculture speaks, politely ignoring the fast. Anti-Mafia posters displayed. Dolci marches grim-faced in 2,000-strong procession; is on his feet 4½ hours. Mafia and Catholic organisations distribute pamphlets denouncing Dolci. No incidents. At night Vincenzina brings his slippers. He says his trousers are too loose and asks for a smaller pair.

I'm not exactly content. Today was a confirmation. You see, in Italy all the political parties are eaten away by rhetoric. I think at the conference they were moved by a desire not to remain alone.

There's one thing: they say I'm out to line my own pockets, that we stand to gain eight per cent of the value of the dam—that's about £480,000. It's absurd. Some people think the money for the dam is coming from the President of Switzerland. They haven't even all got the same *mistaken* idea. But the whole town is talking, that's good. I don't think the Mafia will risk anything now. The Mafia strikes in darkness, but if you throw a sheaf of light on it there are always reflections.

I feel fine, still fine. Something's moving . . .

FOURTH DAY Mafia whispering campaign, joined by Archpriest, gathers force: 'Dolci's getting half-a-million . . a million pounds.' Messages from Moravia, Levi.

A pity hatred's being worked up . . . Last night my eyes felt dry inside—better now. Several things moved me. At first people just came, like that. Now they're hugging, kissing me—strangers. A man came, factory worker, from Palermo. I'd never seen him before. He brought a melon, for my children.

You saw Giustina. The woman from Trappeto whose baby died. She wants help for the passport, to join her husband in Germany. She's terribly sad—leaving four children, farming them out to sisters. Doesn't want her husband to be alone. When husbands leave their wives behind they forget them. This large-scale emigration, it can be harmful in the long run. Did you know the resources of this area are sufficient to provide an extra one and a half million working days a year?

The doctor is giving me anti-toxin injections—lack of sugar. But look, I can still hoist Cielo up with one arm.

FIFTH DAY Government intervention assured within a week. Dolci still able to sit up at a table writing for two hours in the early morning. Acidosis worsens, but he refuses sugar solution. Mail includes letters from strangers in America and a London postman.

You have to get up, staying in bed makes you weak. Last night I went to sleep with a sort of tension. So much activity. This place is practically a public office. This arm's all numb. The injections help. The only thing I don't like, I know I've got bad breath—it worries me a bit when I talk to people.

My father wrote. He hasn't understood. He talks of 'irresponsibility', and . . . why am I telling you this? It caused me great pain. His generation—it didn't hesitate to leave wives, children, to go to war. They felt *this* to be right. And now my father says to me, 'This is tragic irresponsibility—you're not thinking of your wife and children.' But *how* I think of them! And we—I—others—do this, which isn't going off to kill anybody . . . because we, even the children, are living in a new world with a new morality. In a short while it won't be possible to live if people haven't acquired this new morality . . .

SIXTH DAY In the night Mafia destroys all crops on property of a dam supporter. Injections no longer control toxic condition; doctor orders 5 per cent sugar solution, otherwise coma within one day and death within three.

The rumour that we're speculating is growing yet. Now I understand that people can feel wounded, thinking we're getting thousands . . . And when you think of the conditioning of Sicily it's quite legitimate they should think a person acts only for self-interest.

You asked about Don Zeno. He used to read—for example, the Bible. Had a fantastic ability to suck the essence out . . . Used to read three lines, then close it and put it away, and I used to say to myself: 'Why doesn't he go on?' Then I realised. When he found something important he'd make it a part of his life before he went on—the highest tribute to truth. He couldn't admit the possibility of knowing a thing without acting on it. That was the most powerful lesson I learned at Nomadelphia.

Franco's gone to investigate this new crop outrage.

Franco returns and types his report: 'The man is a smallholder, open and courteous. He said: ". . . why did they cut down those vines? Couldn't they cut down the ones I've got at Giancaldara, where it would have been easier to cut them? We've got a saying —it's the gentle ox that pulls the heaviest load. They say that Danilo's getting 18 per cent on the dam. Is that right?" . . . 580 vines and five peach trees destroyed. The property borders on Centineo's . . .'

My thoughts are of work. Above all, work. And decisions. Nothing from Rome. I'm content, not happy. Content.

It would have been better to do without sweetened water. But if I got a cold I'd take aspirin. Still feel strong . . . You know that when you 'die of hunger' you don't die of hunger at all? It's a kind of poisoning you get. In itself a fast doesn't prove a cause just—no. At the bottom is a desire for purification, implicit; and it's true, that a man is purified by fasting. (*Chuckles*.) It's enough to try it. But really it's a comradeship, an act of faith—that others won't let you die without listening to you.

The following letter comes from a woman in Tyddyn-Angharad, Merionydd, North Wales: 'I wonder if it has occurred to you to get Danilo Dolci to take some of the Exultation of Flowers which I sent for the agricultural experiments . . . You can spray the face, eyes, anywhere you fancy, but particularly the solar-plexus . . . Take the drops from the pipette frequently—if he will not drink that then spray very often . . . When seriously ill give the drops every few minutes, if unconscious moisten the lips with it . . .' *

SEVENTH DAY Questions in the House. Pastore, asked the reason for the 'frightful state of affairs' in Partinico, replies: 'There is a halo of mystery.' However, he says he will do something.

The heat and glare of lamps is affecting everyone. Franco, a scarecrow, is almost a hospital case. Dolci's voice is a croak, his sentence structure periodically collapses. Peasants seem despondent and, out of respect, do not smoke. Dolci calls in children and has them sing.

Strange, this business . . . The atmosphere changes. Even the people change, physically—every day they seem more beautiful, especially the women with babies. There's a new light in their eyes, a special tension. They understand. There's a profound humanity in them.

News comes that the Sicilian President, the Regional authorities, the prefects, the mayor, have left suddenly for Rome.

This was one reason for the fast, that all the responsible people should get together. I've still got a doubt inside me. Someone asked

---

* Later Eyvind replied: 'Our agricultural worker in Menfi reports that . . . no result at all can be noted. He has therefore decided to discontinue the experiment; also because he fears that the local farmers, whose confidence is of prime importance to us, may fail to grasp the distinction between this product and H^2O, and so believe that we are losing our sense of proportion. The bad need for water in this zone, they rightly think, must be met on a somewhat larger scale.'

if this will be the last fast. I think there will always be difficulties in the world and for the rest of my life I'll go on trying to solve them in the most perfect, most non-violent way possible. A fast is part of a way of living. I always come back to thinking this, even if nobody knows about it.

Every so often I happen to take hold of one hand with the other, against the light, and it's thinner. One hand doesn't seem to know the other any more.

EIGHTH DAY In Rome the *Cassa* confers with all interested parties. Dolci keeps children out of the room.

Last night I calculated everything again. I thought, 'Shall I stop fasting?' And then, 'But they mightn't decide anything.' Words aren't stones. We don't want promises, we want precise guarantees.

This morning I could only sit up writing for ten, fifteen minutes. Still think though, make notes . . . Generally I write three or four pages a day. It's easy to express yourself, difficult to make yourself clear. But I've an advantage over most people—my colleagues. They re-read, look over things, and then the small miracle of men thinking together happens again.

Evening: Unofficial word comes that an agreement is reached in Rome. Dolci is sitting up, working on draft statement to Pastore, when I arrive at 10 p.m. to bunk down alongside, and insists on getting up, shifting beds, table, to make room. Continues writing, discussing thoughts aloud until 11.30. He dreams; at 2 a.m. sends Franco scuttling outside at sound of police car, calling to make an arrest a few doors away. Dozes fitfully.

NINTH DAY Wakes at 5.30 as usual, rouses Franco; shaves. Polishes draft. Awaits morning papers anxiously; when they come reads Pastore's published statement: *Cassa* guarantees fresh valuation surveys, immediate compensation and start of dam construction within five months.
After six minutes his voice goes altogether. He lies back.

I've called a meeting. Whatever happens we can't let up now. The Mafia will try and get in on sub-contracting, try and wriggle in everywhere. The thing's not finished yet.
I think I've got a cold . . .

10 a.m., all workers gather in fasting-room. Doctor orders Dolci to lie down. Dolci refuses and sits at meeting table, wearing a tartan choker. Meeting approves Dolci's statement and urges him to start eating again immediately as an 'act of responsibility'

216

towards the Government. At noon he breaks the fast with milky coffee, biscuits and fruit juice, and goes home with Vincenzina 'to sleep and think'. Vincenzina is smiling.

Dolci had won, with a day in hand. In nine days he had forced decisions and actions from above which in the normal course of events would have taken years.

Bruno Zevi, one of the planners 'from above', said: 'Things are changing. Once I couldn't get the meaning of this "fast" Danilo talked about, the mysticism and so on. Now he is deeply changed. He is grown-up. This fast was planned. It was the perfect mediator between the faith and belief of the population below and the apathy of the politicians above.'

Eduard said: 'Danilo transforms others. It's a kind of moral strength which can transform even politics.'

The campaign drained the Centre in the traditional way. In a letter to the Dolci Trust in London, requesting a loan, Eyvind described 'our people here who are now making an involuntary fast because the voluntary one cost us half a month's budget . . .'

Dolci did not appear to notice the discrepancy.

On 16 September, the day after the fast ended, the people of Spine Sante threw a *festa* in his honour. Dolci came, wearing a blazer, played the accordion and went home with flu. Vincenzina said he was 'so weak he nearly fell on the floor'. The following day, Monday, he rang the Centre several times and worked by telephone. That evening he was seen driving, and on Tuesday was all day in Palermo. At five o'clock on Wednesday morning he was back at his desk. About noon he walked off in the direction of the sea, reappearing at two-thirty, having swum at a rock inlet halfway round the coast to Palermo airport, walked twelve miles and back, uphill, as far as the Trappeto turn-off, where he had felt a bit tired and hailed a lift the rest of the way from a passing motorist. He worked all that afternoon. The next day he went to Rome . . .

The *Cassa* had pledged that work on the dam would begin by the end of February 1963. Dolci, in his statement of 15 September, warned Pastore that he would fast again if there were further delays.

On 27 February 1963 the contractors moved on to the dam site and work began. One of the first unemployed to be taken on was Sariddu, Dolci's former neighbour, who had been waiting sixteen years for a regular job. When I was last in Partinico scores of men were working in shifts round the clock. Soon the face of the dam would start to rise.

TWENTY-SEVEN

On Being Anti

THE fast had a curious effect on Dolci's father. His is still an average Italian reaction, and it underlines the thorny—many would say the impossible—nature of the task Dolci has set himself as a political and moral educator.

During the fast Signor Dolci wrote to his son: 'Millions have gone to fight wars, ethics don't come into it . . . the idea of destroying yourself in order to create is absurd.' Waiting on a railway platform, between trains, Dolci wrote a long reply (later published in Clara Urquhart's anthology, *A Matter of Life*) in which he said, '. . . it is through ethics alone that humanitarian standards will finally be achieved, by feeding on the consciousness of each one of us.' He added that public fasting was an ultimate weapon, to be used when all else failed.

Their friendly battle had been going on ever since Dolci left home.

Four months later, in February 1963, Signor Dolci came to Partinico, as he put it, 'to scold my son'. Franco drove him from the Centre to Trappeto, to see Borgo di Dio, which Eyvind and his wife, Kerstin, have converted into their home and one of Sicily's more relaxed villas. Kerstin describes a smallish, restrained man 'with a certain nobility and a beautiful soft-keyed voice; a little white hair, and no impression of violence. You liked him immediately.' Signor Dolci wore a suit, silk tie, salt-and-pepper overcoat, and remained standing. He stayed ten minutes. He told Kerstin and Franco:

'Everyone congratulates me for my son. But I'd be happy if he weren't my son, if he were somebody else's. I always come here to scold him.

'It's fantastic how the eucalyptus trees have grown. And how beautiful the iris blossom is! The almonds are finished, I see. It's ten, eleven years now since he came here to live among the poor. I thought he'd get over the idea. He had a blanket. He slept on it— there, in that corner. The blanket was too short, his head stuck out one side, his legs on the other.

'He's never had any money. He never learned to stick to it when he got it. When he had the Lenin Prize I told him to make sure and keep half for his own children. Of course he gave it away, all of it. "The money belongs to everyone's children and the children of everyone," he answered.

'You can't imagine how my wife and I have suffered—him living in all this dirt, the poverty, the disease. The danger. Yes, yes—he's survived. We used to sit up there in the north reading about it, and . . . Why did it have to be *him*?

'It's true they're building the dam now. But, bah! Look at the sacrifice it's cost, the troubles; all this anguish. Of course, the work's organised now, there must be forty or fifty of you in your "Study Centre for——" whatever it is. We're thinking of his children. At least they're now living in a comparatively modern apartment, even if it is spartan. But children of eccentric parents will always have difficulties. How will it be for them later on with a father who has offered his life to helping others?

'The work *is* important for Sicilians. I understand that. Only I wanted someone else to do it. Now if it had been you, Franco—or you [Kerstin]—I would have encouraged and admired you. As it is now, I can only scold.

'I tell you one thing: when I read in a Christian Democrat paper that Danilo was fasting to earn thousands of pounds out of the dam, then I thought, "Ah, at last! Finally a *sensible* reason for starving himself." But, of course, it wasn't true, it was only newspaper bluff. I might have known. He's hopeless.'

On this evidence alone it is not difficult to imagine why Dolci will remain an enigma to the Italians.

The fast did not confound the critics. But it won new friends—an exhibition in Milan to which leading national artists contributed raised £5,400 for the work—and blew away a little scepticism among still doubtful allies. Earlier Nino Sorgi, the lawyer, had remarked: 'I respect Danilo very much. But have you ever seen any change brought about by one of Danilo's fasts? Never. He abandons struggles.' This misunderstanding reflects merely on Dolci's bad public relations. Sorgi added: 'The trouble is, he mistrusts political power.' I doubt if Sorgi would say this now.

Dolci had now fasted seven times. His grass roots approach, 'begin at the bottom' (pure Gandhi), had broadened; he was swaying the politicians as well as the people. He was protesting effectively for the first time. He was doing what his more conservative advisers, Eyvind and Eduard, had long wanted him to do—using the fast as political mediation while remaining uncommitted himself. Their only previous doubts had overlooked his instinctive genius for action. Now they were won.

Outside Sicily experts began to talk about 'the Dolci Group'.

Inside Sicily the unexpected happened. The Mafia made a mistake. On 30 June 1963 the Mafia booby-trapped an abandoned white Giulietta limousine in a Palermo suburb and blew up seven policemen and soldiers by accident. Even Sicily was shocked. At last the Parliamentary Anti-Mafia Commission woke up: it formed emergency police squadrons and began a purification offensive which continues today. Its latest victims include Gaspare Centineo who attempted to gate-crash a sub-contract for the Iato Dam construction, was arrested, tried and is now on parole under strict police surveillance; and Luciano Liggio, of Corleone, the youngest and most vicious *capo-mafia* in history. Officially credited with ten murders, Liggio had been at large for sixteen years. When arrested in May 1964 he was bearing false identity papers in the name of Gaspare Centineo. At his trial he said he had been using this name for sixteen years. Liggio is now in prison.

After eleven years Dolci's lonely battle had been joined by a nation.

Returning from a trip to Norway in July 1963 Dolci found that in his absence the Centre had been raided. But nothing was taken. His Mafia dossier was safely hidden, elsewhere. The Commission prepared to call him as a star witness. When it did so he set off an impressive chain reaction by presenting, as a test case, sworn evidence of electoral complicity between the former gangster, Coppola, and the Partinico senator, Girolamo Messeri. There are some thirty affidavits, testifying to the help given Messeri by Coppola during the 1958 and 1963 national elections. The Commission thanked Dolci and invited him to testify again. Messeri called Dolci 'a cad' and placarded the island with thousands of posters to emphasise the point. Shortly after this he was made Under-Secretary for Foreign Commerce in the Moro Government. Coppola has maintained silence. Dolci has not met Coppola, 'though I dreamed about him once. I don't remember just what happened, but I know we didn't hug each other.'

The Commission has yet to make a full report to Parliament.

The Messeri–Coppola case made a furore in the press, and died. But it had created a new climate, and it seems fairly clear, as a result of other testimonies coming forward, that the Mafia's role as a vote-getting masonry for the Christian Democrat party will never be the same again.

Dolci went on writing, lecturing, purifying. In the winter of 1963 he was in Britain, in the summer in Norway, in the autumn in Yugoslavia. His technicians watched the dam, giving the peasants free advice, doing the Government's work. *Waste* appeared in English. *The Times Literary Supplement* gave it half a page. Gavin Maxwell, writing in *The Observer*, said: '. . . to encounter anyone who found *Waste* boring would be to meet a moron.' Norman Lewis in *The Sunday Times* wrote: 'Dolci's resistance movement to the terrific story of exploitation told in this book is the one bright chapter in Sicilian post-war history.'

Dolci turned more and more to his pacifist writings, clarifying his theory about group protests. 'What's the use of working towards non-violent education when a war will probably break out long before?' an Israeli economist said to him. Dolci replied: 'The greater the popular voice, the greater the chance that those at the top will think twice. And even if there is no hope, *we* must act as sane people.'

'For better or worse all my problems are problems of quality,' he told me. 'I'm all right in the big things; it's the little things that worry me.' Little things irked him. Conferences at which delegates 'smelled of onions and old underwear and talked of "purity"'; fanatics who abused language and said things like 'We must *work the masses up* into non-violence.' He sat at meetings in unflinching concentration, making marginal notes, despairing of small-talk, smiling wanly at jokes, never getting ill. Once he had flu for half a day. 'Not longer?' a friend said. 'No,' he replied, 'I don't let it last longer.'

Some people thought his task as a writer, as a poet of denunciation, was over. Basically it was. But he could not afford to relax. The social stagnation of Sicily had its counterparts all over the globe, in central and southern Spain, in Greece, the Middle East, in Latin America and many parts of Africa. The idea of codifying a non-violent technique with far-reaching influence preoccupied him. It was important, while maintaining an education framework, to knit his organisation into a tight yet flexible pacifist propulsion-centre.

'Dolci is no longer a Gandhi, he is more a Nehru,' observers began to say. It was a fallacy. He did not have Gandhi's mistrust of technology nor was he the complete ascetic; but in all other respects he was more Gandhian than ever. He admired Nehru—'He is a man, a block'; but Gandhi was greater—'Gandhi had no need of guns.'

Christopher Driver has written that the reason the British anti-Bomb movement failed to develop organically is that the movement 'never found a Gandhi'. After many years the Dolci movement was evolving creatively precisely because it had one. But it was evolving in a way few realised.

There is a dogma that development agencies can work effectively hand-in-glove with established authority and with the people, without ever touching politics. When an issue becomes political they tend to retire. This is the conventional approach.

The dogma, Dolci's colleagues say, is 'bunk'. Dolci is more polite. 'Deep change is not possible this way,' he says. He believes it possible for a technological agency to work in a political mould, towards a series of democratic explosions, without ever aligning itself. Put another way, it is quite possible, even desirable, to obtain democratic results by entirely undemocratic means. This was the lesson of the Iato fast.

Having drawn the lesson, Dolci now proceeded to drive it home.

In September 1963 he ticked off the irrigation map. There were three dams—Carboi, Bruca, Iato. One was there, one was coming and one was wanting. The missing link was Bruca, on the River Belice behind Roccamena, the dam in the geographic middle.

Dolci fasted again. This time action did not come quite as quickly as it had for the Iato. It took a day longer.

The bald facts are as follows:

Bruca, one and a half times bigger than Iato, had been projected since 1930. Promises and plans all the way, but no hint of action. Money had been set aside, only to vanish—diverted, during the 1963 election campaign. Dolci discovered this in August. In September Roccamena peasants said they would fast for one day. Dolci said he would join them and fast for ten. He then went to Yugoslavia. When he returned he had less than three weeks to plan the campaign. Roccamena was a ghost town. Three-quarters of the able-bodied population had emigrated. The administration had been in crisis since 1959. Ignorance was such that peasants did not even have a word in their vocabulary for 'dam'—they called it 'the big lake'.

Dolci stopped eating on 26 October. Peter Moule, secretary of the British Committee of 100, fasted with him. Small groups fasted in sympathy all over Europe. Dolci called for 'precise guarantees' from Rome by the tenth day, 4 November.

The intellectual world backed him as usual, but for nine days the authorities kept their distance. Pastore was noticeably cool. On the eighth day 150 peasants began a 24-hour fast; at night half the square was filled with starving people. Dolci and Moule slept with them, lying out on a bed of hay. On the ninth day the whole village walked in symbolic procession four miles to the dam site. Women carried babies in their arms. Dolci and Moule went with them, still fasting and mounted. 'Like Roland on horseback,' an old peasant said. He was thinking perhaps of the folk-hero Miraglia who led a mounted cavalcade of peasants to occupy the Sciacca fiefs in 1947 and was shortly afterwards machine-gunned to death by the Mafia. This time the Mafia did not interfere. That ninth evening the Regional authorities appeared in Roccamena and guaranteed support. Rome came to life the following morning. At five minutes to ten an official car drew up in the square and two Government representatives alighted and walked into the fasting-room with the pledge the villagers had requested. Dolci had called for action 'by ten-thirty a.m.'.

The jigsaw was complete.

Had I not seen it myself, day by day, I would have thought, as many must think after reading this, that it was all 'arranged'. But a moment's thought will show that no Government in the world *wants* to appear foolish.

I have no doubt that Bruca will be built, as Iato is now speedily being built. In a few years' time the Italian Government will boast an enlightened twenty-million-pound irrigation network from the steppes of Partinico to the Mediterranean coast which will be the envy of bigger states. And 'how' it all came about will doubtless be forgotten, which in the long run is as it should be. For the moment, however, it should be remembered.

There is probably no man living who can galvanise deadened or recalcitrant human material as creatively as does Dolci. It is not so much that he makes the Government look sheepish. Rather, that he has perfected a technique of civil resistance which enables the people consistently to shame the Government into action.

It is a gentle way, the way of the peace-builder.

It enables poor folk to become men first and subjects afterwards; and it allows foolish politicians to act at last and retain their dignity —and also the credit for the operation.

It shows that Gandhi is still the strongest part of him and that the French journalist's phrase, '*le Gandhi de la Sicile*', is not a bloated phantasy. Gandhi pioneered passive resistance to external authority. Dolci has successfully extended it to internal authority.

He has repolarised the Gandhi system and given it a potential universal meaning.

One asks, how?

Dolci's policy is active non-violence. This means positive development work, the work of the centres. But when sane development is blocked this also means positive action. Dolci's role changes to political catalyst. He calls up a kind of emergency pincer-group.

It compresses dormant or corrupt forces towards an inevitable clash so that sparks fly out and a democratic transformation takes place.

It is a risky method, open to fire on all sides. In a way it is absurd. But it works. One suspects that it needs supermen, but Dolci and his colleagues claim that, as a method, it can be passed on. The Service Civil International, one of the biggest development networks in the world, agrees: it has begun to use the method in Africa, working closely with Dolci's advisers.

The next step is the founding near Partinico of an international teaching institute for development workers which Eyvind plans to establish, symbolically, in Montelepre country. The institute will be an ideological extension of the Centre, but a separate unit in which—desirably, I think—Dolci would not have singular control. It would draw practical sustenance from, for example, some of the very real community development begun in Partinico in the last three years (four co-operatives working) as a direct result of the presence of Dolci social and agrarian teams.

At present his Centre is the only place where any reliable information on the sociological anatomy of the south and on Mafia as a social phenomenon are available. But this primitive archive is neither designed nor tempered to teach.

The Centre is now a magnet for social scientists the world over. They have long argued the need for a pilot institute. It makes sense. One has only to glance at Southern Europe, and the depressed emergent nations in and below the Mediterranean Basin. Sicily, in fact, is already a focal study point for the Basin where, excluding Africa, twelve millions still live in conditions of total or semi-destitution. Sicily itself is changing faster than at any time before. But there are yet no deep changes. The malaise of 'outlawry' remains. The last of the big estates, Bronte, has only just been handed over to the people. The Church sleeps on. The *per capita* income is still only half that of North Italy. Half a million Sicilians, ten per cent of the population, have emigrated in the last ten years; the emigrant trains to Switzerland, Germany, France, Belgium, are still full. And, while Mafia as a business racket may crumble, Mafia as a cult—as an ideology of silent respect for 'keeping oneself to oneself'—will persist: the cult of the lonely and the backward and the proud. Because of this the island will continue to provide the most disturbing, as well as the most fascinating sociological pattern of the age. Other countries contain one or two of the major ills of backwardness. Sicily, awaking fitfully from the wreckage of sixteen past civilisations, contains elements of them all.

'We even venture to suggest,' Dolci says, 'that some of the basic social problems of our more evolved societies could be resolved more easily through a clear analysis of the tasks we have set ourselves in this developing region.'

A teaching institute, divorced from the Centre but based on its methods, has long been Dolci's dream.

'We like to throw a lasso to the stars,' Eduard says. But Dolci, unlike some reformers, does not seek refuge in dreams. He has always been a builder of dreams; but he has always been also an extremely practical visionary. He is one of the few pacifists who realise that to achieve a moral revolution you need organisation and precise aims.

He is not ambitious in the normal way, neither for money nor social prestige nor political power. He *would* like to construct a world-wide pacific revolution in the hearts of men. It is consistent with everything he has ever said or done.

Paradoxically, Dolci's very consistency makes the future uncertain.

The illusion is that his Centre will become respectable. The fabric of Italy's 21 development organisations has officially acknowledged its role. Angela Zucconi, the master-mind of CEPAS, the prestige Italian social welfare school, visited the Centre in 1958 and was appalled; but recently she came again and revised her opinion. She is now an enthusiastic supporter. Vice-Presidents of the Common Market and Italian Ministers occasionally drop in.

However, the visitors seldom come officially, and when they do there is usually a row. La Malfa's 1963 visit, for example, earned him a rebuff from Rome, presumably because in an impromptu speech he praised the Centre and said he would like to join its heroic band. (The speech reached Stockholm where Ingrid, secretary of the Swedish Dolci Committee, distributed hundreds of copies to friends, including the Italian ambassador there. Next day the ambassador rang her, furious. 'It's a mistake!' he said. 'No Minister of the Republic would *ever* say a thing like that.' He told her to get a denial from La Malfa. Ingrid passed the message to Partinico. The Centre cabled back: 'La Malfa speech tape-recorded.') Nor is Rome ever likely to admit that its sudden dam-building activity south of Partinico, for instance, has anything to do with a man who fasted. And even if the Government does offer some official funds, Dolci is unlikely to accept. He will take nothing 'with strings'.

It is safe to assume that in twenty years he will still be leading a rebel outpost, aloof, independent, beggarly and—when necessary—agin the Government.

Dolci's dogged anti-authoritarianism, the key to his character, puzzles almost everyone. One result is that, given his reformer's autocratic temperament, it makes for obedience, not innovation: a surround of disciples rather than a welcome inclusion of scientists with ideas as original and as valuable as his own. In practice, however, this is not a grave disadvantage. Dolci no longer attracts the ubiquitous Pasqualinos, the anarchical Doglios, the unorthodox Gerrits, but instead less brilliant, quietly qualified people who are more constantly in tune with his working methods. They are courageous, talented, hard-working, sometimes enterprising—they are not yes-men. But they are mostly Italian or Sicilian, and they are disciples. They understand Dolci as no northerner (without chagrin) readily can; and he, them; and they are not tempestuously upset by his foibles. Significantly, where once there were two foreigners in the group to one Italian, now the ratio is reversed.

Dolci's preferred outlaw status is really a good thing. The arguments in its favour, in favour of non-respectability, far outweigh any disadvantages.

One is the pincer-method. In the final analysis only a closely knit rebel group can exploit it.

Another is that there is strength in being uncommitted to either Church or political party. To keep his revolution open and flexible Dolci has never, amid the hothouse of Sicilian temptation, succumbed and crossed into any political camp. This is one of his more remarkable achievements, though it puts him on an uncomfortable tight-rope. He knows that if he aligns himself, he stands to lose useful contact with at least half the population and runs the risk of being smothered by political embraces. Non-aligned, he thus remains open to varied commitment. His enemies call it 'duality'. But Dolci is in a rare position. He cannot remain strictly neutral either. If he sits on the rope, on the Sicilian political fence, he becomes by the very act of non-doing, committed. He plays directly into conservative (i.e. Mafia) hands. Fence-sitting of itself becomes a political attitude. Neutrality is impossible.

It is this openness of revolution, the continual experimenting, which has led to the pincer-method. One really has, I suppose, to thank the Mafia. It would be welcome irony if it turns out that a criminal body with a vested interest in social stagnation should have fostered a major advance in global humanitarianism.

There is a final argument for rebel status. Official chaperons require hard results in a given time. Development work is a more primitive field than sociology; it is excruciatingly slow; results cannot be measured in the normal way.

226

Three years ago, in 1961, there were three big development projects in southern Italy. One for the Abruzzi, one for Sardinia and one for Sicily. The first was state-subsidised. It collapsed. The second was sponsored by the state and the OECD (Organisation for Economic Co-operation and Development). It was flourishing, but it was on a time-expiry basis. When the time expired, it collapsed. The third was Dolci's private development project for 35 rural communes in West Sicily. This is the socio-economic excursus (the *pianificazione*) elaborated by Faber, Doglio and Co. in 1961–2; among other things it has helped shame the national Government into admitting the need for starting its own regional planning. Meantime it remains as a testimonial, the only one of the three which survives.

TWENTY-EIGHT

Dolci's Travels

DOLCI is an incurable traveller. On tour he sows the whirlwind. He takes no luggage, save a satchel, no entourage, no secretary—the interpreter does the lot—and if there is no committee to stand the expense he pays his way by writing a series of newspaper articles, usually at white heat, on his return to Sicily. If there is no interpreter available, he goes anyway.

One is reminded of Churchill's penetrating judgment of Lawrence: 'A rare beast; will not breed in captivity.'

Travel is necessary to Dolci. It is his safety-valve, the only time he can let off steam (he nearly stopped the Carlisle express in 1963, trying to pull the emergency cord with his head), have fun, be a boy again.

Apart from the fund-raising aspect which is necessary to keep his organisation afloat, he is driven chiefly by a restless empiricism. Part of him believes, with the folk-hero Miraglia, that 'a man should understand everything, know everything, comprehend everything'; and Dolci is an activist as well as an experimenter. He will not take 'Yes', or books, or 'Well, they do it this way there' for an answer, but must go and see for himself. So he goes to England to peruse the miracle of adult education, to Sweden to study the neuroses of over-civilisation, to Israel to extract the benefits of communal farming, and so on. He meets community leaders, thinkers, planners, asks endless questions, allows the results to flow and fuse in post-tour discussions with his colleagues, and finally distils the essential experience into his life's pattern. The rest he forgets. If he sometimes carries this questing to the wildest extremes of time and space it is none the less Dolci at his most honest, most down-to-earth and, his interpreters remark, his most human. A postcard from one of them is likely to read: 'Danilo bright as a button—very huggy—singing in the street.'

This chapter is mainly about that *other* Dolci, the side seldom revealed, even to friends. He keeps his friends blocked off, compartmented with the facets of his personality. There are scores of Dolcis. It is one reason why he is so elusive, why one can never presume to know him.

Since he got the passport back in September 1959 Dolci has been to Britain (twice), India (twice), Israel, the United States, Russia (twice), Scandinavia and the West European countries (frequently), Yugoslavia, Africa—every continent, in fact, except Australia and South America. That was until January 1964. He is sometimes away two months.

In 1960 and 1961 he took Vincenzina with him to Britain and Russia. She was not very happy with English food—someone took them to a Chinese restaurant for a 'traditional English meal'—so at Manchester Professor Waller gave her the run of his kitchen. She had 'a whale of a time'. In Moscow they went to the Bolshoi every night, and also to Lenin's cottage in the Kremlin, where Vincenzina broke down because 'none of the crockery matched'. She was surprised to discover how big Russia was. 'I thought it would be like Palermo,' she said.

In Russia Dolci had trouble with his trousers again. He lost them in a hotel. Now when he is away Vincenzina writes regularly, begging him not to lose any more things.

British reporters liken him to a tweed teddy bear, a jumbo-sized Pickwick, a giant film star. In 1963 he arrived at London Airport wearing dark suit, habitual white shirt buttoned to the neck, no tie, beret, tweed overcoat and thick woollen scarf. 'Oh, isn't he *sweet*!' the *Daily Mail* woman said, jumping up and down. 'How much do you weigh?' the men asked. 'I don't know,' Dolci said (he doesn't). His benign crispness and occasional patting gestures—he may clutch his listener just above the elbow and shake him, gently, to get the point home—endears him to the flintiest pressmen. Reporters are told his eldest child is nine and are perplexed when he says, seriously, that he is a grandfather (Vincenzina's eldest boy, Turi, has a child).

He is unfailingly courteous. Once in Sweden, arriving to address a meeting of Quakers, he found his audience sitting in silence, apparently praying. He tiptoed in at the back and sat down. After about half an hour somebody gave a violent snore, and the rest of the hall woke up.

He travels as he works, breakneck all the way, leaving a trail of shredded warm impressions which have magnified the myth. The saint legend is necessary, he realises, but it embarrasses him. He studies his cuttings assiduously, but the question he always asks the interpreter is not 'What do they say?' but 'Have they understood?' His authentic *mana* is difficult to capture. But in Russia, eastern and other delegates to the 1962 World Peace Congress knelt down when he arrived; in London taxi-drivers send crumpled pound-notes to the Dolci Trust in Gt. James Street and refuse to take any fare; in Switzerland railway porters do the same and slip money into his pockets; elsewhere exiled Sicilian barons turn up to his meetings and collect money at the door . . . One is likely to be buttonholed in the most unlikely corners of Europe and offered hospitality merely because one happens to know him. People who meet him socially for five minutes become lifelong supporters, and BBC actresses donate their fee on the strength of slighter connection. Sometimes he has merely said 'ciao'. Dolci has a way of saying hullo which makes it seem he is inviting you to a party. It is partly his books, translated into ten languages, but largely the alchemy of his epic personality. Even in a motor-car he has stage presence. He holds audiences by a simple presentation of the realities. His voice is effortless. He stands stock-still on the platform, gazing benignly about and nods imperceptibly while the interpreting is going on. He has the knack of projecting his personality through an interpreter to the back of the draughtiest hall. Women tend to go ga-ga. Lionising only troubles him. He withdraws from what he calls 'the facile laugh' and 'the non-violence of the limp handshake' and says such things as: 'You'd think it wouldn't matter, this saint business, but everything produces a reaction, and it's impossible to tell what the result of these inexactitudes may be.'

It is normal for him to travel, second-class, three thousand train miles in a fortnight, with appointments timed to the minute every day and lectures on twelve nights out of fourteen. He burns up interpreters regularly. They adore him for it. Diana Fussell, his last interpreter, writes: 'The best part was just talking in the train for hours and hours. I learned things about him I'd never even suspected—his sharpness, charity, humour, and especially a kind of wholeness that he has . . . I started the trip observing him, but finished up loving him.'

Occasionally, at exhaustion or crisis point, when the interpreter breaks down and weeps, Dolci seems bewildered and offers a large white handkerchief.

He will shop, but only for music. He never buys gifts or indulges a weakness for good food, though he enjoys it when offered; in the provinces he eats in modest back-street Chinese restaurants.

A tour may bring a committee five hundred pounds. The 1960 British tour brought nearly three thousand pounds, enough to staff the centre at Menfi for one year.

England seems to be his favourite country; he has been there five times. He hates English beer and fashions and claims—this in the West End—that the most beautiful head-covering for a woman is a scarf. He loves the churches, suspension bridges and especially

the system of local government. The last he discovered under the
aegis of the Mayor of Carlisle. Dolci thought the mayor had invented the system and asked for 'a blueprint'. The architect in him
despises provincial red brick and he finds it difficult to believe that
new housing communities, like the Sheffield Park Hill project, have
actually been designed. 'Draughtsman's architecture,' he mutters,
stamping his feet. He is never afraid to ask a silly question. 'And
what do you do?' he said to his host at a dinner in London given by
the Marquess of Anglesey, who is treasurer of the Dolci Trust.
Lord Anglesey replied: 'When I fill in a form I put Peer of the
Realm.' Dolci read him peasant conversations from his latest book
with the coffee. And for one who is the arch-enemy of ignorance,
he is remarkably patient with mayors who introduce him as 'Do
Dolly' and 'Danillow Dolcillae'. In Glasgow a university professor
presented him with the words: '. . . this country, Italy, which, as
you all know, has given us those two great men, Machiavelli and
Dolci.'

In Glasgow he saw the Gorbals, and wept.

In Carlisle some Partinico emigré tailors came to the meeting.
One had decorated the hall with an Italian flag 5 yards long, instead
of 5 feet, because he didn't understand his instructions very well.

After meetings he likes to stroll up hills, to see the view. 'Which
hill?' his hosts inquire. 'The biggest hill.' His hosts usually drive
up and wait for him on top.

Like the film director Fellini he has a passion for water. A Bristol
hostess said: 'What would you like to do?' 'See the sea,' he said.
'Would the river do?' she asked anxiously. At Stavanger in 1963,
between sessions of the War Resisters' International Conference, he
was usually to be found by the beach. He went deep-sea fishing and
late one night was approached on the wharf by a strange Norwegian
fisherman. They stared at each other. 'Do you believe in Jesus
Christ?' the fisherman boomed. 'I hold him in great esteem,' Dolci
replied pleasantly.

Before meetings there is a ritual 'quiet time'. He wanders off,
immersed. In Belgrave Square, before addressing the Italian Institute, he paused in the middle of the road to consider a plane tree
outlined against the night sky. A taxi missed him by inches. His
attitude to British motorists may be inferred, perhaps, from a
remark made to the assistant-secretary of the Dante Alighieri Society
in Glasgow. She was driving him to a meeting in Downhill Street
at the time. 'Madam,' he said, leaning across, 'you drive just like
Carlo Levi.' She flushed with pleasure. (Dolci did not explain that,
until someone corrected him, Levi used to start in third and drive

everywhere round Rome in that gear—'I thought all these modern cars went that way,' Levi said.)

Trains soothe him. He writes on them about non-violence with the same ease that a well-known English writer compiles thrillers commuting on the southern line. He gives his notes—an upright scrawl on scraps of paper—to the interpreter to mug up, and sighs for a good Italian newspaper. 'When I can't get the papers it's worse for me than it is for you when you can't get a cigarette.' He travels in reverie and bursts of boyish curiosity. For example: Crewe junction, the train-spotters' mecca—his companions (Trust secretary, Robin Dixon, and Diana) ill with fatigue—10.30 on a desperate Sunday morning:

'Where's everybody?' (*brightly*)

'In bed,' Robin says.

'They can't be. They must have gone away for the weekend—they've left the milk bottles out.'

'They're in bed.' (*firmly*)

'Well, what are *they* doing?'

'Taking down the numbers of trains.'

'Don't be silly—of course they're not!'

'They're called train-spotters. I used to be one.'

'Oh, yes, but you've stopped.'

At breakfast next morning he was shown a small boy at the table. 'Danilo, there *is* a train-spotter.' The boy nodded. Dolci looked at the boy for a very long time, amazed.

Expressionistic attitudes and faces, like facts, revive and stimulate him. On the last British tour, numbed by a succession of eighty lectures and appointments between the West Country and Dundee in eleven days, he brightened immediately when taken, secretly, to a late afternoon game of bingo in the North. He stared at the head-up head-down tension of hundreds of puddinged women, many in overcoats and curlers, playing furiously. 'Look at that, look at that!' he exclaimed. '*Mamma mia*—it's pure film material!' He asked for a bingo card as a memento and became engrossed. Some time later a policeman tapped him on the shoulder. 'Are you Dannylow Dolchee?' the policeman said. Dolci nodded. 'Come along, you're wanted urgently at the meeting.' Dolci put the bingo card in his pocket and went.

Exhaustion does not affect the steam-rolling rhythm of his programme. He forbids interpreters to tell organisers when he is upset, angry or tearful with tiredness, and at worst forgoes his late-night stroll, gets a taxi to his lodgings and climbs the stairs for bed, very slowly, leaning heavily on the interpreter and murmuring: 'If this

'Child, why do you starve yourself like this?
Fasting for water, Partinico 1955 & 1962; Roccamena 1963 →

'*They seem to understand . . . There is a pro-found humanity in them*'

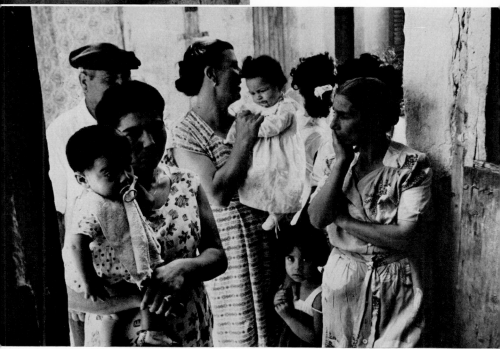

'*Even the people change, physically—every day they seem more beautiful, especially the women with babies*'

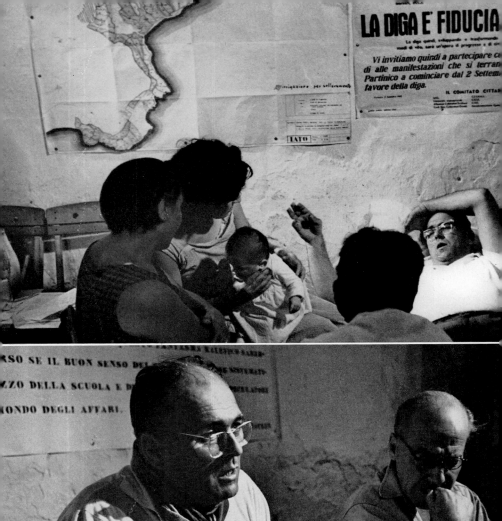

1962, FOURTH DAY: *Giustina visits Dolci in fasting room (upper). The poster reads, 'The dam is faith in the future'*
NINTH DAY: *Rome capitulates. Dolci, meeting with colleagues, agrees to start eating. On right, Eduard*

TENTH DAY: *Victory celebration in fasting room. Dolci borrows an accordion*

1963, ROCCAMENA. FAST FOR BRUCA DAM: *After starving for nine days Dolci and Peter Moule joined a mass fast of friends and 200 peasants, sleeping out in the village square. The following morning they rode four miles to the dam site. The whole village walked behind*

keeps up I'll get to the stage where my mind wanders while I talk,
and that's horrible, horrible. You become a machine, not a man.'
In 1963 friends smuggled coramine drops, for the heart, into the
various liquids he drank round England—until, forgetting Vincenzina's advice, he left the drops in a kitchen in Carlisle. He would
retire about eleven-thirty and be alert at four. In London he woke
at three-thirty and sat up until breakfast-time reading music scores.
He had bought these the day before at Peters in Oxford Street. He
called for the complete stock of Bach organ music and then turned
to Diana and asked her to inquire how much discount there would
be. 'Danilo, you can't ask for a discount *here*,' she reminded him.
(In Sicily it is standard practice.) 'Never mind,' he said. 'Go on—
ask them.' She did. Peters gave him a discount of 25 per cent.

He nearly bought an organ as well, but modified his enthusiasm
and left word for a bowler hat to be sent to Partinico instead—'for
the children, so they can play at Charlie Chaplin'. Dolci took the
organ music, his biggest item of luggage, round Britain and on
return to Partinico scoured the town to find an organ; he was offered
the use of an instrument in a neutral church.

Meeting him, days after a tour has ended, is still to experience
something of the whirlwind. About the time the bowler hat came,
I drove into Partinico from Cammarata and passed him driving the
other way, by the music podium. He swerved to a stop, narrowly
missing a baker's boy, jumped out, straightened his beret, hugged
me and gave a crisp shorthand version of the trip in the middle of
the Corso—'Tremendous, tremendous,' he said. 'And you,' I
chafed, 'were pulped when you got back.' I think he beamed. 'Not
pulped. I didn't exist. For three days I didn't exist.'

Interpreters *say* that travel is his way of relaxing.

TWENTY-NINE

Conversation in Roccamena

MANY people would like to see a *rapprochement* between Dolci and the Catholic Church in Italy. This would appear to be about as likely as the idea that he may one day be canonised. The gulf is not merely wide; the two sides are light years apart.

Cardinal Ruffini's Easter message for 1964 is a pastoral letter which opens with a warning to his flock to beware of the three deadly sins which plague Sicily: the Mafia, *The Leopard* and Danilo Dolci. This is His Eminence's first public statement that organised Mafia is in any way to be deplored—or indeed even exists. So it appears at first glance. In fact, the letter smears Dolci, and comes close to whitewashing the Mafia.

Dolci's last public remark about the Church, deemed provocative, was at Lugano in March 1960; nowadays he does not bother to mention its opposition to him, unless pressed, and then is at pains to say nothing which might create further enmity—indeed, he recently defended the Vatican so hotly to Lord Russell that the old man, who is truculently anti-Catholic, rattled his teacups in surprise. Yet Dolci is still regularly accused of attacking the Church. On balance it seems to be the Church which does most of the attacking.

A head-on collision is almost inevitable, considering the man who has been in the Palermo See for the last two decades and the general backwardness of the Sicilian clergy. Men like the ardent young Jesuit, Father Noto, who denounces Mafia connection with the Church party and wants to enlighten the fixed old-world attitude which blights Sicilian seminaries, are unhappily still rare. Most Sicilian clergy are from labouring or artisan stock. The spirit of St. Francis or the parable of the Good Samaritan have no part in their preaching. Backwardness is such that in rural areas priests have yet to learn the news of Pope John's encyclical, *Pacem in Terris*. Not long ago one told me that Dolci lived in Russia. It made no difference when I corrected him, saying I had just come from Dolci's house a few miles away. The priest interrupted: 'No, no, he's an out-and-out Communist; he lives in Russia.' These men *preserve*. Their opposition to Dolci is human. In their eyes he wants to destroy most things they hold dear. Thus, they call him a

234

'swindler', and refer to that grand old preserver, the late Mafia Head, Don Calò Vizzini, who was a murderer, as a '*galantuomo*'—a man of respect, and '*la buonanima*'—the good soul. (Don Calò had the right connections. One of his uncles was a bishop; a cousin was titular Bishop of Noto and founder of the monastic order of Maria Santissima del Carmelo; two brothers were priests, one a monsignore. Among the many mourners at Don Calò's funeral in 1954 were priests from far and near, in lines, chanting and swinging bowls of incense.) It is not only Dolci. Pastor Tullio Vinay is having a worse time in Riesi; he cannot buy another acre of land to expand his Christian Service there. Father Duynstee was forced out of Palma di Montechiaro by the Church, and he is a Catholic. But he is also a sociologist. And it is not so long since a young poet-priest, Alfonso di Giovanna, was quietly extracted from his country parish and muzzled in Agrigento because he dared champion a politician who broke away from the CD party.

Cardinal Ruffini's reference to *The Leopard* leads one to suppose that Lampedusa's prelate is not a wholly fictitious character: 'He was not a Sicilian . . . and many years before he had tried to leaven with nordic activity the inert and heavy dough of the island's spiritual life in general and the clergy in particular . . . But soon he had to realise that he was, as it were, firing into cotton wool; the little hole made at the moment was covered after a few seconds by thousands of tiny fibres and all remained as before, the only additions being cost of powder, ridicule at useless effort and deterioration of material.'

Cardinal Ruffini is not Sicilian. He is from the Po Valley in the north-west alps, the son of a haberdasher. He was a brilliant scholar and came to Palermo as archbishop in 1945. Pius XII made him a Cardinal the following year. He is handsome, with a fine patrician face and roving beady eyes, and still looks a young man, though he is 76. At the height of his powers he bestowed largesse, opened churches, oratory schools and old folks' homes with a panache reminiscent of Mussolini dedicating one of his monolithic post offices. In 1959 Ruffini returned from a trip to Spain a Franco enthusiast, rejoicing in the union of Church and State there as a model for the Catholic world. Statements to this effect earned him a snub from the Vatican. (Ruffini later denied he made them.) In 1960 after a series of harrowing Mafia murders involving some of Sicily's proudest families he is reported as saying: 'We may be a little backward as regards hygiene, but statistics show that crime and moral dissolution are far worse in the north.' (In 1959 there were 254 murders in Palermo, eight times as many as in any city in the north. Not very long ago I picked up a Sicilian newspaper and saw, on one page, the following headlines: 'Palma di Montechiaro, mother and son killed by neighbour after quarrel; Agrigento, 21-year-old carpenter stabs young wife eight times; Messina, aged peasant hangs himself; Altofonte, corpse of forty-year-old found in wood; Enna, vandals destroy six hundred vine plants and two hundred almond trees; Partinico, masked youngsters rob six cars and seventeen passengers; Germany, Sicilian emigrant stabs brother to death.')

'Prisons should be penal settlements,' Ruffini told an Italian editor named Osmani. 'But visiting prisoners is one of the seven corporal works of Catholic mercy,' Osmani observed timidly. 'Visit them, yes; but allow them enjoyment, no,' the Cardinal replied.

Between the prelate and the apostate it would appear that anti-pathy is mutual. 'Don't talk to me about Danilo Dolci!' Ruffini interrupted when Osmani introduced the name in conversation. At a fairly recent concert in Monreale Cathedral, when a friend remarked to Dolci that Ruffini, who was present, had an intelligent face, Dolci's features darkened. Dolci's last mention of Ruffini, in 1960, was that the Cardinal would like a form of Government along the lines of that in Franco's Spain. This was reported accurately in a Lugano newspaper. Ruffini sent the paper the following cable: 'I deny the affirmation attributed to me and I pray you not to heed pseudo-benefactors who bring nothing to Sicily but dishonour. I bless you.' One suspects nowadays that the Cardinal is a disappointed man who rather enjoys basking in his self-cast role as one of Italy's more aggressive reactionaries.

In Rome there is 'no such thing', I was told, as an official Church opinion about Danilo Dolci. But the present Pope, Paul, has sent his gratitude and blessing to Ruffini for the sentiments expressed in his latest pastoral letter.

However, it is not Dolci's actual split with the Church, I think, which is so interesting. He is anti-clerical rather than anti-Catholic. As humanist spokesman for an entire cultural bloc in Latin Europe, he seems to me to symbolise a widespread discontent with what is most decadent in modern Catholicism.

In the beginning it was the lay culturalists of the north who criticised Dolci, when he signed himself 'Yours in God'. Nowadays, a statement like 'All his principles derive from the Gospels' is enough to make reasonable Jesuits bang tables and to blight friendly conversation with intelligent Latin Catholics. (*Waste*, which has a deep Christian message, was banned in Ireland.) A BBC programme

'Danilo Dolci and his Critics', in which I leaned so far to the Catholic view that the Dolci Trust itself was annoyed, brought a flood of complaints from Catholics in England. Only one of the many Italian priests I interviewed for this programme had read any of Dolci's books (though Cardinal Ruffini's secretary thought His Eminence had once heard a poem recited); a Jesuit editor in Rome whose journal had published two bitter attacks observed that the Vatican was 'indifferent' to Dolci, but agreed to be interviewed only if his identity were concealed. The commonest remark was 'What a *shame* Dolci isn't a good Catholic.'

A glance at the surroundings in which he lives does not readily yield an insight into his beliefs. At home one is likely to surprise him in shorts at the piano, playing a Bach prelude and singing lustily in a mellow bass accompaniment. The house is roomy and under-furnished. Cielo's bike sometimes strays into the kitchen. If a common burglar broke in he would be disappointed; the place is devoid of material possessions. Dolci's office is equally utilitarian. The floor is stone-flagged, and the feel is of space and hard brown furniture. The rafters are pitted by dry rot and a frayed light cord dangles from a beam. The cold wall-face is broken by posters, peasant pottery, a handwoven mat from Erice and some pot plants. Everything is well dusted. There is a plain wooden table, seating ten, for minor meetings. His desk reveals a pile of papers, a few architectural doodles, a telephone, a lamp and little else. Alongside it, glassed in, is a small select library—Gandhi, Tolstoy, Jungk, Capitini are there; no fiction. In a flyleaf of Gandhi's *Autobiography* is written: 'Please! This is the only copy! Return it to Danilo's bookcase after you have read it. Thank you!' Pride of place is taken by three images: faded photographs of Gandhi and Epstein, and a tapestry sketch of Lenin sent to Dolci by Russian workmen. It is very much a man's room. The impression emerges of one of life's uncontaminated travellers, whose sustenance comes from somewhere beyond the rotting rafters.

He is called Christian, heretic, mystic, atheist, pantheist, evangelist, theist and various other 'ists'. His religious belief, like his method, is expanding all the time. Dolci is profoundly religious, but more now in the honest-to-God than in the mystical way. Perhaps Father Bruno Scott James, who is a Catholic convert, is nearest the mark when he says, 'I think he is a humanitarian—a humanitarian who puts us Christians to shame.'

Dolci finally defined his own attitude during the Bruca fast in October 1963. Various circumstances had interrupted earlier attempts. We had begun to talk about religion in September, but first Yugoslavia, then the Bruca campaign intervened. On 16 October his father died of heart failure. On 25 October we were continuing the conversation in his office when he complained of a heart pain. He stood up, breathing in gasps and leaning heavily on the desk. He took a couple of steps and fell forward on top of me. I took him home and later, when I called to see how he was, he launched back into the theme without preamble. But he tired quickly and it was only after three days of fasting at Roccamena, when he was more relaxed and cheerful than he had been in weeks, that the conversation was completed. What follows is an amalgam of these talks. He said:

'People get the wrong idea about fasting. These aren't medieval fasts any more.'

'There's no death-wish now, you mean?'

'If you like, yes. There's no masochism. What would it serve by dying?'

'You wrote to Eduard last year about taking fruit juices.'

'That's right. Gandhi took citrus juices. This confirmed to me that he didn't have the "taste of dying" either. I took juice in 1957, towards the end, when the poisoning got serious. Last year a five per cent sugar solution. This year, too, if the doctor orders. In 1956 nothing; I came through well that time. I'd never take sweetened water on the first few days—what a charlatan I'd be! That would be reinforcing myself, it wouldn't be a fast at all. A fast is a sacrifice, but a joyful one.'

'You've said that Sicily isn't Christian. At your trial Vittorini spoke a lot about castes.'

'I think he's wrong. We're not saints and Sicilians are not Indians. This is *not* India. There are no castes here. It's a blend of paganism, magic, superstition. These cults are still strong.'

'Why did you leave the Church? There were many factors, but what was the real reason?'

'I'll tell you. We of the north always thought that the priests here at least gave alms to the people, but at Trappeto I discovered there wasn't a tradition of charity *even on the alms-giving level*. It's the same today, ask anyone who lives there. Then, I remember two sermons. In one the priest got furious because the people hadn't brought anything for the collection; he called them "a lot of Jews". You remember, the people were starving then. And the other—he said, "Just as you shouldn't approach a leper for fear of getting leprosy, so you shouldn't approach sinners" . . . You understand? Not only that. I didn't leave the Church only because it was uncharitable. But because it was actually a *subversive* element, not only in Trappeto but in the whole zone. What was it that upset me most? After the war throughout that whole rising of the poor, when the people turned "outlaws" in order to live—I realised that the priests could have stopped this, they could have *tried* to stop it. But not one priest stepped in to help the people, to stop the police, to stop the firing, to stop the tortures. Not one.'

'You don't use the word God any more.'

'When I understood that the word "God" was likely to bring more confusion than clarity—we talk to be clear, don't we?—then I stopped using it. I don't believe in a personal God, not in the old traditional sense, any more. For me the key is *creativity*. "To create"—how do we create? It can be "by the will of God", and if there's no fatalism involved then this is also creative in an educational sense. But for me this isn't enough. Man must also intervene to try to change things, to modify and perfect, and this is outside the traditional religious concept. St. Paul says man must be a *co-creator* with God—which is the same idea, though Paul doesn't expand it. Jesus was ambiguous, or rather you find both viewpoints in him. In the parables there is the thought of the condemning God. This is the old world. But he also says, "my God is the God of life" —and, you remember, he talks about the seed having to die before it can bring forth fresh fruit. What matters is that man should be creative. There's nothing higher in man. But is this religious? Some say it is. Here we're trying to graft this possibility of auto-creation on to a fixed old-world attitude. Western Sicily is our experimental field—to try something which may become valid for the rest of the world.'

'You've *almost* answered my question.'

'Look: and in this sense it seems I am religious—for me the *Why?* of everything remains the *Why?* Why are we here? This is something that modern culture largely ignores or eliminates. And I think it's wrong.'

THIRTY

Enigma

I T is one of the eternal riddles of the human condition that the more a man does for it the more he attracts the calumnies of others. Dolci has been called a 'liar' and a 'criminal' by members of the Italian Government, a 'buffoon' and a 'drum-stealing seahorse' by the Church and, at various times by embittered colleagues, almost everything under the sun. Most of these former judgments, together with the people who made them, can safely be jettisoned; few withstand close analysis, and in the long run they merely testify to the largeness of mind of a man who, at bottom, remains an enigma.

One wonders though about the colleague-critics; one wonders, too, about the human wastage, why so many people leave Dolci—why, though he changes them and gives them a stabler purpose, some do not remain so grateful to him. Inevitably their opinions are extremist and highly personal, though this does not invalidate them: Gerrit, who calls Dolci a 'mixed-up social engineer' and 'very Machiavellian', also adds—'This is just my view, influenced, of course, by the fact that he ruined my programme.' The wastage of men (a sad irony, remembering that Dolci is the author of *Waste*) is more serious.

The answer I think, is a very old one—there is an abnormal gap in the spectrum, between the private and the public image; and it has always been apparent throughout Italian history wherever great men, good and bad, from Cola di Rienzo down to Benito Mussolini, have exerted their genius and then been subjected to the detached scrutiny of Anglo-Saxon or nordic eyes. Dolci's dissatisfied colleagues expected or hoped that his diplomacy *in camera* would match his genius at interpreting the hopes of an under-privileged people. They were disillusioned. Dolci was not an administrator—nor will be; he was irrational, unwilling to delegate, sensitive to criticism and (like Nehru) a strange failure in management; and perhaps for this reason alone he will always lose good men. It was always possible to work for him, under him, alongside him or even without him, but never actually *with* him. Many left out of sheer frustration.

It is happening again. The organisation (mid-1964) is in fresh crisis; helpers are leaving, complaining of 'Dolci democracy'—i.e. his autocracy and interference with work programmes.

Dolci's crises, like his books, seem to come at regular two-year intervals—this is the third schism since 1958—and, just as regularly, he manages to mismanage them until the morale at the Centre is so pinched that a general pique sets in and a whole group threatens to walk out. Dolci appears to watch with a sad, slightly sweating, almost bemused detachment. Or, as now, he will become theatrically dictatorial, imposing his veto on a majority ruling and inflating to breaking point an issue which, handled more rationally, would have fizzled and died. Sometimes he is *schlau* and evasive—as when, faced with an uncomfortable administrative decision, he will ponder, begin doodling, then shrink away, escaping into a sort of sardonic featurelessness—until he shuts off his personality altogether and mumbles 'Thank you' when he really means 'Goodbye'.

He is a man who does not appear to learn from experience. Yet sometimes the 'closing down' is necessary, for him to keep going.

Some of the present leave-takers will give allegiance to the new teaching institute. The idea of a university-type structure, sprung from Dolci, based on Dolci and in Dolci territory, but in which he is not significantly involved, may prove salutary. Some of his more astute admirers in the European universities are almost relieved that, like Garibaldi a century before him, Dolci may not in the end be the man to carry out the moral revolution he has so nobly inspired.

The present crisis, more than any other, throws into relief a big segment of Dolci's character, namely the dichotomy in the man himself of which he is only partly, or subjectively, conscious. He feels this cleavage—the frequent meaninglessness of his theories on non-violence in the face of his authoritarianism within his own Centre—subjectively; objectively he is totally unaware. This is the personal tragedy of Dolci. There is a conflict, at times a raging conflict, within him; and he is to this extent his own worst enemy. The danger is, as in the current upheaval, that hidden defects—personal vanities, pride—may emerge, as when a productive machine, uncoupled from its work-load, will reveal sinister whining notes, before racking itself to pieces. Sensitive ears have many times detected warning notes of catastrophe in Dolci's make-up, and every time he has halted the work output and instinctively adjusted the defective parts before surging on again at full bore. The danger of personal catastrophe, however, always remains; and it may well be that one day he will end by crucifying himself on the cross of his own best intentions. But I do not think so. There has always been a conflict; and Dolci does not give up struggles easily. He goes on fighting himself all the time.

His blunders *in camera* are not excusable. They are limitations and a pity. But they do not mean he is a charlatan. They mean he is ineluctably an Italian. And that much less of a saint. Either that, or a very human kind of saint.

One does not easily get to the bottom of big men; if one did, presumably one would learn from them the more and criticise them less. Legend-knocking seems to be in vogue. I am reminded at the moment of the attempt of Gerald McKnight, a Fleet Street journalist, to demolish Schweitzer in a recent book. It is revealing that Mr. McKnight spent only four days at Lambaréné, Dr. Schweitzer's mission centre in equatorial Africa. It would not be difficult to spend four days at Partinico and manufacture the same sort of book about Dolci, and it would be equally distorted. Armchair biographers of this temper are invariably little men; and Dolci—as Schweitzer—is ten times the man of any of his critics.

He has influenced European thought on the whole question of southern poverty; he has drawn the eyes of the civilised world to a forgotten corner of Europe. This much is fairly clear. The most and the least that can be said of Danilo Dolci is that he is a man of his time who sincerely wants to do good. Any wider definitive judgment is for posterity. He himself makes no extravagant claims to achievement, just as he does not claim consistency of method or originality of action.

And while it may be true that his admirers tend to overlook the changes that are taking place in the south quite apart from his reform-ideas, it would appear none the less that a good deal of the current official activity is a direct result of his stubborn needling over the years. Offhand one thinks of massive rehousing and slum-clearance plans for Palermo, for Palma di Montechiaro, for Licata; of moves to woo northern industry, to snap the gut-string of Mafia monopolies, to overcome illiteracy; of starter-measures towards organic regional planning—towards the sort of awareness, for instance, that if you build housing settlements on remote hillsides you must connect water and light *before* you can expect peasants with large families to live in them. One cannot say that Dolci is responsible for all or any of these changes. He appears merely to have hastened them by a generation or two.

He is now a powerful figure, with considerable pull in Rome, especially at the Left and Centre. Power has not corrupted him. He stands alone, head and shoulders above parties and creeds. As Professor Waller has written, he stands amid the denied and the destitute for what a hundred years of adult education have stood in the more fortunate democracies—'the extension of knowledge so that men and women everywhere may have more abundant life'.

He is a master publicist, a master showman ('masterful' is one of the adjectives his friends use most). His is usually an honest performance, without cant. I think Dolci does like acclaim, more than is apparent. He is quite open about some vanities. He once told me: 'When I see myself listed alongside men like Russell and Schweitzer, this pleases me. I know I'm forty years younger than they are.'

Withal, he remains basically a modest person. A remarkable thing about him is his encyclopaedic knowledge, embracing the entire Italian cultural—and much of the European sociological—world. He is on Christian-name terms with almost all the leading figures, and will pepper a conversation with astute shorthand judgments on each in two crisp sentences. There is never a whiff of name-dropping. If there is an element of megalomania in his character, it is largely unconscious and hardly surprising. He has already done more for Sicily than any man in the island's 26 centuries of recorded history.

Dolci is above all a writer and an *educational* reformer. He seems, for many Italians, the quintessence of the moral and spiritual drive which came out of the Resistance Movement. Equally, for many more people, as the enemy of slum-thinking and the chaos born of nepotism and bureaucratic apathy, he is a kind of universal moral detergent—like that bottle of liver pills we can none of us do without: we keep it on the shelf, slightly to one side, and do not boast of it to guests; but from time to time we are forced to take one and are profoundly grateful for the good it does us.

He is also many other things, and it is part of the riddle, as it is part of his greatness, that there is a paradox behind his almost every quality. He reminds me often of Orwell. He exhibits the same anger at injustice, in all its forms; he has the same obsession with poverty which stops just short of fanaticism; and he brings the same fearless approach to his writing and yet remains an artist, never a mere pamphleteer. In some ways he is a frustrated artist. His accounts have a searing muddled beauty, and at best, for economy of language and naked power of description, no Italian writer can touch him. Parts of *The Outlaws* and of the dialogues on the meaning of living and dying in *Conversations* read like an Introduction to the Gospels. He is deeply Italian in temperament and, within the iron mould of his moral consistency, utterly unpredictable. He makes a splendid mockery of the thesis that only the bad are interesting. Nothing about him is small, especially the failings, but in the end the limitations shrink and it does not seem to matter that he burns up colleagues or meddles or is a bad administrator—one is dealing with a typhoon, not a tally clerk; in the end it is the saga of goodness that takes over, with all the infinite variations he is able to ring on the theme. After a time, watching him biting on the kernel of living, getting rid of obstacles like spitting out the shell, one ceases to be amazed and accepts the fact that time and circumstance have created someone quite heroic. What matters, it seems to me, is the original total sacrifice—this and the courage and the awesome tenacity of purpose. In the end it is not the personality— which can be almost too impressive—nor the achievement, nor even the work which really matter. What carries you along, what convinces, is the living example.

Bertrand Russell has written: 'He carries the burden of conscience for us all.'

President Kennedy read *To Feed the Hungry* which became a direct source of inspiration for his founding of the National Peace Corps.

In a profile *The Observer* said: '. . . for Danilo Dolci must be reserved the applause which always through the centuries has been the desert of the man who, with nothing but the blazing charity of his own heart and the lonely strength of his own wits, has identified himself with the depths of human suffering and, at the cost of persecution and derision, has laboured and laboured to enlighten it.'

Gavin Maxwell writes: 'To the barren clash of ignorant armies Dolci brings solution from a higher, non-violent forum: the education of man by and to active love.'

Kathleen Nott says: 'He is a genuine and profound personality.'

Those who know him best from long association say: 'He has roused the imagination of the world. He is a kind of genius.' (Ross Waller.)

'Danilo is one of the few men I know who can live the word "humble", which other people use: he is the only man, I find, from whom I have been able to learn anything.' (Eduard Wätjen.)

'He is very much one piece of a man, and that man is dedicated to a work and not to anything else in the world.' (Eyvind Hytten.)

'He's the most complex person I've known; the contradictions in him are thousands. But the thing about Danilo is, if he hadn't gone to Trappeto in the first place, nobody would have done anything about Sicily even yet.' (Ilys Booker.)

'Danilo has been a powerful link between the southern populations and some of us in the secluded and stifling university atmosphere in the north, offering to us a larger and better scope in our thoughts and, we hope, our deeds.' (Lamberto Borghi.)

'He is a man who nurtures confidence in others; a man who defies definition.' (Carlo Levi.)

At Trappeto today a cow and a calf live in Giustina's basement where her first baby died, but it has been done up and is in rather better condition than when Dolci fasted there in 1952. 'That's where he did penance for the Lord,' the neighbours still say. People who visit the Centre in Partinico will see the sign *Centre for Studies and Action towards Full Employment* on the outer wall, and if they spend any time at all on the island will discover that it is far from an anachronism. The great barn of a building preserves a farmyard approach; grimy children play in the rucks of mud and beg ten lire from visitors; on a concrete pad by the meeting-room an alien Evangelist group continues to burst into revivalist song at no set hour; upstairs, where the social section is harboured, children throng the *doposcuola* and their wild industry echoes through the spartan corridors; downstairs, Under-Secretary Messeri's* poster, calling Dolci 'a cad', dominates the stone vestibule and the towel in the toilet still smells of vinegar; peasants clump in, cap in hand and exceeding polite, and workers in austerity clothing greet visitors with handshakes of iron and move quickly about the rooms; at the farthest recesses Dolci's voice may be heard booming softly for Franco.

There are thirty to forty workers, half of them Sicilians, living on about six pounds a week. Some earn less than three pounds a week. Salaries take nearly two-thirds of the annual budget (£25,000) which comes more or less equally from voluntary committees in seven countries, from private businessmen (mostly northern Italians) and from Protestant and student bodies in Europe and the United States. There is a strong American committee sponsored by such Establishment figures as Auden, Fromm, Mumford, de Santillana, in fact almost the Parnassus of American culture, as well as people like Norman Thomas, leader of the Socialist party. The biggest committee is in Britain (3,500 subscribers, growing all the time) which reflects Dolci's impact on audiences there. 'When I talk to an English audience,' he told Richard West, 'it is like playing on a violin. They seem to understand what I want to say. The English have a love of culture . . . they understand about underdeveloped countries, and they are excellent organisers.' The British Dolci Trust sends some seven thousand pounds a year to Menfi. Its sponsors include such non- or anti-Communists as the Bishop of

* Resigned Ministry post, December 1964.

Manchester, Sir Laurence Olivier, Count Michael de la Bedoyère, the Liberal leader Jo Grimond, Lord Sainsbury, Professor Sir Denis Brogan and a Jesuit priest, Father Thomas Corbishley. Dolci's British press is generally jubilant, irrespective of political affiliation. In Italy, while he has no blanket support from either Socialists or Communists, the picture is just the reverse. Three of the five newspapers which regularly champion his cause—*L'Ora*, *Paese Sera* and *Unità*—are Communist or fellow-travelling; the others are the Socialist paper *Avanti!* and *L'Espresso*, the tabloid *New Statesman* of Italy. He votes 'for the extreme Left'. His most ardent supporters are among the Communist intelligentsia. 'Why are so many of your cultural friends Communists?' a Sicilian engineer asked him. 'You show me a Christian Democrat who is cultured,' Dolci replied. Naturally enough some Sicilian Communists work in his centres. The emphasis is spread between peace and development work, and politics: in Sicily they cannot be divorced from each other. Outside his centres, many Sicilian people themselves—those who have heard of him—dislike and mistrust him, as they would mistrust any humanitarian who worked in a glow of publicity. 'Once he was humble, walked everywhere and was one of us. Now he lives in an apartment, drives a car and travels the world. Here is another foreigner who has risen on our backs.' This is the line of their reasoning. There is no Dolci committee in Sicily.

Most days Libera, his eldest child, comes along and dusts the office. There are five Dolci children, Maria-Libera (or Libera-Maria: Vincenzina isn't sure) who is ten, Cielo (nine), Amico (seven), Chiara (five) and Daniela (three). It is said that Dolci decided against increasing the population further after his last horrified inspection of the birth-rate in India. Vincenzina wanted to call all the children after him, but succeeded only with Daniela. The other names, chosen by Dolci, are symbolic, especially Amico's. Amico (Friend) has five names—Amico Aldo Norberto Lucio Enrico—commemorating Dolci's 1957 success in obtaining a *rapprochement* between Italian cultural leaders who normally couldn't stand the sight of one another.

Vincenzina remains a stoical, contented, if shadowy figure, nostalgic only for the crusading days of Borgo and the People's University. At home she is often dynamic, shouting at her children as vehemently as the neighbours shout at theirs—but not usually when Dolci or visitors are present. She is probably relieved that her five children by her first husband—all sons and all working in the north—lead normal lives and have shown no wish to become involved in the Dolci movement. She reflects his aura with a quiet dignity, and is naturally humble. It is always from some other person that one learns about her—about how, for example, when she was married to the peasant Luciano and living with his people in Trappeto, she was once beaten so hard for a peccadillo that two ribs were broken and she had to continue making the beds for the entire household on her knees; or of how in 1961 she was expected to prepare supper for thirty people, with the usual alacrity, despite the fact that she had given birth to Daniela only a week before. Vincenzina is a remarkable woman, a blend of uncompromising Sicilian fibre rooted in Greek tragedy and of the slow dawn of the modern Sicilian woman. She remains utterly devoted to Dolci and says, simply: 'I understand I have changed because our life is different.' Once, asked why it was that Sicilians sang so much, she explained in these words: 'When I lost my husband and I'd given all the bread to the children I always used to sing, and the hungrier I was the more I sang, just to have it *here* in my head, not in my stomach. But my sister-in-law knew. When she heard me singing at the top of my voice she would say, "Listen to the wretch, her stomach's full of nothing again." '

Not long ago Tullio Vinay came to see me in Cammarata, on his way from Riesi to Palermo. He is one of the famous pastors of Europe and came to live, and work in Riesi—a despairing town in Caltanissetta province—in 1961. It was early morning when he called. The peasants had long begun their two-hour trek to the fields, Peppino the goatswain was finishing his round, milking from the teat straight into the housewives' bottles, and the narrow inclines rang with the thud of hawkers' mules sliding down, and the pestering cries of women and families threading their way up, towards the hills, for the end of the olive harvest. We stood on the little wrought-iron balcony looking across the village to the Tumarrano Valley and the eight or nine villages, their populations cut in half by emigration, which smudged its broken featureless gullies. The valley rolled in a grey cataract to the far horizon, a ridge of blueblack mountains which mark a confine of three provinces. It was on these feudal estates that Mafia began.

Vinay was not surprised to learn that I had to work in Cammarata anonymously, chiefly because the priests—and therefore the ruling clique—considered Dolci a militant Communist. 'It is the same in Riesi,' he said. 'It is easier for the clergy to condemn Communism than to incarnate the faith they profess.'

After a while he said, in English: 'You know Dr. Müller-Ganghoff wrote an idea about the Third People of God. The First People of God was Israel, and they betray the Lord. And in His Freedom the Lord chose another people, the Church. But the Church is now betraying the Lord. And the Lord is free to choose other men, *sine nomine*, as His people. And Danilo is surely one of the Third People.'

There is something prophetic, almost pre-ordained about these words. It is linked in my mind with Dolci's principle of self-immolation in order to create ('to know how to die is to know how to live . . . all things can be changed'); and with the uncanny nature of his survival. His life is a modern fable.

Since Vinay's visit at the end of 1963, which coincided with Dolci's historic denunciation of Messeri before the Parliamentary Anti-Mafia Commission, there has been a wave of arrests of major *mafiosi*. Previously the Government offensive had managed to detain only rank-and-file members. In February 1964 the feudal king of Sicily and the acknowledged Head of the Mafia, Giuseppe Genco Russo, was jailed. Russo, whose twisted moral code provides a revealing chapter of *Waste*, inherited Don Calò's mantle, was an intimate of priest and politician, and had been regarded as 'untouchable'. At his trial he was convicted for being 'a danger to society' and sentenced to exile in the northern Alps. He is contained there now, without a telephone, an arthritic self-pitying hulk of 71, in a remote lakeside district north-east of Milan where as a boy Dolci once walked with his father and dreamed his first dreams about the gift of goodness. The wheel of destiny has completed a revolution.

Dolci is in the prime of life.

Assuredly he will not be canonised. He may continue to try the patience of his sponsors, but I doubt that he will exhaust it. He will probably not—like Bellini (who died in Paris), like Pirandello (who died in Rome) or like Verga (who lived mostly in Milan), all three of whom have monuments in their native Sicily—be honoured in concrete or marble. But his spirit will carry on.

He told a conference in Norway recently: 'With diligence I am continuing.'

Bibliography

Except where specially significant, the newspaper and magazine commentaries I have consulted are not included, chiefly for reasons of space. Many specialised articles and monographs by Dolci and his colleagues are available in Italian and English from Centro Studi, Partinico, on request. Further information about Dolci's work and aims is available from the Danilo Dolci Trust, London W.C.1.

ABBA, CESARE, *Da Quarto al Volturno*. Zanichelli: Bologna, 1912
ALONGI, G., *La Mafia*. Bocca: Turin, 1877
BARBERA, LORENZO, *La Coscienza di Roccamena*. Laterza: Bari, 1964
BARZINI, LUIGI, *The Italians*. Hamish Hamilton: London, 1964
CAPITINI, ALDO, *Rivoluzione Aperta*. Parenti: Milan, 1956
Danilo Dolci. Lacaita: Florence, 1958
CARLI-BALLOLA and NARZISI, '*Il Grano Rosso*: vita e morte di Salvatore Carnevale'. *Avanti!*: Milan, 1956
CARLYLE, MARGARET, *The Awakening of Southern Italy*. Oxford University Press: London, 1962
CENTRO STUDI *Notes for friends*. Partinico, 1958–64
Convegno sulle condizioni di vita e di salute in zone arretrate della Sicilia Occidentale. Palma di Montechiaro, 1960
DOLCI, DANILO, *Voci nella Città di Dio* (poems). Società Editrice Siciliana: Mazara, 1951
Da Borgo di Dio (pamphlet). Trappeto, 1953
Fare presto (e bene) perchè si muore. De Silva: Turin, 1954
*Banditi a Partinico. Laterza: Bari, 1955
'Volevo scoprire l'anima della vita' (autobiographical soliloquy). *Tempo*: Milan, 1956
Poesie. Canevini: Milan, 1956
Processo all' articolo 4 (with others). Einaudi: Turin, 1956
*Inchiesta a Palermo. Einaudi: Turin, 1956
Series of travel articles in *L'Ora*. Palermo, 1958
Una politica per la piena occupazione (with others). Einaudi: Turin, 1958
*Spreco. Einaudi: Turin, 1960

* Published in English by MacGibbon & Kee, London, as:
   The Outlaws of Partinico (1960), *To Feed the Hungry* (1959), *Waste* (1963), *A New World in the Making* (1965); and by Orion, New York, as *Outlaws* (1961) and *Report from Palermo* (1959).
   The Outlaws of Partinico includes extracts from *Fare presto (e bene)*, *Articolo 4* and *Una politica*; *Waste* includes a portion of *Conversazioni*.

DOLCI, DANILO, *Conversazioni*. Einaudi: Turin, 1962
Verso un mondo nuovo. Einaudi: Turin, 1964
FISCHER, LOUIS, *The Life of Mahatma Gandhi*. Cape: London, 1951
FRANCHETTI and SONNINO, *La Sicilia*. Vallecchi: Florence, 1876
GALTUNG, JOHAN, 'Gandhi, Dolci e noi' (article). *Il Ponte*: Florence, 1957
GANDHI, MAHATMA, *Autobiography*. Phoenix: London, 1949
GANACHAUD, GUY, *Les Bandits de Dieu*. Seuil: Paris, 1957
GENTILE, NICOLA, *Vita di Capomafia*. Riuniti: Rome, 1963
GLIOZZO, CALOGERO, 'Danilo Dolci e gli intelletuali francesi' (article). *Civiltà Cattolica*: Rome, 1958
GRASSO, FRANCO, '*A Montelepre hanno piantato una croce*'. *Avanti!*: Milan, 1956.
HOBSBAWM, E. J., *Primitive Rebels*. Manchester University Press, 1959
KEFAUVER, ESTES, *Crime in America*. Gollancz: London, 1952
LAMPEDUSA, GIUSEPPE TOMASI DI, *The Leopard*. Collins: London, 1960
LEVI, CARLO, *Words are Stones*. Gollancz: London, 1959
LEWIS, NORMAN, *The Honoured Society*. Collins: London, 1964
MACK SMITH, DENIS, *Cavour and Garibaldi, 1860*. Cambridge University Press, 1954
Italy. University of Michigan Press, 1959
MAXWELL, GAVIN, *God Protect Me from my Friends*. Longmans Green: London, 1957
The Ten Pains of Death. Longmans Green: London, 1959
MAZZETTI, ROBERTO, *Memorie di Don Zeno e di Nomedelfia*. Guanda: Parma, 1956
NOTO, GIUSEPPE, 'Danilo Dolci e lo "spreco" in Sicilia' (article). *Civiltà Cattolica*: Rome, 1960
NOTT, KATHLEEN, 'Danilo Dolci: Non-violence in Italy' (article). *Commentary*: New York, 1961
PANTALEONE, MICHELE, *The Mafia and Politics*. Chatto & Windus: London 1964
PITRÉ, GIUSEPPE, *Usi e costumi del popolo siciliano*. Cappelli: Milan, 1961 (first published 1848)
RUNCIMAN, STEVEN, *The Sicilian Vespers*. Cambridge University Press, 1958
RUSSO, PAOLINO and ALIA, TONI, *Due pescatori siciliani raccontano la storia del Borgo di Dio*. Il Gallo: Milan, 1954
SIBLEY, MULFORD, *The Quiet Battle*. Anchor: New York, 1963
STEINMANN, JEAN, *Pour ou Contre Danilo Dolci*. Cerf: Paris, 1959

BIBLIOGRAPHY

THOREAU, HENRY, *On the Duty of Civil Disobedience*. Peace News:
   London 1963 (first published 1849)
URQUHART, CLARA, *A Matter of Life*. Cape: London, 1963
VERGA, GIOVANNI, *Little Novels of Sicily*. Evergreen: London, 1959
VITTORINI, ELIO, *Conversation in Sicily*. Penguin: London, 1961
WALLER, ROSS, *Danilo Dolci* (monograph). Manchester, 1960
WÄTJEN, EDUARD, *Danilo Dolci—his life and work* (monograph).
   Centro Studi: Partinico, 1963
WEST, MORRIS, *Children of the Sun*. Heinemann: London, 1957

Index